A Somewhat Incautious Life

(The Many Near Deaths of John Huizinga)

By John Huizinga

Copyright 2023 by John Huizinga
ISBN: 9798329221800
Imprint: Independently published
First Edition

All rights reserved. No part of this book may be reprinted or reproduced or utilised in any form or by any electronic, mechanical, or other means, now known or hereafter invented, including photocopying and recording, or in any information storage or retrieval system, without permission in writing from the publishers.

These stories are true as remembered; some names have been changed. All photos are either the author's own, or used with permission.

These stories are dedicated to my beloved daughter Sjoukje Huizinga

Table of Contents

Acknowledgements

I wish to acknowledge Dirk Brinkman for his valuable comments and editing on these stories. When I was recovering from a car accident (number 22) in Dirk's house in New Westminster, he had me tell all of the times I could have died. He documented them in an old account book, and that was the first time these stories were recorded and tallied. I want to thank Erik Brinkman for reviewing and editing this manuscript, Evelyn Postgate for allowing some of the photos she took of the Brittany to grace this book, and Dirk Brinkman and Joyce Murray for a lifelong friendship. Thanks to Sjoukje whose podcasts of eight of these stories inspired me to write this book. From the very first story she advised me as the book progressed, formatting, adding photos. I am a bit of a luddite when it comes to computers, and her astute and unstinting assistance was invaluable. There are many more to thank, but it is well past the witching hour, my memory fades and my wine glass is empty.

A Somewhat Cautious Foreword

At Calvin College in 1967, I was in resistance to those who insisted, “You have to meet John Huizinga.”

I usually responded with, “why would a Philosophy of Religion major want to meet a guy driving a red 1954 MG roadster?” Not long after I finally met John, his pragmatic self-effacing, thoughtful, mischief-making, shared curiosity about life’s mysteries set us out together on the kind of adventures that bonded us as best friends, and mutual critics, for life.

You, the readers of these anecdotes from John’s amazing journeys, will soon discover the same thing that I did: John's implacable "it is what it is" stolidity in the face of every unexpected change, combines with his methodical problem-solving nature, cultural/historical sensitivity, and pure relish for adventure, to make him an unmatchable travel companion.

John graduated as a historian despite dropping out of high school in Grade nine to work. In those days only drop-outs became an A-Class mechanics, eminently useful in the adventures of our times together. (PS: I was not with him when he made the following decision, described twice in his book). Who else could calibrate the range of a Kalashnikov against the acceleration of a Land Rover?

Our families remained close and each of our children found John’s Kootenay home and compassionate, pragmatic counsel--when he was home-- a refuge. As John returned from another adventure into remote areas of our world, our family always looked forward to his slide shows and elegantly told, thoughtful, stories. Not only because he is a photographer with a keen eye, but especially because his need to comprehend each circumstance’s local and historic precedents sensitively contextualized his stories. Here too his book brings the reader of his life’s journey around the world into a clearer understanding of times and places.

These stories are of especially unusual times in wonderful places because John’s journey was driven by his boundless appetite for adventure—or as he describes it, 'young men’s sense of invincibility, which is why we send them to war'. The survivor of many more seemingly fatal circumstances than he recounts in this book, we get to share these stores because he made it into his eighties. Well, not only that, but he paused his roaming long enough to write some of his stories because, as he now says, ‘My greatest regret getting old is missing my delusions of invincibility.’

Written at first for his daughter Sjoukje, at her insistence and to all of our benefit, the scope of these stories grew into something larger, that speaks to all of us. Enjoy.

Dirk Brinkman
Vancouver, BC. August 2024

John and Dirk circa 2014

Introduction

I've almost died a lot of times. I've had a great deal of plain old good luck in my life, which means that I have not died yet, and here I am at age 83 able to tell the tales. I've always had a restless curiosity: wanting to see what was on the other side of the hill, what was possible, propelled me forward. I took on what came my way without much thought for the morrow. The world offered ongoing opportunities and my bent was to take them on. An overrated confidence in the sure sense of "I can do this!" (no matter what it was) prompted me to take on new challenges. My life motto became: "Pay Your Money and Take your Chances."

These "near death" tales are, in the end, a small part of a much larger life, but my daughter thinks them remarkable and wants me to write the stories of the many times when, as she says: "you coulda died."

During my lifetime, we experienced a growing sense of optimism. There was a steady increase in money, and we simply "knew" that the next generation would be better off than the present one, in stark contrast to our current age of uncertainty. As well, we had an unprecedented freedom to choose how and where to live our lives. For better or worse, I embraced this freedom of choice and did most everything that came my way. I mostly did what I wanted, with little thought for my own safety or for how my cavalier life played out for worried loved ones. One can question the wisdom of this way of living, but I believe that in the end we each live out the character we are blessed with at our birth. One thing is for sure, my life choices left a lot of stories in their wake. They are true as remembered and I hope you enjoy them.

World War II – Memories of a Five-Year-Old Partisan

Out of the Blue: It's War

May 1940. My mother (Mem) Feikje Huizinga is standing beside the red brick road in front of our house, holding a three-week-old baby (me) in her arms and with three other small children clustered around her. It is a cold, blustery morning with low clouds scudding across the sky and a steady drizzle falling on everything. The children are gathered tightly around her so as to be under the umbrella. She is waiting for the truck that will take us away to a distant refugee camp.

The Dutch army was about to breach the dam and flood the entire area, including our town, De Westerein, to stop the blitzkrieg advance of the German army. After an hour or so, a truck with a loudspeaker slowly drives by, announcing that it is too late, the Germans have already breached our defences, and we can all go back home and wait to see what occupation will bring. She used to say, "John was born and then all hell broke loose." Once back in the house, Mem makes us each a cup of hot chocolate. Little did she know that we would not see chocolate again until May 1945, when Canadian soldiers, riding on top of their Sherman tanks, liberated De Westerein and handed out chocolate bars to the wildly cheering people.

Mem with Vickie, Melle and John in 1940

Pissing for Freedom

Our village, De Westerein, lay in Friesland, the northernmost province of the Netherlands and at the edge of a wild, untamed region of trees, shrubs, heather and swamp interspersed with shallow ponds, quicksand, and vast swaths of 10-foot-high reeds. This wild, roadless region this was known as De Heide (the Heath). The locals travelled their wild homelands on winding footpaths. The people of this watery wasteland were fiercely independent. The "Heide Folk" existed on the fringes, living off the land, catching fish, hunting ducks and geese, and making some money by catching the moles that plagued the wealthy farmers bordering their swampy homeland. These people stubbornly resisted all German incursions into their lands. For German soldiers, it was a dangerous and uncertain place to patrol. It was easy to get lost, and a misstep in the wrong place could send a soldier into bottomless quicksand. As well, these fringe people were not recorded in the meticulous records maintained by the municipalities, so their numbers and location were unknown. The German military wisely tended to stay out of De Heide. The entire region, including De Westerein, was referred to by locals as "Onbezet Gebied" (unoccupied territory). A proud, if somewhat exaggerated, claim. We were geographically and culturally primed to resist.[1]

Friesland was not a strategic region. It was a rural backwater well away from the movements of vast armies and the battlefields of WWII. The German military saw Friesland as a safe place to house frontline troops badly in need of rest and recuperation. On the outskirts of De Westerein, they had requisitioned an entire farm and turned it into an army base. In addition,
German soldiers were lodged in private houses throughout the town. Two soldiers had a room in our house, but they had their own meals provided by the Germans.

---

[1] The idea of the free Frisian goes back to the year 800, when a band of Frisians re-took the city of Rome after a revolt by its citizens. Charlemagne and a grateful Pope offered the Frisians vast wealth in gold and treasure, but their leader, Magnus, turned down the treasure and instead asked for a guarantee of freedom in their own lands in perpetuity. They left Rome with a charter from Charlemagne that read in part, "All Frisians are freemen, the born and the unborn, as long as the wind blows from the clouds and the world stands." Thus, feudalism never took hold in Friesland. Every individual owned their land and did not pay taxes to anyone. To this day, the idea of free Frisians is ingrained in the culture, captured by the common saying, "elste Fries is sien eigen kening" Every Frisian is his own king.

One hot summer day in 1944, the older boys in the village rounded up as many of us little boys as they could find. We were taken to a grove of poplar and willow trees and, one by one, sworn to silence before being let in on the secret. The older boys had found a cache of beer bottles placed in the waters of a drainage ditch to keep them cool. On investigation, they found out that the German officers from our army base had invited officers from somewhere else in the Reich for a weekend get-together. The beer was a prized Bavarian treat for their guests.

We younger boys were led, one at a time, to the submerged beer bottles, where an older boy would take up a bottle, open it and pour out a small amount beer. Then he would hand it to one of us to piss the bottle full again. The bottles were resealed with a wire snap that secured a ceramic stopper with a rubber ring. I left there immensely proud of myself. I had pissed five bottles to full. I was one proud little Frisian patriot who knew he had struck a mighty blow against the enemy.

Knowing Your Enemy

My father was the miller. The feed mill was some distance from the house down a sandy road. Heit (my dad) had changed the mill over from its traditional wind power to electric motors. In the process of electrification, the "wieken," the enormous iconic wings that had powered the windmills of the Netherlands since mediaeval times, were removed. What was left was a round, three-storey, truncated tower with a flat roof. The Germans had placed an anti-aircraft gun on this flat roof, which was the highest point in town. The gun was manned only during flyovers of the thousand-bomber raids from England.

Heit was in the Resistance. The mill served as a safe place where weapons and messages could be distributed. Farm wagons, coming and going, did not attract attention. Most anything could be concealed in burlap bags of grain or flour. The mill also housed a forbidden radio where some chosen men gathered every evening to hear the "real" news from BBC, as well as coded messages broadcast to the Resistance. It was a dangerous decision my parents made to defy the might of the German army from within occupied lands. The two German soldiers billeted in our house never twigged to what was going on under their noses. The same can be said for the soldiers who manned the anti-aircraft gun on the roof of the mill. The unthinkable consequences of being found out were not something people dwelt on. As a five-year-old, I had no understanding of what was happening all around me, but one event helped me understand why German soldiers were the enemy.

Behind the mill, at the end of a footpath, was a sandpit. It was a favourite place for us to play. One spring day, several German soldiers took over our sandpit and drove a circle of wooden stakes into the ground. After this inexplicable event, half a dozen soldiers carrying tools instead of guns would come to the sandpit every morning. Over the next several weeks, they proceeded to build a miniature Bavarian village with perfectly made half-timbered houses, hinged wood shutters, a town square, a church and cobbled streets made with pebbles. We were enchanted. We were not allowed to come near the toy village, but in the evening, after the soldiers were gone, we would inspect every nook and cranny of the growing, changing work of art. On the last day, the men painted their handiwork. The house timbers, painted brown, were now framed beautifully against the white clay background, and the miniature window shutters were painted green.

The following day a group of German officers, all in full dress uniform, came to the sand pit. The officers from our military base had invited officers from elsewhere for a social get-together. We were well hidden behind an old farm wagon a ways away from the sandpit, and we watched as they inspected the cobblestone streets made with pebbles and the half-timbered houses. They opened and closed the green window shutters, apparently as charmed as we were.

Heit Huizinga at age 19.

The entire group then walked to the edge of the sandpit and lay down behind a small berm of sand. All the officers took up their rifles and took turns shooting at the beautifully made miniature village. After what seemed like a really long time, the shooting stopped. The German officers shouldered their guns and walked away laughing and joking. We cautiously walked back into our sandpit and looked at the wrecked houses, the scattered pebble streets, the splintered green shutters. We stood there stock-still with tears in our eyes. At that moment, I understood why Germans were the enemy.

A Thousand Bombers

I have memories of nights when our whole family would be hurried down the stairs into the basement. It was a cold, dark, slightly damp place lit by a single candle. Mem had us well bundled in blankets, but the chill and the damp seeped through. We were there because a fleet of a thousand bombers was passing by overhead. The fear was that the Germans, who manned the anti-aircraft guns on the roof of our mill, would shoot at the fleet of bombers, at which point fighter escorts would peel off and direct a hailstorm of 50-calibre bullets, or bombs, at the mill and perhaps our house. Who knew?

These were the infamous thousand-bomber raids launched from England to destroy German cities. A thousand bomber planes, loaded with incendiary bombs, were required to close the circle and make a deadly ring of fire around the city. The resulting fire storm would create searing hot winds that would utterly destroy everything inside the ring of fire and suck all of the oxygen out of the air. Families in Dresden died huddled in their basements and bomb shelters, breathing superheated air deprived of all oxygen. We did not know that our family, huddled in the basement of our house in De Westerein, were the lucky ones.

John and his best friend, Heddy Bylsma, just before leaving for Canada in 1948

Bevrijdings Dag (Liberation Day)

I am not sure which memories of the war are my own or which come from the stories adults would tell about the war for years to come. But no matter. Some of these are indeed my own recollections, and some of what I remember comes from our collective memory of those desperate and traumatic times.

It was May 5, 1945. Everyone in De Westerein, men and women, old and young, children of all ages, was lined up along the red brick road that ran in front of our house. The air was an electric hum of expectation. People were all jostling, talking, gesturing, laughing, crying. Some craned their necks to be the first to see the Canadian soldiers coming down the Rijksweg.

For the previous two days we had watched as thousands of German soldiers streamed by all day long and into the night, heading east towards Germany on foot, on bicycles, some on horseback, in stolen farm wagons, driving hijacked trucks, and officers in staff cars.

Many of the fleeing soldiers had discarded their rifles and were carrying their personal belongings, wrapped in blankets or stuffed into makeshift backpacks. The mighty German army, the pride of the Third Reich, in total disarray. The much-vaunted discipline, gone. It was each man for himself. Everyone knew the Canadians were coming!

The children were not allowed outside. We watched in amazement and sheer delight from the safety of our front room as the seemingly endless chaotic stream of men and the odd selection of vehicles passed by. Mem had sternly forbidden us from opening the windows so we would not be tempted to yell out our childish insults for German soldiers, "Rott Moffen! Dutse kaffer!" At the end of the second day, the stream of men was reduced to a few stragglers, and then they were gone. It was unbelievable!

"The Canadians are coming! The Canadians are coming!" These words were on everyone's lips. Friends, neighbours, strangers – everyone came by with the same message. "The Canadians are coming! The Canadians are coming!" The whole family went out to the red brick road. It was lined with people as far as we could see in both directions. It seemed that the entire town was there, on our street. Way more people than I had ever seen in one place, even at church.

Suddenly, there were the Canadians. First came enormous tanks and army jeeps. Heit was riding on top of the first tank holding a Sten gun. He was wearing a white arm band that identified him as a member of the resistance, out in the open, for all to see.

The crowd cheered and cheered, people hugged and kissed and jumped with joy. I noticed that Mem had tears in her eyes. I remember wondering why she was crying and thinking that she must be very sad. I had never seen Mem cry before. People ran out into the street, and Canadian soldiers leaned down to hoist the girls onto the top of the tanks and into jeeps. People threw flowers till tanks and jeeps were covered in all the colours of the rainbow. Then came the troops on foot, marching in fours. It seemed that a soldier could just break rank whenever he wished – to shake hands with people, to hand out chocolate bars, to kiss a pretty girl. The bolder girls would join the ranks of soldiers and march, or skip, or walk with the troops. These girls were also covered in the blizzard of flowers thrown by an ecstatic crowd. This was so different from the disciplined German troops we had lived with for five long years. It was a day of total celebration, a day of unrestrained joy for all.

I now know that this day, May 5, 1945, was a truly historic day. It was Bevrijdings Dag (Liberation Day), a day that is remembered and commemorated even now in every village, town and city in the Netherlands. As a five-year-old, I lived an incomparable day that has been fixed in my memory for a lifetime.

Number One: Wie Bougje Woll Maar Breake Nooijt! (We Bend but Never Break)

It was the summer of 1945. We had survived the war and the German occupation. During the war, the boast was that De Westerein and its swampy environs were unoccupied territory. That boast was now true.

We had a small Fiat car. It was one of two cars in our town. Gasoline was finally available again, and our previously horse-drawn car was running on its own steam once more. When my father stepped into the car to drive to the mill, I jumped onto the back bumper to hitch a ride. Unexpectedly the car, rather than going forward, backed up. Since my feet were touching the ground, I fell off the bumper. I grabbed at it and got turned over before falling flat on the ground. The car kept backing up, and a wheel ran over me. The car lifted and dropped back down. My father then drove forward, running me over a second time. He wanted to pick up whatever he had run over – easier to do if it was behind rather than under the car. What he saw was his five-year-old son on the ground, crying, with a muddy tire print across his stomach.

I was taken into the house. My clothes were taken off, and I was placed stark naked on the kitchen table. All the neighbourhood kids crowded into the room to see. I was quite embarrassed to be on display naked. The doctor arrived on his bicycle, and he prodded me with his finger in a dozen different places, saying, "Does this hurt? Does this hurt?" My replies were honestly, "no, no, and no." The doctor stepped back and said, "The boy is made of rubber, there's nothing wrong with him." I got dressed and went outside to play. The only thing that hurt were my feelings.

Already, at the early age of five, I was a good little Calvinist. I knew shame and guilt. We learn to hide such feelings to protect the image we construct for ourselves, of ourselves. My self-image, of being indestructible, stayed with me and directed how I acted out a life for the next 78 years.

Immigration

May 1948, Quebec City

Family portraits were a serious, formal affair. This was the last photo of the family, together on Frisian soil, frozen in time by the camera. We went by train to Rotterdam and looked up in awe at a ship bigger than our house, ready to take us to Canada.

Why did we go? Why did we leave behind our ancestral homeland, our familiar social village life, our language, and our people? My dad was restless and willing to take a risk for a new, freer life. Holland was struggling. The Marshall Plan and post-war recovery was still just a faint hope. Emigrating to Canada was in the air we were all breathing. It was a movement. It was infectious. During the ten post-war years, one hundred thousand people emigrated from Holland to Canada, and many more emigrated to the USA, Australia, New Zealand, South Africa. The war had unmoored the world, it would never be the same. The costs of this move were not apparent to my parents at that time. They were to learn that immigration was an earthquake. Our familiar Friesland, with its cobbled streets and verdant green fields was forever lost.

The black slate cliffs of Quebec City wowed all us flatlanders, the biting cold not so much. I was with Mem and my fifteen-year-old sister Vicky in a small bakery. Inside the bakery, it was warm and filled with the familiar yeasty smells. Vicky was the only one who could speak some English. She was having little success understanding the woman behind the counter, who obviously was not understanding my sister either. Mem sternly berated Vicky. “We paid good money for you to have lessons in English and now you can’t even buy a loaf of bread?” We did not know that the Quebecois woman behind the counter spoke only French.

Family photo taken in 1948, just before emigrating

"TABINTA" MAY 22 - JUNE 1st 1948

The Dutch Emigrant Ship, Tabinta- the ship that brought the family to Canada

The Taste of Canada

Toronto Union Station, an enormous nineteenth-century colonnaded edifice, was built when railroads were the measure of a country. Dutch, Italian, German, Belgian and more immigrants disembarked and walked into the cavernous great hall with its 88-foot-high domed ceiling. Individual families claimed a place by spreading out blankets, bags of stuff, and suitcases. It felt like camping. Mem sliced a huge loaf of Quebec City bread and passed out sausage sandwiches to her ever-hungry children. Then we, the four brothers, set out to explore this huge exotic place. We saw other Dutch kids along with Italian, German, Belgian, and Polish boys all checking the place out. It was a bewildering mix of languages, nationalities seemingly representing the whole world. This was in fact a snapshot of the Canadian mosaic that, more than anything else, defines Canada to this day.

When we approached the end of the great hall, a Dutch boy we knew from the boat came running up with electrifying news. "Ice cream! Free ice cream!" He took us to a small, hole-in-the-wall store where immigrant kids were licking real ice cream cones. Hesitantly, we stepped up to the counter and said "Ijsco!" (ice cream!). A man in a white chef's hat handed each of us an ice cream cone. We ran back to our parents clutching our ice cream cones to tell them of our amazing discovery; ice cream is free in Canada! In spite of our irrefutable evidence, Mem was sceptical of free Canadian ice cream. So, we took her to the store to see for herself. Rather than go inside to get an ice cream cone herself, she just stood and watched. What she saw was two nuns, wearing their black-and-white habits, sitting side by side on a small bench at the back of the store. There was an empty coffee can between them. Each time the man in the chef's hat handed over an ice cream cone to an immigrant kid, the nuns would drop a nickel in the can. That was the end of free ice cream for us. This was accepting charity and, even worse, it was accepting charity from the Roman Catholic Church. Four hundred years had passed since John Calvin had revolted against the corrupt Catholic Church, but old world people have long memories.

A New Home

Our farmer, John Wolfe, picked us up in a huge station wagon from Union Station in Toronto and drove us to our new home near Owen Sound, in Southern Ontario. After the war, Canada took in large numbers of immigrants. For people from the Netherlands (commonly called Holland then), the deal was that a family would be sponsored by a farmer. It was a mutually beneficial arrangement. Canadian farmers needed cheap labour for their expanding agriculture, and war-torn Holland had surplus people, farm labourers nearly all. An immigrant family would be given a house to live in, the use of land for a garden, and generally a milk cow as well as be paid $75 a month for the head of household to work six days a week for the farmer. After three years, they would be free to go. We were twentieth-century indentured servants. We were fortunate to have John Wolfe as "our" farmer. He was a generous, open-hearted man who was willing to do what he could to get us established in this new country. Other immigrant families were often not so lucky.

We dove down a rutted, half-mile-long driveway to arrive at an old Ontario farmhouse set back against a copse of tall birch trees. The house was the colour of weathered wood with an equally well-weathered wood shingle roof, some multipaned windows, and one door. To us boys, it looked like a house from Medieval times, tucked in the woods and out of one of our fairy tale books. In De Westerein, all the houses were brick. The front door led directly into a kitchen with a wood plank floor, a table and six chairs, and odd wallpaper with the texture and look of cooked oatmeal. The most arresting thing in the kitchen was a grand Findlay cookstove, made in Guelph, with nickel-plated trim, a flat black cast-iron cooking surface and an overhead warming oven. True to its nineteenth-century origins, the house had no running water and no electricity. It was provisioned with eight kerosene lamps, some burlap bags of flour, and cupboards stocked with store-bought food. The corn flakes stumped my mother, who finally boiled the entire boxful in a pan of water for dinner. Our first Canadian meal was memorably weird and tasteless. Outside, there was a sagging barn on a foundation of hand-squared rocks and a two-holer outhouse. We were so excited, all four of us boys wanted to go at the same time.

Heit and Melle fixing the water pump at the family's very first house in Ontario.

Four Boys – Life in a New Land

The four boys, Melle, Cecil, George and I, had an irresistible urge to explore. The next day we set off and discovered an unimaginably vast country of open meadows and huge, rolling hills. It seemed an impossible landscape to four flatlander boys to whom a hill was home to an ant colony. We explored dark forests with trees so enormous that they did not seem real. We wandered this vast and varied land for days on end and saw not a single house or a foot of red brick road. We were the Swiss Family Robinson marooned in the exotic wilds of the Canadian wilderness.

From left to right, John, George, Melle and Cecil, in 1948

In a portrait of us four boys taken before we left Holland, Melle is the tall thin boy second from the right. His lips are beginning to pucker up as if he had just swallowed something sour, or is it a smile? My brother Melle; a mysterious nine-year-old Mona Lisa. He very early on called himself Wobe. The self-declared name stuck. Wobe became Melle's affectionate nickname. My brother was a mere sixteen months older than me, but to me he was always the older brother. The role of the eldest was thrust upon Melle. Our oldest brother, George, was physically handicapped. I only ever remember Melle as the oldest brother – the serious, responsible, reliable one who was always ready to do what was needed, who also felt it was his duty to keep a wary eye on the younger brothers. Melle was a cautious boy, thinking before he acted and slow to anger, but once aroused Melle was one scary sight. Consumed by rage, he would throw all caution to the winds and, regardless of the odds, charge into the fray. A throwback Frisian berserker. Beneath Melle's steady and stoic exterior beat a heart the size of our John Deere tractor.

George was the slight and frail one in a family of large strapping boys. He was born with a deformity of the spine. According to doctors, he was fated to slowly become a doubled-over hunchback. George was extensively studied and evaluated by doctors in Leiden. They decided there was nothing that could be done. It was during our third year in Canada, in 1950, that George was admitted to the Sick Children's Hospital in Toronto. The doctors at Sick Kids' performed a series of experimental surgeries to correct his slow growth towards a hunchback. In the process, they collapsed one lung and somehow displaced his right shoulder blade so that it looked like he had a small fin growing out his back. The result: George was smaller, less robust, and less strong than his brothers but stood as straight as any of us. He more than made up for his physical limitations with a quick and agile mind. George was a gifted child; this term, bandied around so frequently in our brave new age, perfectly fit my oldest brother. George had a photographic memory. He would quote entire passages of Shakespeare from memory. George had a natural ability to draw. He would paint lifelike scenes from our new surroundings. A creek meandering through a meadow with a wavering green cedar tree reflected in the ripples of the clear running waters. His subtle shadings of colour made this painting come alive. George made a masterful India ink drawing of a Hudson Bay fort with native Indians trading sumptuous furs for axes, cast iron pots and flintlock muskets. George was a voracious reader. Our house was a repository for books, and George had read and remembered them all.

Cecil was a beautiful but troubled boy with golden blond hair, bright blue eyes, and the most winning smile. Cecil was born during the war. Mem, during this pregnancy, lived with fear and uncertainty. De Westerein was occupied territory. Heit was in the resistance, we had two German soldiers quartered in our house, and there was inadequate nutrition for a growing baby. Cecil had moods when he was suspicious or fearful and felt that people were against him. His sense that the world was not a safe place became a self-fulfilling prophecy as he got older. My younger brother was a silent causality of war. I was the middle child, a place that allowed for a life freer of expectations. I was quick, restless, and curious about most everything. I was not cautious, and at times plain reckless; a risktaker with little thought for consequences.

The barn with all its animals was our second dwelling. It was the place where we played, we worked and we ruled. Twice a day, early morning and late afternoon, we did our chores: milking the cows, mucking out the stables and feeding the pigs, calves, chickens. My first official chore was to collect the eggs.

The occasional broody hen, intent on keeping her clutch of eggs, would fluff up to twice her normal size, mutter low threatening clucks and peck the hand that took the warm eggs from under her. Not so nice. No longer wanting this job, I would swing the basket, filled with newly collected eggs, back and forth as I walked back to the house. One day the inevitable happened: The swinging basket collided with a post. A basket of broken eggs, oozing yellow egg yolk, was delivered to Mem. At this point, the job of collecting eggs was given to the more reliable brother, Melle. From the beginning, Melle picked up the slack when others would not complete a job.

We four brothers grew up together, living and working on the farm. We played and worked and sometimes fought, but in the end, we were brothers who stuck together when it mattered.

Our new home was a great adventure for us. We would wander the open fields, climb hills for the first time in our lives, explore the forests, the creek, the ponds, climb trees, and find enormous granite boulders. There were no stones of any kind in Friesland. We caught a snapping turtle big enough to ride. The turtle could snap a stick the size of a broom handle in half with its fierce beak. We danced and yelled when a crayfish with wicked claws would not let go of the fingers that had picked it up out of the crystal waters of the creek. We caught fish that would leap out of the water to bite at a homemade hook. We chased killdeers, who ran away dragging a wing, until we were breathless. We would get so tantalisingly close but never close enough to capture one. We did not know that these perfectly capable and uninjured birds were engaged in a pretense to lead us away from their nests. We picked up a fearless little creature with white stripes running along its black coat. Afterwards, Mem washed and scrubbed us until our skin was raw. Going against her notions of thrift, she ended up burning our clothes. We hunted wild cats in old barns and made a punishing raid on a honeybee nest in a hollow tree. We were living the life. But this first free, wild, untroubled summer came to an end.

Come September, our lives changed. We had to go to school. Every day, we walked or biked a mile and a half of gravelled country roads to the Dobbinton school. This was one-room country schoolhouse with one teacher for all eight grades. The standard for rural Ontario at the time. The first day, we all came home with new names. "Jaring, that's not a name. You are George." "Mellie, that's a girl's name, you are Melvin." Jan became John and Sietse was now Cecil. Mem, upon being told of our new names, would have none of it. "Jimmi bluiwe allejer de selvde" (you are all staying yourselves).

The teacher, Mr. Maclean, spoke no Dutch. We spoke no English. The solution: all four of us were put in grade one. Two desks had to be added to the grade-one row. Mr. Maclean would write a word from a Dutch dictionary on the blackboard along with the English equivalent and then read out the two words. We would giggle and nudge each other at his inability to pronounce even the simplest of words in Dutch. Mr. Maclean was not amused.

The Canadian kids were curious but wary of the new boys. Over time, we began to learn some English. We learned to play baseball and showed the Canadian kids how to play marbles. Our glass and ceramic ones were the envy of the other kids and later became important trade items. We eyed, with envy, the lunches that the Canadian kids brought to school. Metal lunchboxes filled with exotic gourmet delights like buttered ham sandwiches, homemade bread, potato salads, boiled eggs, cookies, apple pie in its own separate container, and a thermos that poured out hot chocolate. We came to school with our lunch in a paper bag. Lunch consisted of four sliced tomato sandwiches made with white squishy Wonder Bread buttered with lard and sprinkled with sugar. A carrot was desert. The Canadian kids would swap lunches with each other. We knew that we would only get one chance to swap a lunch. When we finally persuaded one of the other boys to swap a lunch, he first couldn't believe the contents of our paper bag, complained bitterly, and then wanted his own lunch back. Too late! We knew how to eat fast.

However, they envied the tall, all-black bicycles with leather chain guards that we had brought from Holland. Sometimes one of them would trade a lunch for a chance to ride one of our bikes. In the end, the elegant Dutch bikes did not stand up well to the rough, gravel back roads of Canada. Since we had no spare parts for repairs, the stately Dutch bikes had short lives.

After a month or so, the Canadian kids were less curious and more intolerant of the Dutchies. The older boys began to push us around, to bully us. One fine day, the older boys blocked the outhouse door to prevent one of us from going. Melle came to the rescue. He charged straight into that group of boys, hurtling a grievous Frisian insult: "Greate Verekelingen!" With arms and fists flailing, yelling at the top of his voice, he waded in. Within seconds they all turned tail and ran. That ended all attempts at bullying the Dutchies. At the end of the school year, we left Dobbinton School forever.

In April of 1949, we moved onto our own farm, the first of three that we would own in Canada. It was a nearby fifty-acre farm and John Wolfe, our farmer, helped Heit to buy it. We worked the farm with equipment borrowed from the Wolfe farm. As well, we got two huge workhorses to use, much to the delight of us boys. The new farm had a great classic Ontario two-storey brick and stone farmhouse. Inside, there was a sweeping wide wooden stairway with curved oak banisters. The banisters sometimes served as a kind fireman's pole for a fast, exciting descent. After I collided with little sister Pat standing at the bottom of the stairs, Mem put a stop to this.

Melle loved the old, weathered wood barn that sat on massive stone footings. It was inhabited by our own animals: milk cows, pigs, laying hens and, most important, the two huge workhorses, Charlie and Barney. There were two other Dutch immigrant families, each with the requisite six or eight children, living on the next concession.

Life for us boys, on our own farm, was a time of unrestrained play, trying new things, figuring stuff out, learning what was possible and what was not possible. We rode the horses everywhere, falling off and getting back on till we learned to stick like burs to those wide bare backs. We learned how to harness the horses, rode on top of wagons piled high with loose hay, and rounded up the cows on horseback, sometimes two of us to one horse. Barney, the younger horse, we harnessed to an all-black cutter with high slim runners, left by the previous owners in the hay barn. After a heavy dew we had a stagecoach, filled with whooping boys racing cross the wet grass and with little whooping Indians in hot pursuit to cut us off at the open gates and clamber onto the careening stagecoach. It was a high-speed king of the castle. By summer's end, the elegant nineteenth-century cutter with its delicate red pinstriping had suffered injuries beyond our cobbled-up repairs.

We found an old buggy with all of its wheels intact, but no traces. Charley would drag the old buggy up the barn hill backwards and, once all aboard, we would delight in careening down the hill with accompanying shrieks and victory yells, coming to a stop in the apple orchard. Two ropes, each tied to an end of the front axle, were fastened to the driver's seat. The one in the seat steered the buggy by pulling one rope or the other. It was a lot like steering a horse. One fine day, Melle was the proud boy in the driver's seat with Cecil and some neighbour boys as passengers. He yelled "here we go!" As we began going down the hill, a steering rope came undone. Melle got out one loud "Ferrek!" before the buggy hit a solid old apple tree, lost two wheels, tipped over, and died an ignoble death. Menno Sietsma broke a tooth. Ralph De Vries said he broke his head, but since there was no blood we did not believe him. Cecil cried but would not say why. The buggy was chopped up for firewood.

This was the summer George came home. George was in the Sick Children's Hospital in Toronto the entire winter of 1949 where he went through a series of radical experimental surgeries. They took one of his ribs and used it to support his spine. They collapsed one of his lungs. He lived with shortness of breath for the rest of his life. George was in a plaster cast that encased his entire torso and one leg. The leg was held up at a 25-degree angle by a rope attached to the ceiling. His arms were free, but otherwise he was immobilised and in bed for the entire summer. He was quite unable to move, but he could read. After he had gone through our own extensive collection, people brought books from the library in Paisley. We would sit by George, and he would tell stories gleaned from the books. When he would itch under the cast, we would try to reach the spot but almost always to no avail. George never, not once, cried or complained. In that small, surgically altered body beat the heart of a true Frisian hero.

It was a fun, free summer but, come September, we went to our new school. Dunblane school was another one-room country schoolhouse with the teacher's desk and long blackboard in the front and a wood stove at the back to heat the school in winter.

We liked Dunblane better than the last school. There were more kids in this school, eighteen in all, and there was more to do. A high set of swings made for some dodgy acrobatics. With two boys standing on the swing, the idea was to use our legs to pump the swing higher and higher and then stop just short of going over the top. A sense of self-preservation restrained us enough to play another day.

Just outside the fence was a fast creek with green snapping turtles living on the muddy bottom and foot-long trout holding still in the clear waters. The trout we learned to snare by ever so carefully passing a thin looped fishing line over the fish starting at the tail and, once at the gills, you would jerk the line up and have a flopping fish land on the grass. This took precision and patience and would succeed once in three to six or more tries. We would gamble marbles, boys' treasures, lunches etc. on the outcome.

Whenever we caught two snapping turtles, they were taken to the schoolyard. When we shoved them together, sometimes the turtles would fight. The fight, which could go on for a half hour or more, was to the death. This was also an occasion to gamble on the outcome.

Life on the farm went on and things happened. Menno Sietsma, the 10-year-old Frisian neighbour boy, wiped his ass with poison ivy. Menno suffered grievously. One look at Menno's red and blistered ass taught us everything we needed to know about poison ivy.

Jigs, our German shepherd, ran in front of the mower and lost his right front leg. But before long, Jigs was as good on three legs as he had been on all four.

Heit, along with Dirk De Vries, bought an old horse from a Canadian neighbour, Loren Mills. It seems that the Mills thought the old horse was for us boys to ride. The next Saturday, Heit and Dirk DeVries shot and butchered the horse. Some of the meat was cut into thin strips and dried to make long, paper-thin strips of dried horse meat – "lijre," a much sought-after Frisian delicacy. A few weeks later, Lorne Mills saw Heit and asked, "how's the horse, Jake?" Heit patted his stomach with his huge hands and replied, "good!" The Mills never forgave us.

There were monthly meetings at the schoolhouse. It was the occasion for the locals to discuss farming issues. The women brought scrumptious goodies to eat, and at the end they would show a film. The meetings began with singing "God Save the Queen." Dirk De Vries, to demonstrate his newfound loyalties, would belt out, in his booming voice: "God Shave the Queen!" He then would proudly proclaim, "Ik zing uit volle borst." But in his broken English this came out as "Ja. I sing with big breast." This delighted the teenage boys.

On Saturday evenings we all went to Paisley, the small town that served the area. This was the occasion to buy supplies and for the people from the farms to see their far-flung neighbours. The main street was crowded with people exchanging the news of the week, catching up on events, talking and shouting across the street to someone so's not to miss anyone. It was as if they met up only once a year.

One wintry Saturday there was a dead wolf hanging from a telephone pole in Paisley. There were all kinds of stories about how this rapacious wolf had torn Mr. McDonald's cow to pieces. The wolf looked like a rather sad raggedy dog barely bigger than our border collie. Heit said Canadian men exaggerate just like Frisian men.

Before going home, we would always go to the creamery where our cream became butter. The cream went into a long stainless-steel vat with huge shiny rollers and stainless-steel paddles that would slowly turn and rotate. The cream turned into great gobs of yellow butter. The highlight of the visit to the creamery was when we each got a five-cent double scoop ice cream cone. Every time, as he handed us the ice cream cone, Mr. Grant would say, "made from your own cream."

The Saturday evening trips to Paisley stopped once our own Christian Reformed church in Owen Sound had been organised. This was where we socialised with our own people. I had a crush on 11-year-old Betty De Vries. During a Saturday at the De Vries' place, Betty and I hid in the threshing machine. This was the ultimate hiding place. The others were never going to find us. The stuffy and close confines were worth it because, away from prying eyes and the derision of the pack, we could hold hands. Until we heard a tractor start up and the threshing began to move. It creaked and rattled, and clouds of dust near choked us. We scrambled out the straw chute and fell to the ground, right where everyone was gathered in the front yard for an outdoor lunch. Our secret was revealed to all. We were mortified. Our crush evaporated like chaff in the summer wind. We never held hands again.

Melle, age 11, worked for the summer on a farm a few concessions over. The wage was a dollar a day. The farm was owned by an older couple, Wilf Grant and his wife Dorothy. They had no children of their own. Melle came home on Saturday afternoons and went back on Sunday night. The money he made, a dollar a day, went into the family pot. This was the norm for Frisian families at the time as it still is today for immigrant families coming from poorer countries.

One summer day, Cecil and I set off on our bicycles to visit Melle. The Grant farm was about four concessions away (a concession was one country mile). The gravelled roads were hard going for a bicycle. The full-on summer sun was baking hot. We went on for what seemed like hours before we realised we were lost. We stopped at a farmhouse and knocked on the door. A woman wearing an apron opened the door. We asked her "where Wilf Grant live?" She cheerfully said next door and disappeared back into the house. Cecil and I walked along the house until we came to the next door. We knocked, and waited, and knocked some more. When the very same woman with the apron opened the door, we again asked for Wilf Grant. She laughed, took us by the hand, walked into the yard, and pointed to a house in the distance, saying, "Wilf Grant's house." We were pleased to have our own clear example of what we so often heard the grownups say: "Canadians do not say what they mean."

Melle got the afternoon off until it was time for chores. He proudly showed us around the farm. Cecil and I were introduced to new ways to do chores. A chain-driven conveyor system that, with the flip of a switch, took the manure from the gutter outside to the manure pile. We did this with a shovel and a wheelbarrow pushed up wobbly planks to the top of the manure pile. A shiny, brand-new milking machine that sucked the milk directly from the cow's teat, all four teats at once. Wow! These were marvels beyond our ken.

Mrs. Grant, a rotund motherly woman, called us in for apple pie topped with whipped cream and a glass of orange juice to wash it all down. "Lekker." This was a glorious send-off. For the next week, we salivate like Pavlov's dog at the mention of her name. Cecil and I came away proud of our big brother. He appeared to be so at home with these new Canadian ways. We envied Melle all the way home.

September 1950 and another school year, but we now spoke pretty good English. We had a new teacher. Twenty-year-old Miss Parker. She was a high-strung, exceedingly nervous young woman, just out of high school. This was her first teaching assignment. She soon lost control of the older boys and then lost control of herself. Miss Parker would lose her temper and threaten and scream and then break down and cry. One day all the boys, except for grades one and two, got the strap. One bad day I got the strap seven times. The strap was a regulation leather school strap about two inches wide and a foot long. The next year, Miss Parker did not come back.

The low-level intolerance of "foreigners" experienced at school was a feature for Dutch kids at rural Ontario schools in the 1950s. We were told, "you've come here to take our land." This opinion obviously came from their parents. Farmers in southern Ontario had come from England over a century earlier. They established their small, fifty to 100 acre, farms and lived isolated, backwoodsy lives. We were the first foreigners to move into their turf in over a century.

The first house in Ontario.

A Ghost from the Past Makes Waves

It was in the second year living in Canada that a ghost from the past caught up with the family.

Back in the spring of 1948, the Netherlands was bankrupt. The German army had raided the Netherlands taking our foodstuffs and much of the country's industrial machinery. They had destroyed the vast harbours in Rotterdam and in the end taken even our church bells to feed Germany's voracious appetite for war materials. In 1948, Holland could well afford to lose some of its unemployed population, but it would not allow money to leave the country. Consequently, each emigrant family was allowed to take only the equivalent of 500 Canadian dollars with them.

Mem was not eager to leave Friesland but agreed to emigrate with the understanding that we would use the money from the sale of the feed mill to buy a state-of-the-art dairy farm in Canada. Heit was restless and just wanted to go. He wanted to leave his hollowed-out country. He wanted to leave the war and its ugly aftermath behind him. Some of the heroes of the resistance became the self-serving bullies who briefly ruled the newly liberated nation. There were rumours of another war on the horizon. This time it was to be with Russia and the fanatical Bolsheviks. Seventy-some years later we now know that Russia, and its war-weary people, were in no state to begin another war.

Heit had decided to short circuit the system. The money from the sale of the family feed mill was deposited into a Swiss bank account. It was the equivalent of several million dollars in today's money. From there it was to take a circuitous route, via South America, and eventually arrive in Canada. By the spring of 1950, it became evident that this money would never arrive. It was lost. The dashed expectations, the recriminations and the stress took a severe toll on both Heit and Mem. Their plan to have a state-of-the-art dairy farm was undone. The dream had turned to ashes and dust. Heit and Mem were 50 and 47 years old, respectively. Not so young in the face of starting over. And there was no going back. No one knew that the coming Marshall Plan would resuscitate the economies of Western Europe much faster than seemed conceivable. A few years later the staged release of monies, left behind in Dutch banks by immigrants, began slowly to flow to its rightful owners.

Heit was of average build, six feet tall, and quick on his feet. However, belying his size, he was enormously strong with hands the size of dinner plates. When he gripped your arm with those huge hands you knew that he could crush it, bones and all.

This gave Heit a unique kind of confidence. Before we left Holland, a team of runaway horses, pulling a carriage with a terrified woman and her small child hanging on to the seat, came clattering down the brick road in front of our house. People on the street scrambled to get out of the way. Heit walked down the middle of the street and stood his ground. As the two horses were about to run him down, he simultaneously grabbed both bridles and commanded the horses with a booming “Whoa!” The wild-eyed horses, heaving and white with sweat, stopped.

Heit was a very capable guy who could do most anything he took on and could do the work of two men. He had a quirky sense of humour, and he was a good dad who was proud of his boys. He was a man who commanded respect. I admired my father immensely. But underneath all of this he harboured a restless soul, one that always wanted to move on.

Mem was a strong, no-nonsense mother. In the house she ran a tight ship. We would rarely see Mem with empty hands. In the evenings, she would be darning socks and knitting underwear till it was time to go to bed. She quietly took care of everything. Mem took the church and the bible seriously and demanded we do the same. She would write sermons, well-written and well-thought-out sermons, on the finer points of reformed theology. The sermons were acknowledged as remarkable by no less than the dominee. But, because she was a woman, she was never allowed to deliver her sermons to the congregation. People loved to visit our house. Mem had strong opinions, always had things to say and was a born storyteller. As young boys we suffered Mem’s often tough discipline but, after I left home, I came to appreciate and then to really love my mother.

In Friesland, Mem was in her element. She was the proud daughter of landowning farmers, who occupied an elevated place in the social hierarchy. She did the bookkeeping for the feed mill and had a maid for the housework. In De Westerein, she was known as "Vrouw Huizinga," a well-known, well-regarded woman in the community. Heit was a capable man who had transformed an old, failing feed mill into a thriving business. They were both persons of status who were known and respected in De Westerein and beyond. Now they faced a huge setback in status and the prospect of starting over, of living by nothing but the sweat of their brow. Both Heit and Mem went a little crazy, each in their own way.

It was a hot summer day. We were walking towards the barn, the cutter loaded high with green corn, when we saw Mem running across the muddy barnyard. Her clothes were dishevelled, her hair hanging loose and partially covering her face. She had tears mixed with streaks of dirt running down her face and a wild look in her eyes. She tripped and fell. When she got up, her dress was torn and covered in barnyard muck, her hair hanging in muddy strings. One shoe remained embedded in the mud. She ran towards us screaming, "ik bin de Duivel! Ik bin de Duivel!" Was this apparition our neat, tidy, well-spoken mother?

We were all rooted in place, so shocked, so afraid, so not understanding what was happening. Just as Mem reached us, we turned and ran. She came after us across the fields screaming "Ik bin de Duivel!" We hid in the high corn where she could not find us. We could hear her weeping, all the way back to the house. Just before suppertime, with great trepidation, we quietly crept back into the house. Mem was at the table wearing clean clothes, her hair back into a tidy bun. She was completely back to her normal, tidy self. She turned to us. There was a minute of complete silence. Then Mem, looking us each straight in the eye, said, "niks tsyn Heit sizze" (do not say anything to Heit). Heit came home, we had supper. He told stories about his day at the Wolfe farm. Mem darned socks. Life was back to normal.

Heit had his own breakdowns. A few weeks before, I came into the barn and saw Heit yelling at the top of his voice, cursing and chasing my brother Melle with a pitchfork. Melle was dodging in and out of the cows stabled for milking and scrambling over the sides of the pig pens. A 12-year-old Melle was quicker then Heit. I ran to the house shouting at the top of my voice, “Heit meaket Melle dea!” (Heit is killing Melle!) Mem ran out of the house, all the way into the barn. She got between Heit and Melle, and it immediately stopped. Melle fled the barn. Heit threw down the pitchfork and hung his head. His shoulders shook. Mem took his hand and led him to a hay bale where they sat for a long time. We all waited in the house. They came back, and we had a late supper. When supper was finished, Heit read his customary chapter from the bible. Life was back to normal.

Heit and Mem. Left: in 1952. Right: with Pat in the winter of 1949

Number Two: A Canadian Winter

It was the winter of 1950. Every morning, Melle, Cecil and myself, ages eleven, ten and eight, walked two miles from our farm to school. George mostly stayed at home and Vickie and Betty had already gotten sewing jobs in the nearby small town of Chesley. Our school was a one-room building for all eight grades, one row of seats for each grade ran from the front of the building to the back. Every school year we graduated and moved one row to our right. Every afternoon the three of us walked two gravel county roads and a half-mile-long laneway to get back home. We knew every curve and hill and tree and shrub of this familiar path. One day in early March, Lorne Mills, a local farmer, stopped at the school to warn the teacher that a severe snowstorm was on the way. The teacher, the motherly Mrs. McDonald, was concerned for the safety of her brood and sent everyone home early, all fifteen schoolchildren. However, the three Dutch immigrant kids stayed. It was our job, for 50 cents a day, to clean up the schoolhouse. We put things away, swept the floors, cleaned the blackboard, filled the inkwells, split firewood, and filled the stove with kindling and paper to have it ready to fire up in the morning. By the time we were finished with our work, the temperature had plummeted, and the north wind was wailing.

We began the long walk home with the wind at our backs. It was a capricious wind that would, with no warning, suddenly turn and swirl and whip up a whirlwind of fine snow that would sting when it hit exposed skin or find a sleeve end or any small opening in our clothing to get to us. The mounds of snow on either side of the road were six feet high. They had been pushed up over the long winter months by county trucks with huge, double-wing snow blades mounted in front. It was impossible for us to lose the road. However, we knew that in the blinding snow we could easily miss our turn onto Fifth Line, the side-road that would take us home. Or we could just as easily walk past the narrow laneway into our farm. This was our second winter in Canada, and we had heard stories of how Canadian farmers often strung a rope between the house and the barn so's not to get lost and perish, cold and alone, in a blinding blizzard.

Within a half hour, the rising wind wailed like a banshee and tore at our clothing. It pushed at our backs like it wanted us down on the ground. The driving snow obliterated everything, and we could no longer see each other. We stopped in a huddle long enough to tie ourselves together with a length of binder twine that Melle had in his pocket. Before we left Holland, a friend at school had told us that if you are out in a Canadian blizzard, you must always keep moving. If you stop, very soon your legs no longer work and then you freeze to death. We quickly carried on, heads bent low into the driving snow. The howling wind was a living demon that wanted to rob me of breath itself. Melle, the biggest, was walking in front but in the shrieking wind and whirling snow of the blizzard, it was the blind leading the blind. Suddenly, our little train stopped, and we stumbled into each other. Melle had walked into a horse. It was Charlie, our faithful farm horse, pulling a sleigh. When the blizzard began, Heit had harnessed up the horse and sleigh and set off to find us. The moment we saw Charlie, the sleigh, our dad, we felt cold and tired and afraid and happy all at the same time. Heit picked us up, one at a time, and heaved us into the sleigh. He turned the horse and sleigh around between the walls of snow. Dad's voice momentarily drowned out the sound of the wind when he boomed out "Home, Charlie." We all, including Heit, crawled under a heavy buffalo robe on the floor of the sleigh behind the buckboard. We snuggled out of the wind, warm, tired and safe, thinking how good life in Canada could be after all.

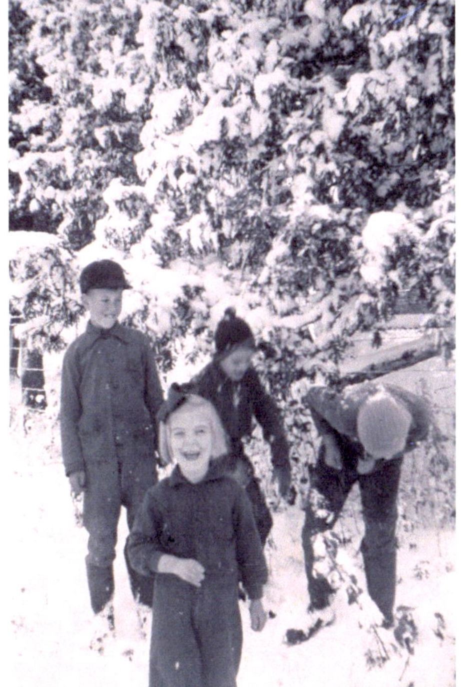

Huizinga children with Pat in front, circa 1950.

Surviving

Number Three: Don't Take Your Guns to the Swimming Hole

In 1951 we bought a 100-acre farm near Forest. There was a large Dutch immigrant community in Forest that Mem longed to be a part of. Our farm was the typical mixed 100-acre farm of the 1950s. We had eighteen cows as well as pigs, chickens, horses and two dogs. We had everything. In the summer, after farm chores were done, my brothers and I would head straight for the swimming hole at the back of the farm. We had energy to burn. We never walked. We trotted everywhere. Melle carried our newly acquired 12-gauge shotgun, the pride of our young lives. All the other farm kids on our concession were dangerously envious. As we got to the wild brushy land closer to the creek, we scared up a cottontail rabbit that darted into a large round shrub. I began to walk around the back of the bush to flush out the rabbit. Another rabbit, coming out of nowhere, ran away from me. Melle swung the barrel as he tracked the fast-moving rabbit. He pulled the trigger, and the rabbit did a somersault in midair. I felt a sharp pain in my left side. A trickle of blood seeped through my shirt. I had been hit.

When a load of buckshot, as many as 100 pellets, leaves the barrel it immediately begins to spread. This pattern gets wider the farther it travels. This is what makes a shotgun so useful for hitting moving targets. I was standing about 100 feet away at the very edge of the buckshot pattern and caught two pellets.

We were at a loss. What to do? We couldn't go home to Mem. She would tell Heit and we would lose the shotgun. We couldn't go to the doctor; he too would tell Heit. So, using a flat piece of sandstone, we stropped my knife till it was razor sharp. Melle began to probe with the point of the knife for the pellets buried somewhere 'tween two ribs, all the while telling me "You gotta stay still. Stay more still!" Melle's "surgery" was way more painful than being shot. After a few minutes, I stood up and refused any more of it. We carried on, went for a swim, and washed the blood off my shirt. We arrived home with a plump rabbit, skinned it, and Mem cooked it for supper. We all sat around the kitchen table and told of the day's events. Heit said, "Ja mine jonge, he is a Canadian Nimrod!" Melle beamed with pride. With Dad reading the bible to us every day, we knew that Nimrod was the great Old Testament hunter. It was a good day!

I was lucky to be standing at the very edge of the buckshot pattern. Had I walked one more step forward, the full load of buckshot would have torn a hole several inches in diameter in my rib cage. Melle woulda bagged a brother. We never told anyone. The pellets stayed put. Seventy years later they are still in there.

The Farm in Forest, Ontario

A Crow in the Family

A bird dropped out of the blue summer sky like a bolt of black lightning. It landed on my right shoulder, rocked back and forth to catch its balance, folded its wings, and uttered a soft, throaty "caw." I smiled and said, "hello, Jimmy, where you bin?"

We saw my older sister Vicky leaving the house. She was wearing her long, sky-blue Sunday dress. The crow left in a flurry of wing flaps, rocketing into the sky. I watched with an expectant grin. The crow swooped down like a peregrine falcon. In one fluid motion, his outstretched wing whacked the top of Vicky's head just as he swooped back up into the sky. The raucous "CAW!" at her ear and the hit on her head came out of nowhere. Her knees momentarily buckled with fright, and she ran back into the house. "I am going to kill that evil bird," she yelled through the screen door to no one in particular. I grinned, happy that my big sister had not seen me. I was in enough trouble with my mom and did not need an angry confrontation with my sister. The crow, the love of my eleven-year-old life, was creating waves.

Several months earlier, Melle and I were on our way back from the swimming hole. Melle was the more serious and reliable brother who followed all the rules. The adults liked to hold him up to me as an example. As boys we seldom walked – we mostly moved at an easy trot. Some crows were making a big ruckus a ways farther into the trees. We headed for the noise and saw a young crow on the ground huddled in last year's fallen leaves. The parent crows dive-bombed us as I picked it up. We looked at the baby bird. It was mostly naked, with some pale fuzz and the brave beginnings of four little feathers.

The adult crows sat in the lower branches of the tree, waking the entire forest with their outraged cawing. The baby bird opened its beak impossibly wide when it detected motion. The inside of the beak was yellow, the same colour as my baby pigeons. My heart did a flip. I saw a totally helpless creature. I immediately knew it would become a friend. I dropped a crumpled piece of old bread that I found in my pocket into the yawning mouth, and the beak snapped shut. Melle said, "Now he is yours." All the way home I cradled the baby crow in my palms. I was carrying pure happiness in my hands and in my heart.

The new addition to the menagerie was kept in the barn where it was warm year-round but also where a dozen or so barn cats prowled for their next meal. A cat-proof cage of wood boards and chicken wire was hammered together. The cats liked to sit outside the cage licking their lips as they looked longingly at the edible little critter. Yummy, no feathers.

The little crow demanded to be fed whenever anyone walked past. It had developed a thin, squeaky "caw," its insistent plea for more more more food.

It was a bright, sunny summer day, and us four boys were in a field halfway back to the back of the farm blocking (thinning) sugar beets. During summer holidays, everyone worked on the farm. There was never an end to farmwork, there was no light at the end of this hundred-acre tunnel. I ran to the barn every hour to feed the crow, who cawed for food as soon as the barn door cracked. After a few days, I got permission from Heit to take on the work near the barn so I could keep up my hourly vigil.

I weeded the family garden, mucked out the pigpens, fixed the fences that kept the chickens in their place. I took on the annual mucking out of the two-seater family outhouse, the farm's least desirable chore. It was enough to make anyone gag. The crow was exacting a steep price, but an innate Frisian stubbornness kicked in. It is my crow, and I will do whatever I have to keep him alive. I told the crow, "I'm your mother, and mothers never give up."

The crow was fed a diet of crickets, potato bugs, flattened June bugs, caterpillars, and other insects, as well as bits of bread and pie crust pilfered from Mem's cooking pots. He refused to eat worms. He clearly considered himself above regular run-of-the-mill crows. Everyone decided the crow needed a name. He became Jimmy the Crow. "Jimmy" for short.

As Jimmy's coal-black feathers grew, his squeaky "caw" became a mature, boisterous "CAW!" The other farm animals soon learned to ignore his full-throated "CAW!" at their own peril. Jimmy had a beak like a steel dagger. He twisted it sideways as he drove it into the skin or fur of his target. This stab was always punctuated with an unrestrained "CAW!" so whoever was at the receiving end knew exactly who inflicted their pain. It was Jimmy's version of psychological warfare. Now that he could defend himself, Jimmy strutted about the barn like he owned the place, a habit he retained long after he learned to fly. He became a barnyard presence, one hard to ignore.

A month before they calve, cows are given a special flaxseed cake. Jimmy loved this cake. He would leap into a cow's manger and move the piece of seed cake to the far edge, where the cow, restrained by a chain around her neck, couldn't reach it. She'd reach for the cake with her amazingly long prehensile tongue but fall a few, frustrating, inches short. Jimmy would then hide the seed cake under some hay so that we would give the cow a new one. Jimmy soon had a secure stash of cake for whenever he felt like a snack. Dad was the first to notice what Jimmy was up to and was impressed. Once a cow got a sharp stab on the nose, she was happy to ignore the obnoxious creature that invaded her manger.

Jimmy selected Lucy's manger from which to steal most of his seed cake. Lucy was our one Jersey cow. All the other cows were big, black-and-white swaybacked Holsteins with udders so enormous they nearly dragged on the ground. Jerseys, on the other hand, are much smaller, with caramel-coloured hair, delicate legs, and an udder in proportion to their size. Lucy gazed out at the world with impossibly large, brown, liquid eyes. She had a spring to her step and looked like an overgrown deer. A Jersey does not give as much milk as a Holstein, only half a pail full, but it's so rich and creamy that it has a yellowish sheen. Lucy's milk went to the house for our own use.

We had eighteen milk cows. The skim milk was fed to the pigs, the cream was removed by a separator. The separator had two spouts – one for milk and one for pure cream. The cream was sold to the creamery in town, where it was made into butter or ice cream.

Mem had become a capable, no-nonsense farmwife who could pitch in to milk the cows or midwife a sow. She was no-nonsense raising her children as well, collaring the nearest boy to help as needed. We tried to avoid her on "dangerous" days like wash day, when tubs of water had to be heated, and butter-churning days, when we had to pump the ancient wooden churn until our arms ached. Work for farmwomen never ended. In the evenings we read books or played boardgames, and Mem would join in, but she would not put down her knitting or the socks she was darning until she went to bed.

In the barn, summer or winter, it was always warm. The musty, alive odour of the animals, the sweet smell of new hay, and the slightly sour breath of our cows mingled together. Each cow had her own distinct personality. Some were gentle and placid, others bad-tempered and quick to bunt a neighbour with their horns. Some were really stupid. Dora was the leader, and all the other cows would follow in her footsteps. The cows went out to their pasture in single file, always walking a well-worn cow path with Dora in the lead. Some cows we liked a lot, others not at all. Just like people at church.

The barn was filled with life. The soft, satisfied grunts of a sow as she nursed her dozen little piglets. A cat silently padding by on its own mysterious errand. Our loyal border collie, Tipp, asleep, with one eye open, on a straw bed behind the separator. Jimmy in his eyrie atop an eight-inch, hand-hewn black walnut beam that held up the roof, watching everything. He could leap straight up over six feet high, using his wings to help gain elevation, but he had not yet connected this with the next step, to take wing and fly.

The barn was a welcoming place where animals and people all knew one another. We were a single interdependent entity. The barn was home in a way that Mem's tidy, clean, rule-bound house could never be. It was alive and intimate and felt like the warmest, safest place on earth.

From the beginning, Jimmy had it in for cats. Jimmy, no doubt, had memories of the cats eyeing him when he was a helpless baby bird. When he could catch a cat off guard, Jimmy would drive his beak into whatever part of the cat was in range and then return to his eyrie. Grown cats learned to stay out of his way. To remedy this, Jimmy would grab a kitten by the tail and drag it backward as it frantically dug its little claws into the floor and mewled loudly for help. At some point, its mother would rush to the rescue. When the mama cat was close enough, Jimmy would let the kitten go and stab the mother with his beak. Then, from his safe perch in his eyrie, he would scold the cat for being a cat with his repertoire of loud, obnoxious caws.

Jimmy had his own crow language, which involved different caws as well as body language for emphasis. There were soft greeting caws, loud greeting caws when he was talking to a group, good-morning caws when he woke up, warning caws to alert us if a stranger showed up, nonstop insistent caws when he wanted something, scolding caws when he was displeased, harsh, loud caws when he was angry, curt “fuck you” caws when he was disgusted, haw-haw caws when he felt something he had done was funny, and a kind of rolling caw to reassure that he meant no harm. There was a “What’s this?” caw in his vocabulary, which included a sideways turning of his head so that he looked directly at you. It was flirtatious and always prompted a response. There were different tones that matched each caw. These tones carried his emotions and could change mid-sentence to let you know how he felt, how well he liked your response. In time, we learned to decipher his language. I believe the farm animals also learned to understand Jimmy when it mattered.

Jimmy had the dignity of a bewigged judge on the bench. He hated being laughed at. One day he was in the barn as we were running milk through the separator. He was sitting on the edge of the milk can to catch the milk in his beak as it streamed out of the separator. He stuck his beak too far into the stream of milk, lost his balance, and fell into the milk can. We heard a loud squawking and flapping of wings and rushed over to fish him out of the tall, narrow can, which was half full. We all laughed when we set him on the ground, his wings drooping, every black feather dripping with white milk. Jimmy went silent, stood up straight, clamped his sodden wings against his body and strutted away, his head held high, tiny rivulets of milk dripping from the ends of his long wing feathers. Without a sound or a backward glance, Jimmy walked out the door. He was gone all night and returned the next morning when we were milking the cows, every feather glistening black, preened, and perfectly in place. He greeted each of us with his usual, friendly good-morning caw. His message was clear: “That indignity never happened." Jimmy waited, displaying some consideration, until Heit was finished milking Lucy to invade her manger for his breakfast.

After his ignominious dunking, Jimmy would leap up to sit on the edge of the smaller cream can and delicately put his beak into the smaller and safer stream of cream to take small sips. He was a fast learner.

One bright, sunny day I set out to teach Jimmy to fly. The flying lesson consisted of taking a pigeon in one hand and Jimmy in the other and throwing the pigeon into the air. The pigeon would flap its wings and launch itself into the air. Now that he had seen how it was done, it was Jimmy's turn. I threw him up in the air. He fell like a stone and hit the ground with an audible thump. Jimmy gave out a loud, "What's this?" caw as he looked at me. I attempted one more lesson before Jimmy would not let me pick him up. Any attempt to do so was met with a sharp peck. He gave his curt "fuck you" caw, walked into the barn, and refused to leave his private perch.

The next day I took Jimmy up into the hay barn and, from a height of forty feet, tossed him into the air. About halfway down, he began to flap his wings, and just before he hit the ground, he levelled out. His landing was a bit rough, too much forward motion. His feet hit the ground running like crazy to keep up before he tumbled head over heels. But he got the concept. On the next try he spread his wings and flew.

Once Jimmy could fly, he became the undisputed lord of the barnyard. He was quick to enforce his mastery. Flying gave Jimmy some serious advantages over the other animals – he was the only one who could take to the air to escape, or to launch a surprise attack from above.

His first clear declaration of "I am in charge" came about a week after he learned to fly. First thing every morning, the huge Barred Rock rooster made his rounds. He would strut about like he was the Lord of the barnyard. Hens in his path either ran or crouched down in servile obeisance to their lord and master. He would leap on an available hen, dig in his spurs, hang onto her little red comb with his beak, and have at her. When done, he would swagger off to step up onto a high point, usually the salt block, push out his chest until he was precariously unbalanced, strain to stretch his neck straight up as far as it could go, throw his head back, and crow to the heavens. He was proclaiming, “Look at me, the grandest king ever of this barnyard, I takes whatever I wants!” This obnoxious display was a challenge to the entire world. It seems that that was exactly how Jimmy interpreted the rooster’s behaviour.

One day when the rooster was finished crowing and pompously sashaying back to the hen he had violated earlier, Jimmy landed on his back, drove his beak into the rooster’s glorious red comb, and hung on. This broke the rooster’s proud strut and he began to run full out, his wings flapping, bouncing up and down across the barnyard with Jimmy firmly latched onto his back. The rooster seemed to think he could leave his attacker behind by running faster. Jimmy rode like a seasoned rodeo rider on a bucking bull. He just kept hanging onto the comb and extending his wings for balance. He rode that rooster well beyond a bull rider’s eight winning seconds.

The rooster got clear across the barnyard before Jimmy launched himself into the sky with a series of loud caws, leaving no doubts as to the author of this public humiliation. His dignity shattered, the rooster retreated to the henhouse. We did not see him outside it for the rest of the day. I was proud of Jimmy and felt a rush of affection. Jimmy shared my dislike for bullies. We were soul brothers. I would have liked to take down this vain bully myself, but that would have made me the bully.

A week later, we were given a banty rooster. Banties are small and feisty with black and bright red feathers and iridescent breast feathers. They have long sweeping tail feathers and wicked spurs on their feet. Compared with the run-of-the-mill white leghorn chickens he was a runt, but he was a runt that looked like a Mexican fighting cock. A wilder version of a farm chicken, he had retained some of the original jungle fowl’s ability to fly; he could get a few feet off the ground and fly short distances.

After his encounter with Jimmy, the big Barred Rock rooster set out to reclaim his pride of place by taking on the newcomer. After puffing out his chest to new dimensions, stretching his neck to new heights, and crowing so that it echoed off the barn, he headed straight for the banty rooster. With his comb standing straight up, he launched himself directly at the little rooster so that his superior weight would overpower his smaller opponent. The banty leaped straight up in the air, raked the big rooster's head with his spurs and landed on the Barred Rock's back. His long spurs dug in as he latched onto his opponent's comb and proceeded to peck, his head moving up and down like a feathered jack hammer. It was no contest. After this encounter, the big rooster would skulk around the periphery of the banty's new harem of "his" hens. He was a sad picture of a broken barnyard bully. We named the banty Piet Hein, after the heroic Dutch privateer who raided Spanish treasure ships and thus made Spain contribute to Holland's war of independence.

Jimmy made enemies, but he also had allies. Jimmy and Piet Hein developed a mutual understanding. It seemed that each recognized a compatriot's wild soul in the other. They did not avoid each other but kept a respectful distance when they met in the barnyard. By the end of the summer, Jimmy and Piet Hein were eating from the same feeder, real buddies.

Jimmy befriended our workhorse Charlie. He would land on Charlie's broad back and ride high up where he could dig his claws into Charlie's long mane. Jimmy would utter soft rolling caws that said, "Charlie, you and I are friends." Charlie understood. They were an incomparable pair making their rounds of the barnyard, a proud crow riding his giant steed.

Charlie would sometimes attempt to lift the latch on the wooden gate beside the big, round, wooden water tank. He had seen us lift the latch to open the gate a thousand times and knew what was required. He would grab onto the wooden latch with his lips, but the latch was made for long human fingers not for short horsey lips. He could never get a firm hold. At best, he would lift the latch an inch or so before it fell back into place. Jimmy watched Charlie's failed efforts and realised he could help. Sitting on the gate, he could get a good grip on the latch with his beak and lift it up to where Charlie could get his teeth on it and pull it up and out of the way. Beyond the gate was a small mountain of newly harvested sugar beets. Charlie would nibble to his heart's content on his favourite treat while Jimmy snacked on horseflies.

A mountain of sugar beets, ripe for stealing.

A daily ritual Jimmy never missed was his bath. He took his bath seriously. Every day, we set a pan of water out for him. He would take a beakfull of water and work it into his feathers. Then, using his beak, he would carefully flatten and straighten his feathers and in so doing squeeze the water out. He did this repeatedly until every feather shone. The last thing, his long wing feathers, received special treatment. He would extend a wing and preen each feather with great care. He walked away with gleaming black feathers and not a speck of dust to be seen. At lunch, we would watch from the kitchen table as Jimmy took his bath on the grass outside. Jimmy was quite vain by our farm boy standards. His bath took twenty minutes to half an hour. Even Mem applauded Jimmy's meticulous bathing routine.

Jimmy's world revolved around people and the farm animals. We figured that Jimmy did not know he was a crow. He thought he was human, one of us. He considered us boys his own folk and accepted that we couldn't, or wouldn't, fly and so walked with us everywhere we went.

He had his favourites and tolerated most everyone else. He mostly hung around us four boys. When we went into the house for dinner, our border collie Tipp would want so badly to join us, but the house was Mem's domain and she had an ironclad rule: Animals belong in the barn. Tipp would lie on the ground with his nose just over the doorsill, looking longingly at his humans. They were the very purpose of his life. Tipp would carefully creep forward on his stomach, slowly inching farther into the kitchen, as if he were stalking his human family. When he gained a little distance he would look up guiltily, but his tail would wag with pure doggy happiness. He would often make it over halfway by the time Mem noticed and shooed him out. Ever the optimist, Tipp would begin his stealthy crawl over from scratch. We would make bets on how far he would get each time. Mem was nearly stone deaf so we could make these bets at the table. It was just another part of dinner conversation.

Jimmy, on the other hand, once walked into the kitchen, proclaiming his arrival with loud "hello, all" caws. Mem was not quite deaf enough for Jimmy. She grabbed a broom and swept him out like he was just more dirt. Jimmy, thinking no human being would ever deliberately treat him with such disdain, picked himself up and made his grand entrance again, only to be swept off his feet again and tumble out the door backwards.

Jimmy was humiliated and angry way beyond usual. This was not a dignified exit. People, even little feathered ones, were simply not to be treated this way! Rather than try a third time, he stood in the open doorway, scolding and scolding incessantly. He was so noisy that Heit's after-dinner bible reading was stopped halfway through the daily chapter. (He read one chapter of the bible out loud at each evening meal. It took three years to get from Genesis to Revelations, and then he began all over again.) Jimmy had interrupted a sacred family tradition. Mem was not amused. We all giggled at this valiant show of righteous indignation.

Jimmy never forgot the humiliating treatment he had received at the hands of our mother and had his winged revenge. The next week, Mem was outside walking to the garden when a black-winged missile silently streaked down, one wing thumping her head as Jimmy let go with an ear-splitting caw and swooped back up into the sky. Mem, not a woman who is easily disturbed, fell to her knees in fright. She was mortified. After this, Mem protected her implacable dignity with an umbrella when outside.

While our sister Betty was still unmarried at the ripe old age of twenty-four, her younger sister Vicky got engaged at age nineteen. Way more normal, we all agreed. It was obvious to everyone that Betty was headed for spinsterhood. Even more worrying was that she didn't seem to care. Both sisters worked in Chesley doing embroidery in a 1950s Canadian sweatshop and came home on weekends. Vicky's presence brought levity to the house. She would sing as she went about her chores and played the old pump organ. Most important to us, when she was home she would bake real Canadian pies with fruit and sugar, something we had never tasted in Holland.

Unfortunately, Vicky had a phobia about birds. She was terrified of silent flying objects darting out of the sky. For her, Jimmy was a nightmare come to life. She was a victim of Jimmy's revenge against women folk twice, and for a while she refused to go outside. However, it was soon discovered that when she wore jeans Jimmy ignored her: his was a war against skirts not against women. Mem, on the other hand, refused to wear pants. "Never!" she'd say. "I will dress how I have always dressed. I am not wearing men's pants for anyone and certainly not for a crow."

The family became quite divided about Jimmy, who had another habit that added fuel to this fire. He was irresistibly attracted to anything shiny. Anything that glittered was his. Jimmy, from the depths of his heart, was a Gypsy crow. Gypsies believe that it was a wandering Gypsy who gave Jesus to drink when he thirsted on the cross. After his drink from the sponge, held up to him on a long stick, Jesus blessed the Gypsy and said that he and his descendants could now claim ownership of everything that was lost in the world. Wherever they found a lost object, it was theirs by divine right. To Jimmy, the shiny glittering objects he found were clearly lost. To others, Jimmy was a flying kleptomaniac. Anything shiny lying around disappeared. Bits of tinfoil, small silver spoons, polished brass buttons, Mem's tiny scissors, shiny new dimes laid out for the church collection plate – and then one day Vicky's engagement ring! This was a disaster of biblical proportions. Our severely distraught sister's despair was such that wearing sackcloth and ashes seemed the next step. After her wails, floods of tears, and death threats directed at Jimmy, I promised to get the ring back and recruited my brothers to help.

Jimmy stashed his treasures in a secret place. It was only a matter of finding it. But this was not so easy. Jimmy was one wily bird. I put out irresistible trinkets – polished, stainless-steel ball bearings. George was stationed on the roof of the house, from where he watched Jimmy select a treasure and fly away with the bauble in his beak. The other boys were stationed outside to see which way he went. He flew in an erratic fashion, like he was not sure where to go. At the far end of the apple orchard, flying close to the ground to avoid detection, he circled back to the barn, swooped in through the big open wagon doors, and disappeared into the haymow.

Melle, hiding in the haymow, watched as Jimmy flew high up where two beams met and a moment later left again. We closed the big barn doors to keep Jimmy out. With ladders and a rope, Melle and I climbed up. There was a concave section between two beams that did not completely meet. There we gazed upon an eclectic treasure trove that would have done a dragon proud. Marbles, brass buttons, a hair clip, silver spoons, a gold ring, painted beads, four dimes, Mem's small scissors, a piece of mirrored glass, a cow's ear tag, two safety pins, George's shiny new pen – and Vicky's engagement ring! The treasure hunt had taken most of a day, but we saved our sister from heartrending grief. Vicky was relieved to the point of shedding tears of gratitude but not placated. As she clutched her engagement ring she said, "I will be happy when I get married and leave this madhouse where my brother keeps this evil black bird."

Jimmy was so upset that he followed Melle and me, in turn, for the rest of the day, shouting out his outrage at this betrayal. We had raided his private treasure trove. How could they take his stuff!! Later in the day, from his perch in the barn, he would utter a low cry of fury every few minutes until the evening chores were done and we left the barn.

Early the next morning, Jimmy began moving his stuff. All day he flew back and forth with his booty in his beak. If he knew one of us was watching, he would deposit his plunder in a temporary hiding place and move it to his real hiding place when no one was watching. A pirate would not have been more circumspect about burying his treasure. During evening chores Jimmy was back in the barn, his normal garrulous self. His loot was safe, all was forgiven. Jimmy had moved on.

Jimmy ignored the wild crows. He had no desire to stray from his adopted home. We were the centre of his life. He considered us not just his benefactors but his equals. If the freedom of wide-open spaces beckoned, the price of leaving his flock of humans was unthinkable for Jimmy. For us boys as well, life without our clever and endearing feathered friend was unimaginable.

Most of the day he would stay close to us. One day we were in the garden picking cucumbers. We would lift the long vines to reach the cucumbers growing on the underside. Jimmy would run under the vines to eat the crickets gathered in the little shady place. Once, Melle dropped the vines on top of Jimmy. It took twenty minutes of struggling and furious pecking for him to get free. We were all sitting at the end of the row laughing at the sight of a crow's head slowly emerging from under the tangle of vines. Jimmy was angry, squawking in a loud, angry voice as he walked up the row. He did not take kindly to being made sport of. He walked around the four of us, giving voice to his grievance. Then he stopped in front of Melle, looked him over, and suddenly let go with a well-aimed peck. He had spotted a tear in Melle's coveralls and landed the sharp point of his beak on bare skin. Melle yelled out in pain as blood oozed from the broken skin. Jimmy moved into the centre of our little circle and greeted us with soft garrulous caws. He was happy. Justice had been served, his pride restored.

Jimmy realised early on that his family could not, or would not, fly. He accepted their plodding way of life. When he was with us he also walked, although he was not well adapted to this way of getting around. One hot summer day we were working in a beet field a long ways from the house. We had left Jimmy in the barn. Sitting at the end of a row we could see a distant black speck walking down the middle of the dusty lane. When Jimmy finally arrived, he was covered in dust, his tongue hanging out the side of his beak. He croaked a weary hello. We gave him a bowl of water and made a great fuss over his heroic trek.

On the way home Jimmy reverted to his usual mode of transport, riding on my left shoulder. I was Jimmy's favourite human. His next favourite was Melle. He was a bit more indifferent to George and Cecil. Heit was accepted as some kind of superior being of whom he was slightly wary. Our mother was an outright enemy.

Tipp was jealous of Jimmy. This pleased Jimmy, who strutted back and forth in front of the dog while uttering soft "I dare you" caws. Tipp was the only other animal that was with us all the time. Sometimes as Jimmy walked by, Tipp would raise his lip and bare his teeth in a silent snarl. We admired Tipp's restraint as he lay there in the sun tolerating this obnoxious bird, when what he really wanted to do was clamp his teeth around the arrogant little interloper. But Tipp knew that Jimmy was not to be harmed. Jimmy was the definition of mischief in the making. He always had a wicked gleam in his eye and possessed an almost devilish fondness for practical jokes, a quality I identified with. Poor Tipp was often the victim of Jimmy's jokes.

During the heat of the day Tipp would usually have a nap in a depression he had dug beside a lilac bush. He would turn himself in a complete circle several times and, once satisfied that this was the perfect place for a nap, lie down with his nose on his paws and his tail tucked against his back legs. For Jimmy this was the signal that his quarry was now vulnerable. Jimmy was a born risktaker and had his own sense of what was and was not sporting. He was also immensely patient. He would wait twenty minutes before he began his stalk. He would stalk his victim only on foot, not taking advantage of his powers of flight. He proceeded slowly and deliberately, one step at a time. He would stop, turn his head sideways, and carefully view his quarry before he took the next step. If Tipp stirred in his sleep, Jimmy would freeze and remain motionless for several minutes with his unblinking eye fixed on his objective: Tipp's nose. It took a half hour for Jimmy to get within striking distance. He would then raise his head with his beak held directly over Tipp's nose for much longer than needed, as if to savour the delicious next moment, and then let go with a harsh "caw!" as he drove his beak into his soft, unsuspecting target.

Tipp would wake up with a high-pitched, most un-dog-like howl as he leapt straight up off the ground. It looked like he had achieved powers of levitation. He would land and whirl around to punish his tormentor, but Jimmy would be gone. From the top of a nearby fencepost would come a series of quick, short caws. With murder in his eyes and teeth bared, Tipp would frantically leap at the fencepost but fall short of his goal by a few maddening inches. Jimmy would lean forward, uttering short insulting caws to taunt the dog. To Jimmy's delight, Tipp, blinded by his rage, would repeatedly leap at Jimmy before finally realising that his thirst for revenge and doggy justice was a hopeless cause.

Heit and we boys spent an hour and a half in the barn twice a day, every day, doing chores, early morning and late afternoon. Breakfast was at eight and supper at six. This daily rhythm never changed except on Sundays. Following an ironclad rule in the Dutch immigrant community, no one worked on "the Lord's Day," with an exception for the necessary milking the cows and feeding the animals. On Saturday, preparations were made for the sabbath. The gutters were cleaned, hay and other animal feed was laid out, the pig pens were mucked out and clean straw put down for them, and the milk cans and the separator were cleaned so that on the sabbath we would have only the bare minimum of work to do. The women would make similar preparations for minimal housework on the sabbath.

Jimmy was always in the barn as long as the men were there. He took notice of everything and let us know if anything was "amiss" – when a cow was in the wrong stall or a piglet had escaped the confines of the pigpen. When the sow had a litter of eight little piglets, Jimmy sat on the boards of the pigpen and stared at them. Several times a day the sow would lie on her side and grunt softly, a sound of total contentment alerting her piglets that it was dinnertime. Jimmy seemed fascinated by the sight of the eight tiny white piglets sucking away all in a row, and he never interfered with this touching ritual between mother and her little ones. Jimmy had lost some tail feathers to the sow. Just before the sow gave birth she charged this noisy intruder, and Jimmy missed being her breakfast by mere inches. Jimmy was so mesmerised by all the new activity in the pigpen that he didn't hold it against her.

When a sow was ready to give birth, someone would sit with her all night; sows never seemed to birth their babies during the day. The "midwife" would catch each piglet as it emerged, cut the umbilical cord, rub it dry with a piece of burlap, and place it on a teat for a drink of warm milk. The baby pig was then put in a straw-filled nest, where a 100-watt bulb kept the piglets warm. A litter was usually eight piglets, and it would take four to six hours for all to be born.

Our animals were integral to life on the farm. While milking a cow, I would snuggle my head into the furry hollow where the hind leg meets her stomach. It was a most cosy place to rest your head and listen to the musical thrumming of two streams of milk alternately hitting a pail full of milk. It was a place to be lulled into a dreamy kind of state where everything else fell away. It was just a boy and his cow, and a primal kind of contented warmth.

Entertainment was found in simple everyday things like milking a cow. You could bend the cow's long teat sideways and direct a stream of milk at a passing cat. You could train the cat to catch the stream of milk in its mouth. We would direct the stream of milk higher and higher so that soon the cat was teetering on its back legs to catch the milk. The trick was to then squeeze the teat hard so that the last of the stream was forceful enough to knock the cat over backwards. We would chuckle while the fallen cat got up and walked away. Cats were addicted to fresh, warm milk and quickly forgot their injured pride.

Jimmy liked warm fresh milk as well. Once, I directed some milk his way, and Jimmy realised he should open his beak. The next day, Jimmy jumped up on my knee, uttered a soft caw, and opened his beak. I aimed a stream of fresh warm milk into his open beak. When he was sated he left, a happy crow.

Several mornings later, when Heit was milking a big Holstein cow, Jimmy jumped up on his knee. He cawed and then opened his beak. Heit, thinking this was Jimmy's new "good morning," greeted him back with a proper "good morning." Jimmy would become quite put out if you ignored his morning greetings and could remind you to mind your manners with a sharp little peck. Heit kept milking and Jimmy again opened his beak and uttered more soft caws. This went on for several more rounds, until Jimmy leaned forward and pecked the cow on a hind teat. The cow gave a mighty kick, sending Heit and the pail of milk flying into the gutter. We walked into the barn with loud Frisian curses hanging in the air, just as Heit, drenched in milk and cow shit, scrambled up out of the gutter. For Jimmy, there was no mistaking Heit's state of mind. He wisely departed for safer environs. At the evening milking, I showed Heit Jimmy's new trick, but he was not impressed with such "dangerous nonsense."

One morning, Jimmy was sitting on his perch and woke up to a strange sight: a shiny bald pate right below his perch. This was a frightening apparition for a crow who normally woke up to see only a straw-covered barn floor seven feet below. His own private retreat had been invaded! Jimmy was not slow to react.

We had no bull, so the cows were serviced by a man from the artificial insemination service. He wanted to be addressed as the Lambton County Veterinarian and wore a badge to this effect. To us, he was the County Cow Fucker. He was a six-foot-five bully who did not like small boys. In return for his dislike, we would tell jokes about a cow's stolen love life.

As Heit greeted the "vet" and saw what was about to happen, he yelled, "Look out!" It was too late. Jimmy screeched as loud as all get-out and drove his beak down into the middle of the shiny dome. The vet turned white as death, his eyes bugged out, and uttered a strangled scream as he made a mighty leap in the wrong direction. His head hit a beam with a solid thump, and the county cow fucker crumpled like a felled ox. When he got up, his pants had a wet stain. He stormed out of the barn, forgetting all about why he came. We were delighted that this huge, overbearing bully met his Waterloo at the sharp "hand" of our little crow. Our hero of the day was presented with a dish of Jersey cream. The "vet" returned the next day, rigidly dignified and with a hat on his head, to perform his delicate mission while Heit did his grownup best to not let his smile show.

Jimmy was an unfailing watcher. He liked to sit high up in the maple tree beside the driveway, from where he missed nothing. Loud caws and an overflight greeted anyone, or anything, that came up the driveway.

Mrs. Kernohan, our schoolteacher, came to the house to register her unhappiness with "the boys." I had thrown a handful of chestnuts into the wood stove, which exploded with loud repeated bangs and lifted the stove lid in a series of satisfying clangs. Mrs. Kernohan thought I had broken a solemn vow made in front of the entire school a week earlier when I had been made to repeat, with my right hand on her bible, that I would never again throw twenty-two bullets into the stove. As she stepped out of her little red Morris Minor wearing a long dress, Jimmy dive-bombed her. She left without completing her mission. Our winged hero was rewarded with pilfered apple pie crust and admiring strokes to his head just the way he liked.

One day Jimmy's dive-bombing met with more serious disapproval. On a sunny Sunday afternoon after church, Vrouw Miedema came to visit Mem. She was a sturdy matron, a pillar of our Dutch Christian Reformed Church. She got halfway across the yard when Jimmy's wing hit her hat, sending it flying. A raucous caw reverberated in her left ear. She gave out a high-pitched squeal and stood stock-still, frozen in place, making squeaky hiccupping noises. An embarrassing dribble ran down her left leg into her shoe. Mem ran outside, took her arm, and guided her into the house. We were immediately ordered outside. It took some smelling salts and some softly uttered words of comfort for her to begin to talk. Her first words, "That black crow is the devil's beast." I locked Jimmy up in the barn, his early-warning duties done for the day.

Later I was told, in no uncertain terms, that it was my responsibility to prevent any more such sneak attacks by my wicked crow. If I did not, I would be punished for each and every such assault as if I had done it myself. The standard punishment for a grave wrongdoing was to go into the woodshed and select the piece of wood that would deliver the blows to your backside. This was a matter of some serious consideration. You did not want to pick a too-solid piece of wood, but you also did not want it to be too switchy. If I did not choose a piece of wood suitable for the purpose, Heit would do it himself. He would exercise no discretion at all, but just grab the piece of wood closest at hand.

Mem agreed to tell me when she expected womanly company so I could lock Jimmy up. She continued to walk with her umbrella to dissuade Jimmy from his ambushes. In our negotiations, however, she refused to change her method of removing "that bird" from the house, insisting on sweeping him outside with a broom. Thus, Mem and I agreed something of a truce on Jimmy's war on humans wearing skirts.

On Sunday mornings everyone would get dressed in their Sunday best and drive to church. We went to church twice every Sunday, once in the morning and again in the evening. The church, Dutch Reformed, was the centre of social as well as religious life. Everyone met their friends. This provided an opportunity for an exchange. One of the boys would often go home with a friend after the morning service and return to the family after the evening service. As new immigrants, we did not socialize with Canadians. The hundred thousand Dutch people who came to Canada after the war were nearly all farmers. They came to Canada to realise what for them had been an impossible dream: to own their own farm. They were a no-nonsense people dedicated to the hard work needed to achieve their dream. In Holland, being a farmer was a position of status. First off, you were now a landowner and as such commanded a place of respect in Dutch society. Secondly, landowners were well off economically. God favoured the farmer.

There was a sad irony buried in this dream. After a lifetime of backbreaking work, a life of not having much time for their family, a life of sacrificing so much in order to be a family of landowners, the immigrants learned that to have a farm in Canada was no big deal. It did not confer any status; it just made you another dirt farmer working a measly hundred acres. But this insight was still far off in the future. It was 1951. We all still lived the dream.

Coming home from church one Sunday morning, the family was greeted with a stony silence. Where were Jimmy's loud, "welcome home" caws? I immediately ran to the wooden cattle tank. Jimmy sometimes bathed in the cattle tank. He had been rescued from drowning once before.

I saw Jimmy floating in the water, face down, his wings spread out wide, an avian parody of the crucifixion. I jumped into the tank, held him upside down and squeezed him against my new Sunday suit coat. A dribble of water emerged from the beak. Tears rolled down my cheeks. I felt a big, black hole somewhere deep inside that tears would never fill.

I buried Jimmy in the orchard under the old, bent-over apple tree. He had chosen its hollow trunk as his last secret hiding place. All of Jimmy's trinkets were placed around him in the little grave. A boy's tears sanctified Jimmy and his treasures. He was then covered with clean black earth while my body quivered with the rapture of sorrow and grief, anger and betrayal. Jimmy had died while I was in church singing praises to God. It is written that "not a sparrow will fall to the ground, but that God wills it" (Mathew 10:29). This same God had then willed Jimmy to die alone and abandoned. This cold betrayal seeped into the marrow of my still-growing bones.

Jimmy's untimely death set me on a path of no longer unthinkingly accepting all I was taught, and I eventually left the church. To my mind God had killed my crow while I was in church singing His praises. It was impossible to worship the God who had committed this unpardonable betrayal. Rather than believing in the omnipotent God of the bible, who is said to notice every sparrow who falls to the ground, I began to see the church and its doctrines as fallible human constructs. This new way of seeing God was a balm for my wounded soul and eased the sense of betrayal. Jimmy lived on in the minds of those who knew him, and now he lives on in this story.

Number Four: Driving to Eternity

My interest in, and close involvement with, cars has been a recurring feature my entire life. At age twelve, I tried to jump onto the running board of our moving family car, a 1938 Plymouth. This was a very heavy car. I miscalculated, and slid under it. A wheel drove over my legs, pushing gravel into and then under my skin. We removed bits of gravel from my calves with needle-nose pliers and the sharp point of a jackknife. On this occasion, Heit did not back up to run over me a second time.

In 1955, Melle had a summer job working on a tobacco farm east of Simcoe. Summer holidays meant no school and, now, the exciting possibility of working somewhere besides on our own farm. It was transplanting time, taking the little tobacco plants from the green house and planting them in the fields. Extra help was needed. On a Sunday evening after church, everyone headed for home. Brother Melle and I went the other way, driving to the Polish tobacco farm. Melle was sixteen so he could legally drive the clunky 1938 Dodge car. Approaching the crest of a long hill coming into Jarvis the headlights went dark, so Melle pulled off the road and then hitchhiked into town to fetch a mechanic to fix the lights. I was left with the disabled car.

Within a few minutes three older guys from our church, driving a 1932 Ford coupe with a flathead V8, stopped. “What’s the problem?” “The lights quit and Melle is on his way to Jarvis to get a mechanic.” “Just drive your car to town, we’ll drive ahead, you can follow our taillights. It’s less than two miles, just stay close behind us.” We were farm kids, so we all knew how to drive.

I started the car and pulled out to drive behind them. But they stepped on it, and the peppy V8 Ford disappeared over the top of the hill. I kept on driving thinking that when I crested the hill, I would see their taillights. Suddenly, there was a car coming over the crest of the hill. A set of headlights coming straight at me at fifty miles an hour. To avoid a head-on collision, I cranked the steering wheel and hit the gas. The other car, a 1951 Studebaker, hit my car with a glancing blow just back of the driver’s door, making a terrible crunching noise. The collision spun my car into the ditch. I sat clutching the steering wheel, dazed by the violence of the collision. An angry man came charging out of the Studebaker and yelled "Where did you get your driver's licence? Out of a corn flakes box?" I replied in a squeaky frightened voice, "I don't have one." He yelled, "don't get smart with me young punk." He went back to his wife sitting in the Studebaker. She was crying. I was sick with anxiety and fear of what Heit would do.

A police car showed up. I sat in the back seat of the police cruiser, not yet knowing that this is an ominous place for a young man to be. The cop asked for my driver's licence. "I don't have one, I'm only fifteen." He took off his hat, hit the seat with it and, with a big sigh, jammed it back onto his head and carried on. No one was seriously injured. I had a sore thumb. Had it been a head-on crash it could have been fatal, possibly for all three of us. Dad had to pay out $500 to have the Studebaker repaired, and he had to buy another car for Melle so that he could get to work. The very plain 1938 Dodge was replaced by a classy, low-mileage, 1936 Chrysler with roll-up rear window shades and a cut-glass vase for flowers, purchased from a widow in town for $200. When dad was outa sight, I grinned and shook Melle's hand. He shook his head and sighed.

Weeks later I went to court. Mem said, "now you will answer to a judge for your sins." Both Dad and Mom came along, the three of us dressed in our Sunday best. I shed some real tears for the woman judge, who decided I had been punished enough. No fines, no talk about what I feared most: not allowing me a driver's licence when I turned sixteen. In 1955 getting one's driver's licence was the rite of passage for teenage boys. Nothing mattered more. On April 22,1956, my sixteenth birthday, I got my driver's licence and joined the world of men. All's well that ends well!

Number Five: Hot Rod Lincoln

It was the fifties, and the car was King. At age nineteen, my 1949 Ford was my pride and joy. I worked as an apprentice mechanic and so had the use of a fully equipped shop to "soup up" my car. The '49 flathead V8 Ford ended up with overdrive, dual carburetors and shaved heads. It had white wall tires, black moon hubcaps, the chrome taken off, holes filled, and painted flat black to make it look menacing. I was proud to claim the fastest car east of Simcoe and willing to take on all comers to defend an unofficial title. The Car was King, and I was in the driver's seat. Charlie Ryan's hit song "Hot Rod Lincoln" was blaring from the radio.

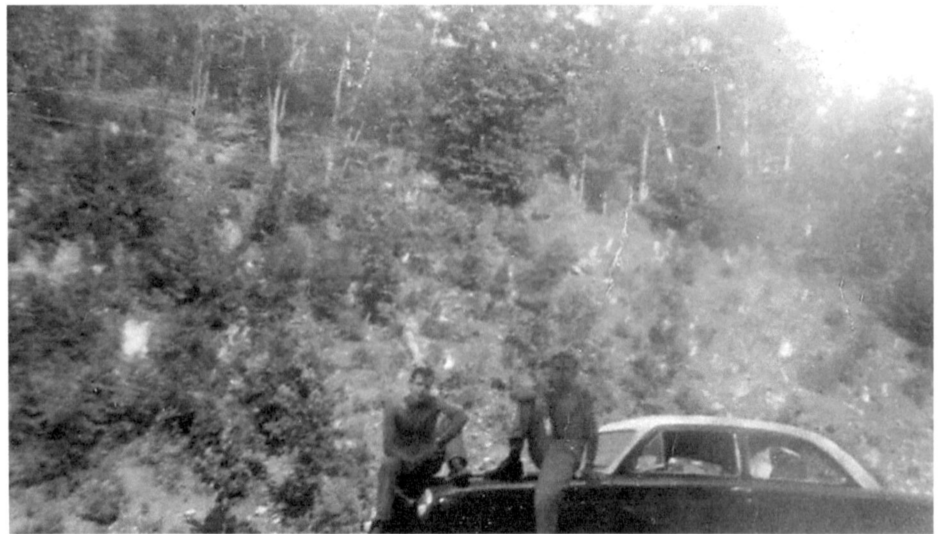

John and Cecil with the 1949 Ford

Bart, the owner of the shop, asked me to drive his very pregnant wife to her sister's house in Watford. He said, "drive slow!" "Will do." I drove the speed limit, safely dropped Anneke off at her sisters' and proceeded to drive back. I was driving due east on a dead-straight gravel road at seventy miles an hour. The early morning sun was on the windshield. I did not see the stop sign for Cockshut Road until it was too late. I hit the brakes and as the car skidded into the intersection. I saw a five-ton truck barreling down on me. The last thing I remember is stomping the gas pedal to the floor and feeling the Ford surge ahead. The truck, heavily loaded with green peas, hit the car just behind the driver's door at seventy miles an hour. The car spun like a top and went airborne. There was a little country church on a corner of the intersection. The front end of the car ended up propped on a tombstone. The front wheels were three feet off the ground, still spinning. The lid of the trunk ended up on the church steps. The incredible force of the collision took off both rear wheels leaving the wheel nuts still attached to the hub. We later marvelled at the oversized holes in the steel rims and that the tires were still inflated. The truck lost its front axle and skidded along on its frame rails until it was stopped by a bridge abutment.

Four farm boys, working in a sugar beet field close by, came running to see the accident. After looking everywhere, they were completely mystified. There was no driver to be found for the car, although the truck driver insisted there had been one. They sat down for a smoke when someone noticed blood dripping from under the left front fender. Someone put a hand up into the wheel well and felt a body laying on top of the front tire. They took off the wheel, pulled me out and laid me on the grass. A few minutes later a car stopped. It was a priest. He took one look at me, put on his priestly robes, and proceeded to administer last rites. Just as he had me at the pearly gates, another car stopped. It was a doctor. He took one look and immediately loaded me into the back seat of his car, a brand-new 1959 Buick. He had one of the farm boys sit in the back to prevent me from rolling off the seat. I came to and knew right away I was in a car moving really fast. The kind of floaty feeling that you experienced in cars going at a very high speed was the giveaway. The doctor was heading for the Simcoe hospital, hell bent for leather. I looked up to see one of the boys from church and said, "Hello Ralph." His mouth fell open in disbelief. He had not recognized me or my car. We hit a bump, and I passed out.

At the Simcoe hospital they patched me up. Both ears were attached by only a bit of skin. There is just enough room for a head to go into the wheel well of a 1949 Ford if you are perfectly centred, but there is no room for the ears. So they were pretty much torn off. The acid from a busted-up battery had dripped onto my badly abraded right arm, eating into the flesh. This was the worst injury. It took half a year for the skin to begin to grow back. There were no internal injuries and not a single broken bone. Within a few days I felt quite OK, what with a flirtatious young nurse looking after me. On the second morning she asked me if I had had a bowel movement. I had no idea what she was talking about and asked her to explain. Her face flushed with embarrassment, left and came back with an older nurse who abruptly said, “did you shit today?” I was so offended at such a personal question, and besides, it was none of her business. My reply was an outraged “No!” That evening, the pretty young nurse had medicine for me. I asked, “what is this?” “It’s a laxative.” I did know what “laxative” meant and, after she left, flushed it down the toilet. For the next three days I was asked, “did you have a bowel movement?” and then later flushed the pink mixture delivered in a small paper cup. Every day I asked to go home, and every day she said, “no, not yet.”

My friend Jack Kramer came to visit me. First thing I told him: “I wanna go home but they won’t let me leave. You gotta get me outa here.” Jack says, “OK get your clothes” – “they took my clothes!” Jack went to the Sally Anne store and came back with a garish Hawaiian shirt and a pair of jeans, no socks. I got dressed and lay in bed under the covers. As soon as the coast was clear I escaped in bare feet. Jack had a real prize waiting for me. He was driving a 1949 Mercury convertible with an oversized V8 Oldsmobile engine under the hood and twin straight pipes. It was painted flat back. The Merc was a mean machine. It topped out at over 120 mph, enough to move the speedometer needle off the scale. Wow! Never saw anything like it. With two straight pipes blaring, we sounded like we belonged on the Indy racetrack. Jack had gotten the car from a kid who was afraid to drive it because the brakes didn’t work so well at stopping that V8 engine. Later, we worked endlessly to improve the brakes and got them to where they worked pretty good even at 120 mph. It was a perfect and timely, made to order, replacement for the ’49 Ford.

When we got to Jarvis it was my turn to drive. I got behind the wheel, and it was pedal to the metal. The road was straight and clear, we were coming up fast on a car ahead of us. We passed with straight pipes blaring at well over 100 mph. One quick glance told me that the green 1955 Plymouth we were passing was my dad's car. Both my dad and my mom, who is stone deaf, near had a heart attack.

When we got to our house, Jack raced off with the incriminating Merc! I dove under the cover with my clothes on, hoping they did not see it was me driving the beast. A few minutes later Heit stormed into my room with his boots on. He was angry. He ripped back the cover and said, "Du jonge verekeling" (severe disapproval in Fries). You are turning your mother's hair white. My dad was completely bald, so I figured he was OK. I was brought downstairs for a serious talking to. Dad was plain angry, my mother adding biblical texts to illustrate the seriousness of his points. It was all about honouring your parents, "the fifth commandment, honour thy father and mother all the days of your life." This is the only commandment with a reward. If you do this, you will live a long life and then go to Heaven. I could not see how my driving had anything to do with honouring or dishonouring my parents. I wasn't even sure I wanted to be in Heaven and sing praises to God all day, every day. I wisely kept my mouth shut about all that. The hospital had called three times. "Where is John? Did he have a bowel movement?" My immigrant father had no idea what a "bowel movement" was. I explained and Dad phoned the hospital and told them that I was home, I was fine and "Ja myne jonge Jon, hé shit every day." The hospital agreed that I could stay home. I expect that they were glad to be rid of me. I never again had a car that fostered the same sense of pride as my '49 Ford. My very own hot rod Lincoln.

Number Six: Ballad of a Broken Heart

Having lost my first love, my '49 Ford, I was reduced to pedalling a demeaning bicycle. It was a Sunday afternoon. With my brother Cecil chasing me, I madly pedalled onto the road directly in front of a water truck going 50 miles an hour. The front bumper fractured my skull. My mother rode in the ambulance with a blanket folded over five times under my head. By the time we reached the Hamilton hospital the blood had soaked through the folded blanket. Her Sunday dress was soaked in blood. Ten hours later, after multiple blood transfusions, I woke up with my head swathed in bandages. I had survived a fractured skull and had lost copious amounts of blood. I was feeling a bit groggy, but other than that I felt quite OK and ready for whatever came next. What happened next was unlike anything that had ever happened to me.

We were a Dutch immigrant community in Ontario. Our lives revolved around the church. We spoke a mixture of Frisian, Dutch and English and did not socialise with Canadians. This was a Dutch enclave that maintained old country values and beliefs. It was a community with a clearly defined sense of right and wrong.

One Sunday in April, a new girl appeared at church. She had just come from Friesland on her own to live with her uncle and auntie. There was a buzz of excitement in the churchyard after the morning service. She was liquid motion with a river of raven-black hair that fell to her hips. Her body swayed as she walked. She did not look anything like the demure blond Dutch girls of our church. She was exotic and unencumbered. The young men flocked to her like bees to an open honeypot. With a ready laugh and some pointed comments, she easily warded off their eager attention. I was instantly enamoured.

Maaike was the scandalous outcome of a Frisian farm girl sneaking out her bedroom window at night to dance around the fire at a Gypsy encampment close by. In a few weeks, the Gypsies had packed up and moved on. On the same day the German army invaded Holland, this free-spirited Frisian farm girl realised she was pregnant. Her parents raised the baby girl as their own. This was kept a closely guarded secret. The grandparents were afraid the German occupiers would take her away if they knew she was a Gypsy child. The exonerated new mom married a local farmer.

On my third day in the hospital, some time in the afternoon, Maaike walked in the door. My unbelieving eyes rendered me speechless. She sat on the bed, held my hand, and gently stroked my face. There were tears in her large, dark, luminous eyes. As she left, she leaned over to kiss me. The image of those mysterious eyes softened by tears lingered on. I left the Hamilton hospital believing that the water truck, coming down Stone Church Road at just the right time, was a gift from God.

Maaike and I were inseparable for the next heady nine months. The sun, the moon, the stars revolved around her. During a workday I had only to think of her and it was like she was there at my side. Every detail of her face, her deep dark eyes, her soft, sensuous lips. It was pure magic. I could think of nothing else. Nothing else compared. Nothing else mattered.

Our coming together fanned the rebel flame that smouldered in both our hearts. We scandalised our Dutch reformed community with our devil-may-care attitude and flagrant disregard for the community's prohibitions. We wanted to enjoy the alluring pleasures of that other, Canadian, society. We went to downtown movie theatres that showed the forbidden fruits emanating from Hollywood's tents of wickedness. We went to the drive-in theatre, a passion pit for Canadian youth who would pay admission and then pray for fog or rain so they wouldn't even have to pretend to watch the movie. The enormous fifties cars, with back seats like unto a living room couch, gently rocked to an unseen movie soundtrack. We went to stock car races and demolition derbies where profane and blasphemous language hung in the air like gasoline fumes. We went skinny dipping at the local stone quarry and embarrassed ourselves when caught out in a private moment. We drove to Buffalo to see a live cabaret where skimpily dressed women performed funny and blatantly sexual skits. During church service, we sat in the very back row of seats in the balcony where we drowned out the minister's sermon with long, lingering kisses. The open flame of rebellion was a problem for our tight-knit community. We were a dangerous example for their young people. Time and again we were warned that our reckless and wayward ways would lead us to perdition.

One Sunday evening the dominee (minister) invited us to his house. He had prepared for us by laying out on the floor a weeks' worth of two-page movie ads in *The Hamilton Spectator*. He began by telling us that the church does not condemn all movies but when you look at the overall picture, laying here at your feet, what do you see? Mostly lurid advertising, ungodly violence, lascivious freedom, and adultery! There is nothing of value for the spirit here. The love you have for each other is from God and it is to be cherished and conducted according to his wishes. Maaike sat straight up. "Our love is our own miracle; our love knows no boundaries. We are free in ourselves to do as we wish." The minister's wife gasped. She trembled as she blurted out, "it's all true, everything we have heard and more, she is a Gypsy harlot leading our boys astray." The dominee uttered a long, deep sigh. As we left, I said to the dominee "we hope that your sigh is for your good wife." Maaike giggled.

The tensions created in the community infiltrated our relationship. After another argument about rumours, half-truths, and innuendoes, Maaike up and left me. Shortly thereafter, she went back to Friesland. My heart cracked in two. A crushed nineteen-year-old discovered his sense of invincibility could evaporate like the early morning dew. I learned that my emotional self, something largely ignored in our stoic Frisian culture, could take me down in a way that nothing else could. With Maaike leaving me, I felt that I had indeed fallen into something far worse than perdition. I survived the loss of my first love, but I never again experienced the magic and innocence of being totally and irrevocably lost in love.

Maaike in1959

Number Seven: Dangerous Motorcycle Fantasies

In the spring of 1960, for the first time in our lives, my brothers and I had our own money. In our immigrant community, whatever money anyone earned was all put in the family pot. It was the family, not our own personal 'self-serving' needs, that mattered. Over time Canadian norms slowly infiltrated our immigrant community and, by the time I was twenty, the practice was being questioned enough that Mem and Heit decided to let it go – despite their faith that young people would spend money foolishly if they had it. With our own money to spend as we wished, my younger brother Cecil and I immediately proved them right. We bought two used police bikes, Harley Davidsons with 74-cubic-inch engines. These were the biggest, baddest, and loudest motorcycles made. Needless to say, for young men brimming with testosterone, the Harleys were the perfect expression of a dangerously rebellious youth. On Sunday mornings, dressed in our Sunday best, we would wheel into the churchyard and expertly lock the back wheel brake to slide sideways and come to a stop in a cloud of dust, the bikes neatly parked, side by side, facing the church steps. The combination of big powerful motorcycles and youthful bravado spelled trouble. But our luck held, and it was only luck that got us through this three-year motorcycle phase alive and in one piece.

On a sunny Sunday afternoon, we were driving the road that runs along the Escarpment in Hamilton. It's a curvy road with a hundred-foot drop-off along one side. We came around a downhill bend that was nicely banked. Made to take at a high speed, made to lean into until the footpad kissed the pavement. With my body almost parallel to the road, the front wheel hit a small patch of oil and instantly the bike was skidding on its side with a stream of sparks coming from where the crash bar met the pavement. At this point you have no control of where this is going. With my left leg held tight up against the engine, the crash bar kept it off the pavement. You only had to hang on until the bike came to a stop. I had been here before.

The bike headed across the road straight for the edge of the escarpment. It was a hundred-foot vertical drop. Incredibly, the front wheel hit one of the wooden posts and bounced the bike back onto the road. There was one post every thirty feet. These wooden posts had two cables strung between them to stop a car from going over the edge. Had the bike not hit the post it would have skidded under the lower cable. This would have seriously damaged, or beheaded, the rider before he continued hurtling over the drop to the rocks below. We picked up the Harley, no damage other than a more-scraped-up crash bar. Cecil said, "you are some lucky. If you hadn't hit the post your bike woulda been a total wreck." That was more or less the depth of my response as well.

Me and Jack Kramer with our Harleys in 1960

We were young men, we were invincible. We would pass on the yellow centre line regardless of what was coming towards us. A vehicle coming the other way always moved over a bit. A few times when driving the yellow line between two vehicles both going 50 mph in opposite directions, I had a brief flash of "I'm going to die here." However, in mere seconds the cars were gone, and the sense of invincibility was back stronger than ever, bolstered by escaping another close call. This is why they send nineteen-year-old boys to war. Much later in life, I toured the battlefields of WWI with my friend Joyce. There were so many cemeteries, each with row upon row of white crosses, each bearing the rank and name of a Canadian soldier. Almost all the names were those of boys of 18, 19 or 20 years of age. Had I been of age at that time I too would have eagerly joined up, believing that my sense of invincibility would keep me safe. It is a time of life when youthful delusions rule the day.

Heit and Mem in Hamilton, circa 1962

Left to Right: George, Melle, John and Cecil circa 1960

A Wandering Life

Number Eight: Homeland is No Longer Home

By 1962 working on cars had lost its magic. After finishing a five-year apprenticeship, I had my Class A Mechanics licence and wanted to get away from garages. I sold the Harley, then Jack Kramer and I made our way to Friesland. We took a passenger ship, the cheapest way, from New York to Rotterdam. Once back on land we immediately bought a car, a 1948 Renault with the engine in the rear, for 185 Canadian dollars. The car had to be hand-cranked to start the engine, like our Farmall tractor. Life without a car was unthinkable for Canadian farm boys.

Jack and I stayed with relatives. They were delighted to have us and grateful to have helping hands with the farm work. We drove the little Renault like it was the '49 Ford, flying down the narrow little brick roads at speeds the locals had not seen since the wild Canadian soldiers had driven their jeeps full out, pedal to the metal. Eventually we skidded into a ditch. The car ended up partially submerged, on its roof. We crawled out covered in green duck weed. A stern, disapproving Frisian farmer pulled the upside car out with his horse. We flipped the Renault back on its wheels, borrowed a large hammer from the farmer, bashed the caved-in roof back into its original shape, (there was no headliner) dried the ignition, straightened a tie rod and we were back on the road. After two months, Jack went back to Canada. He missed hamburgers. Reason enough to go.

I set out to see Europe the only way I knew how – in a car. For the next several months I was on a European road trip. I almost lost the Renault going over the Brenner Pass. The car had no heater but my camp stove, sitting on the passenger side floor burning merrily away, kept the car toasty warm until I braked hard. The stove fell over, fuel spilled, and the inside of the car was flames from floor to ceiling. I leaped out, placed a rock behind the rear wheel, and shovelled in armload after armload of snow. The fire went out but not before the passenger seat was completely burned. Hitchhikers sat on a raggedy piece of carpet covering bare springs.

In northern Italy, with no warning, the brakes on the Renault gave out part way down a long, steep hill. I careened around a corner on two wheels, still picking up speed. I barely missed a farm wagon pulled by two horses. The car, hurtling down the hill, felt ready to become airborne when in sheer desperation I steered towards a small lake in an open field on the left. The car crashed through a fence, flew across a shallow ditch, and slowed as it encountered the boggy ground before the lake. It came to a stop in about two feet of water. The same farmer I had just flown by at an insane speed, stopped. He swore in Italian and with expansive gestures and whooshing sounds re-enacted my wild ride through the fence and into the water. It was a performance worthy of the best Italian theatre. We laughed and clapped each other on the back like old drinking buddies. “Bravo chauffeur” he kept saying. We pulled the car back onto the road with his horses and to his house not far off. We went back and fixed the fence, and I spent the rest of the day drying out the ignition and kinda got the brakes working (I travelled with a set of tools). After a simple supper of pasta I slept in his haymow, the sleep of the saved.

The next morning I set off, constantly checking the so-so brakes. I came down the Brenner Pass in first gear, driving slow, with an eye out for places to ditch a runaway car. I found a master cylinder at a wrecker, and after a bit of fiddling with it, the Renault once again stopped on a dime. In Berlin I stayed in a camping site up against the new wall with its barbed wire and guard towers, all there to keep people from leaving. To me it was more Nazi military forcing people to do their bidding, just with a different name. In 1962 it seemed the Nazis had changed their name to Communists.

Back in Friesland I sold the Renault for what we paid for it and boarded a Holland America ship going to Quebec City. I hitchhiked home to Hamilton. I had seen life in Friesland where young men did not have their own cars and stayed home on the farm. Both Jack and I were seen as wildly irredeemable Canadian boys. My uncle said, “Jonge alst du jiere blujt, wie mytsje dye mak” (if you stay here, we will tame you). Even though I loved speaking our own language, the price of staying was too high.

What made a lasting impression were the WWI battlefields at Verdun. I found 303-size cartridges and a helmet with a bullet hole in it. This brought tears to my eyes. 45 years after the fact, the horror of this place was still palpable. I stayed two days to wander at will through partially collapsed trenches and the craters left by exploding bombs. I could feel what had taken place in this mangled landscape. The land had not recovered from the most sustained and severe artillery bombardment the world has ever seen. The suffering of the men who fought and died here was real. It was a haunted place.

The Dolomite Mountains, in north Italy, changed my perception of the earth. I was overwhelmed and awestruck in the face of the great limestone crags and cliffs. In my Calvinist upbringing a sense of awe was reserved for God. I was seeing another version of God. Today the word “awe,” to stand in awe of, has been reduced. The most trivial experience is now described as awesome: “an awesome hairdo.” This is how language changes. Our digital age has flattened the human sense of wonder.

The Renault

Portrait at age 23

Mexico – Travels with my Brother

Coming back home and working for four months at the garage only made me more restless. In the dead of the Ontario winter my older brother George and I set off for Mexico. George and I travelled the length and breadth of Mexico in his blue 1958 VW Beetle. We camped out the entire time, in deserts, on beaches, in pine forests, in bug-infested jungles, and at times, we were invited to stay in someone's house, or hacienda or upscale hotel. Lady Luck rode with us in Mexico. When we camped, it would often be in empty desert, miles from the nearest dwelling. People would appear out of nowhere, sit at some distance, and watch us as we cooked and ate our food. George sometimes felt afraid of these diminutive simple peasants dressed in traditional wide white pants, loose, all-white shirts, tire-tread huaraches and a straw sombrero along with the ubiquitous machete. Hence, we bought a pistol. We eventually realised that they were only waiting for our discarded tin cans. This was true third-world rural Mexico. It was well before the freeways and maquiladoras of today's much more prosperous country.

Eventually we made it to Taxco, the fabled silver city high in the mountains of Guerrero. For hundreds of years fabulous amounts of silver from Taxco were loaded onto galleons and sent to Spain. Much of this silver never arrived in Spanish coffers. It was taken, on the high seas, by the Dutch Privateers celebrated in song to this day (Piet Hein en de Zilveren Floot). The stolen silver from Taxco helped pay for Holland's eighty-year war of independence from Spain, the long costly war that bankrupted Spain. A fine example of poetic justice. George told stories of the heroic Piet Hein. I longed to have lived in this age of heroes, and we did our bit to commemorate those times. We improvised a small ceremony of gratitude for Taxco. This involved burning a sheet of paper and some sage in a brown Mexican sun-baked bowl. On the paper, a hand drawn flag of Spain in red and yellow with "Piet Hein" in black letters across the page. We held our ceremony on the central plaza with the majestic baroque cathedral looking on. A curious American tourist asked, "what are you doing?" George explained. We got only confused looks. They didn't get it.

Some of the fabulous wealth stayed in Mexico and paid for an exquisite seventeenth-century town with steep cobblestone streets and an immense stone cathedral with two towering spires. Twin spires on a cathedral were a sign of wealth. Churches with twin spires were designated cathedrals and as such paid an annual tax to Rome; churches with one spire were not cathedrals and thus were not required to pay the tax. As the silver mines played out, Taxco was forgotten by the world. Two hundred years later, in the 1930s, Taxco was rediscovered by William Spratling, an American scholar, adventurer, and entrepreneur. He began making silver jewellery to sell in New York City. He set up a silver shop hiring local apprentices, and Taxco's silver industry was born. By the time we arrived, Taxco was fabled for its exquisite silver work and Spratling, called Don Guiermo by locals, was the centre of quite a scene.

We got connected with Spratling through some American travellers we had met in Mexico City, and for several weeks we were guests at his eccentric country house/museum. Spratling regaled us with stories of barnstorming in the twenties, wing-walking on the canvas-covered wings of biplanes at county fairs. There was competition between the wing-walking daredevils for a beautiful young woman named Anne Morrow. Spratling's best friend, Charles Lindberg, won her over in the end. Spratling told us, "she chose for fame." He left the USA with a broken heart and a hankering to just disappear but instead became the famous, beloved knight in shining armour for the people of Taxco. Spratling put their town back on the map.

Sitting on his porch and drinking the finest American bourbon was a daily morning ritual that often went on into the afternoon and evening. On finishing a drink Spratling would throw the empty glass over his shoulder into the swimming pool. We followed suit. Spratling would yell, "Tonio!" A young Mexican kid would appear carrying three more glasses of fine Yankee bourbon with a shot of ginger ale. The pool, covered in green algae, was home to a pair of ducks that had learned to dodge flying glass missiles. This was Spratling's statement on social conventions. The gesture earned him my admiration and respect. Brothers in shared rebel values.

Etched negative from 1963, commemorating our travels

Number Nine: Murder Most Foul

The state of Guerrero had a reputation for wild, unknown mountainous hinterlands that were reputedly a haven for bandits and anti-government rebels. It was hard to travel these remote areas with few roads and no maps. On our arrival in Taxco, the fabled silver city of Mexico, we stopped in a small bar. Mexican men were always ready to share a drink with a stranger, which is how we met Alejandro and his sidekick, Pancho. We started to talk, using our stumbling mixture of rudimentary Spanish (ours) and English (theirs). Alejandro was a hefty guy with a loud voice and thick hairy wrists. Pancho was a little guy with a baby face, bulging eyes and skinny bow legs. His fingers continually fidgeted, as if he were squishing unwanted insects. Alejandro was obviously the dominant macho man of the duo. This duo – a dominant man and a subservient sidekick – was a holdover from Cervantes' example of Don Quixote and Sancho. It is a universal theme that a strong macho man needs someone to blame, to bully – to reinforce his self-imposed view of being a superior man.

After hearing about our desire to see the hinterlands of Guerrero, Alejandro said, “No problema, I will be your guide.” We could go to his village, deep in the hills of Guerrero, and even farther, if we wished. Since there were no maps of the intricate mesh of Guerrero’s back roads, Alejandro was our Godsend. His village, he informed us, was a two-day drive in our “fine little car.” One more beer, and we set off. There were four of us: George was driving, with me in the front; Alejandro and Pancho in the back.

Our way out of town was up a long, steep cobblestone street that led to the mirador, a lookout with a great view of Taxco. Part of the way up, we stopped at a small tienda for beers to take along. The old woman behind the counter greeted Alejandro like a lost brother. As they talked, the old woman would occasionally giggle with delight. It seems that our guide was a bit of a comedian.

As we got back in the car George (speaking Frisian, so we could not be overheard) turned and told me that he had overheard Alejandro talking to the old crone at the store. George spoke Spanish better than myself. “I want a case of beer and some tequila, but I don’t have money,” George heard Alejandro say. “I’m taking the gringos to my village, but before the village, the gringos will disappear down the warm throat of the caldera. When I come back, in my fine little car, I’ll pay you double.” The old woman cackled like Macbeth’s witches and said, “take a whole barrel of beer. If you need help, my sons are close by.” He was just finishing telling me this when Alejandro and Sancho got back in the car.

“What to do?” asked George, still speaking Frisian. “We need to get them out of our car!” I replied, “when we stop at the mirador, get them out first and then hit the gas.” “Hey, what are you guys saying?” asked a suddenly suspicious Alejandro. “Nothing, nothing, just sharing a childhood joke.” He seemed satisfied. We pulled over at the mirador. From the edge of the lookout we would see Taxco and all of its surroundings. “Come on, come, you both have to get out to admire this view,” insisted Alejandro. Pancho wasn’t moving. Our plan wouldn’t work. Pancho stayed in the car and George took the keys out of the ignition as he got out. We walked to the edge of the lookout. Taxco and its environs lay at our feet: an intact, seventeenth-century city built on a steep hillside with an enormous baroque cathedral at its centre. We were looking 300 hundred years back in time. We all stayed well back from the cliff's edge. It seemed like our sense of distrust had infiltrated our macho friend's mind.

Alejandro stayed close to me as we walked back toward the car, talking all the time about how friendly and hospitable the people of Guerrero were. The folks in his village would all welcome us with open arms. Pancho started to get out of the car. Alejandro yelled at him, "quedate!" As we walked, I opened my jackknife (a long-bladed German-made Herder knife) while it was still in my pocket, and held the blade in my hand so that only the first few inches extended beyond my clenched fist. In De Westerein, Frisian men would fight with knives held this way. The object of a knife fight was to be the first to draw blood, not to kill the other guy.

As we approached the car, I turned and hit Alejandro hard in his ample stomach with my right hand. Pulling back my arm, I shifted the knife so that Alejandro saw the entire seven-inch blade, red with his blood, in my hand. Alejandro deflated like a punctured balloon. He fell in the dirt crying, "Mi Madre, Mi Maria." When he saw what had happened to his general, Pancho scrambled out of the VW and ran away into the bush as fast as his skinny legs could carry him.

We got in the car, stepped on the gas and took off. Halfway back down to Taxco, we met a police car with its red light flashing and siren blaring. They were coming to our rescue. We had been seen leaving town with Alejandro and Pancho. The police knew them as "hombres muy malos." They figured that we were on our way to be disappeared. When I showed the policeman how we got away, he said, "Stupido! Next time, use the whole blade. This is Mexico!"

From right to left: John, George, unknown (in front), unknown (in back), Alejandro (white shirt) and an unknown bartender.

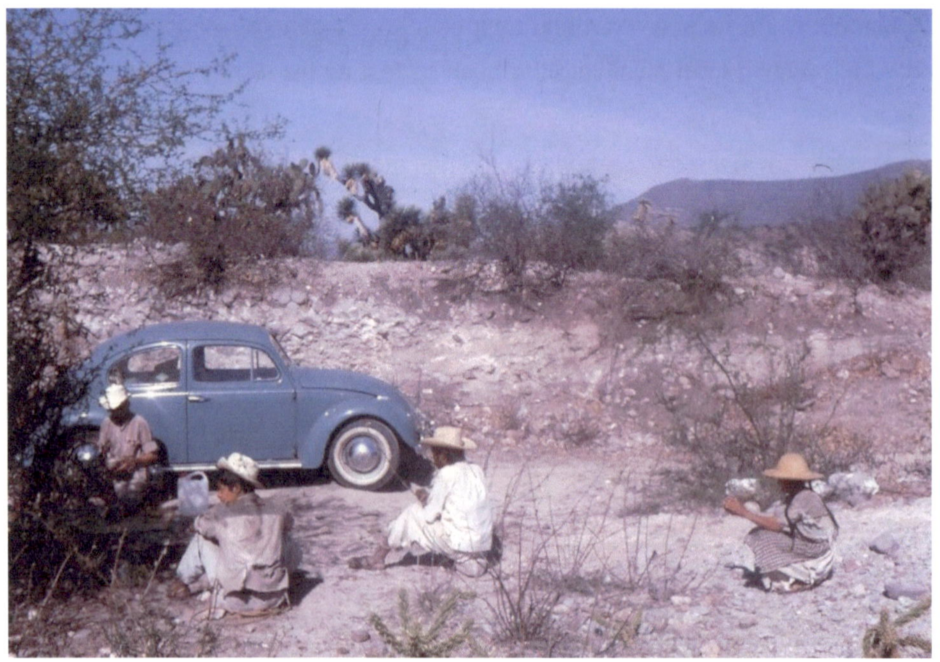

Camping with the Volkswagen in Mexico, with visitor waiting to collect tin cans.

A Wider Wilder World

The impoverished Mexico of 1963 was a real third-world country, poor, hospitable, and full of surprises. We made our way south to Oaxaca, then continued farther south to Tehuantepec, the fabled matriarchy of Mexico famous for its beautiful women. Stately women dressed in brightly coloured dresses ran the stores and market stalls. The men were shy and smaller than their women. We could easily imagine the statuesque women lording it over their diminutive husbands, who drove the donkeys and carried the market produce. A steep winding road eventually got us onto the highlands of Chiapas and to San Cristobal de Las Casas. This was Mexico's southernmost outpost where the five native tribes of the region still wore their traditional clothing. We made camp in one of the old-growth pine forests that flourish at 9000 feet elevation. We slept in hammocks we had bought from men in prison. Every town had a jail, and men would commonly sell things they had made through the bars to any passersby. The blessed cool temperatures and pine forests were a welcome respite from the blistering heat of Tehuantepec.

We spent three weeks in San Cristobal. During our explorations, we found Casa Na Bolom (the House of the Jaguar) This was the home of Gertrude Blom, a famous Swiss journalist, writer, and anthropologist. As a young woman she had travelled to the Lacandon Maya, who lived in remote jungle villages close to the Guatemalan border. Documenting their vanishing way of life and fighting the deforestation of their jungle homelands became her life work. Her house was a museum of Mayan artefacts and old black-and-white photos. Her husband Frans Blom, a Danish explorer who had found the Mayan ruin of Bonampak, had died the year before. George and I stayed at Casa Na Bolom for two days. In the evenings we listened, over dinner, to Gertrude's stories of the mysterious Lacandon Maya. They were a tribe living deep in the jungle who were intimately familiar with the intricacies of the natural world but had retained the ancient Mayan knowledge of advanced mathematics and astronomy. They knew of a portal, hidden in the jungles of Yucatan, to a mysterious spiritual realm that rules all. We asked for directions to the portal, but Gertrude warned that anyone looking for the portal who wasn't Mayan, not initiated, would be killed in the old, sacrificial way of cutting the beating heart out of their living body. This was enough to discourage our search for otherworldly portals.

Gertrude talked of finding the Mayan city of Bonampak, lost to the world for over a thousand years. They had cut their way through with machetes and squeezed into an enormous room in an overgrown temple, the first people in centuries to see the most vivid, colourful native murals in all Mexico. The murals covered the walls from floor to ceiling. It was an intimate window into the royal life of the last rulers of this Mayan city. Gertrude made us see how small our view was of what life can be. She talked of the provincialism of time. Knowing only about your sliver of time is as restricting as knowing only about your own sliver of place.

We were told that it was possible, in the dry season, to drive from the 7000-foot elevation of San Cristobal to Villa Hermosa near sea level by the Gulf of Mexico. It was a one-way drive down some impossibly steep hills that a vehicle cannot get back up. We strapped Jerry cans filled with gasoline to the roof of the Beetle and left San Cristobal and the temperate pine forests of Chiapas, heading for the jungles of the Yucatan. A series of dirt roads led us into a land that time forgot: indigenous villages, with conical grass-roofed houses, unchanged since the time of Cortez.

In two days' time we passed through four villages. Excited groups of barefoot children ran alongside our car yelling and laughing. We figured these kids had never seen a car. The unsmiling adults were dressed in wool serapes with bare legs, all carrying a leather shoulder purse and a machete. In their black wool clothing it was hard to tell the women from the men. They all had long straight black hair and were not welcoming of outsiders. It took us eight days of getting stuck in black mud and clambering down rocky pitches so steep we knew we would never make it back up. So, it was ever onwards, floating the VW across mountain streams and skidding down steep hills with the brakes locked. The VW, with a metal sheet covering the entire underside, was well suited to off-road travel. Unlike other cars, the VW Beetle will float. It was sweltering hot, and ever-present insects were all starved for our blood. We came away from our jungle tour severely sleep deprived, looking like impoverished refugees, wearing unwashed raggedy clothing and faces swollen with bug bites. We made Villa Hermosa with our Beetle slightly battered, with roadside-patched tires and the muffler suspended with hose clamps and bailing wire.

San Cristobal, 1963

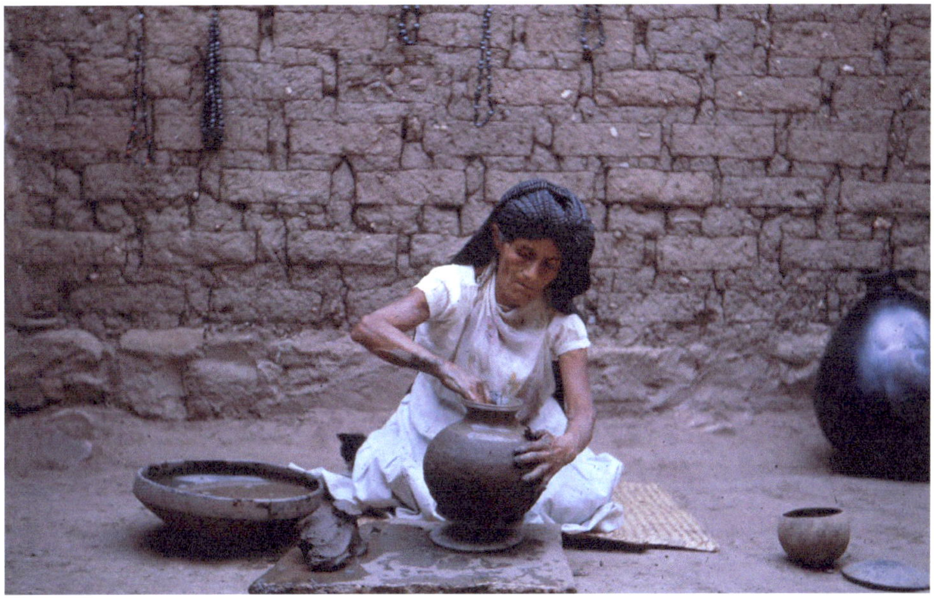

Local potter, Oaxaca, 1963

Number Ten: Terrorists in the Sugar Cane

We pointed the Beetle north. We were on our way home! We intended to drive along the gulf coast from the Yucatan to Vera Cruz, three hundred miles. Our map did not show a continuous road. However, we discovered this drive was all on passable back roads with isolated villages and small towns along the way. Outsiders were seldom seen in this part of Mexico. At the end of one long day, looking for a place to camp well away from people and villages, we chose to go up a sandy, one-lane road running between fields of six-foot-high sugar cane. It felt safer if we slept out of sight of curious, peering eyes. We drove along the sandy road for a mile or so, turned the car around for a quick exit in the morning, and set up camp. We had a system where the VW seats were taken out so that we could stretch out and sleep inside the car. Just as we were preparing our meal over a small, open fire, two young boys came along. We offered them tortillas, but they seemed nervous and soon left with lots of backward glances.

When we turned in for the night, it was dead dark. We were woken up from a sound sleep by sharp raps on the windows. I opened the car door and could just make out a number of men carrying machetes. Whoa! What's going on? One of them had a torch made of bamboo and grasses. They pointed down the laneway and told us we had to go with them, OK? As we loaded up the car, we could see that there were at least a dozen men, one with a long-barreled gun pointed at us. We slowly drove the car with our escort – some of them behind us, some walking in front. One of the two young guys riding in the back seat held a knife with a long blade at the ready.

As we approached the road we were emphatically told to "turn right! Go only to the right! Do not turn left! When you turn wrong, we all die." As we turned onto the road, the car headlights illuminated a scene straight out of the Mexican revolution. There were twenty or more men all dressed in white wearing the wide white pants, loose white over-shirts and wide brimmed sombreros, the traditional dress of the campesinos. Some were holding machetes and some were holding ancient muzzle loading guns. Primed and ready to go, we figured. They were standing shoulder to shoulder, blocking the road to the left as well as the laneway into more sugar cane fields straight across the way. After a drive of about a mile at walking speed with armed men walking behind us and armed men walking in front of us, we arrived at a village.

We were told to stop in the zocalo, our car surrounded by armed men. The jefe, the village chief, now feeling it was safe, came out of his house. We were seated on a wooden bench and questioned, “who are you? Where do you come from? Why are you in our sugar cane fields? Why do you have beards?”

We finally realised they thought we were bearded Cuban revolutionaries come to burn their fields. The Americans, in their frenzy of anti-communist fear and loathing, had convinced Mexicans that Communism and Fidel Castro were the world’s ultimate evils. According to them, these members of Satan’s minions were to be beaten back and murdered wherever you encountered them. Using our limited Spanish, we tried to convince our captors that we were not Cuban terrorists out to burn their sugar cane fields but that we were from Canada. “From where?” No one had heard of Canada.

We were taken into a small windowless adobe hut with a great steel door. The door clanged shut and was then securely padlocked. Ten minutes later someone opened the door and gave us a bucket to pee in. Thankful for small considerations, we slept an undisturbed sleep believing that our innocence would become apparent. George said that in *Macbeth* Shakespeare wrote, “the truth will out.” “He wrote this for us,” he says. I was not so sure.

Quite late in the morning, the door opened. We were momentarily blinded by the sunlight. During the night someone had taken our passports and gone to a bigger town, far away we were told, to check if Canada was a real place. It was! Once satisfied that we were not Cuban terrorists, the jefe invited us to have a breakfast of tortillas and frijoles with him. His wife, a plump motherly woman, encouraged us to eat, have some more, have more tortillas. She beamed with pride while we devoured her tortillas like starving men. The jefe took us on a tour of his village. He pointed out two mounds by the river and said, “This is how we welcome Cuban terrorists in San Sucre.” One small, misunderstood move and we would have ended our journey as two more mounds on the banks of an unnamed river somewhere in the back roads of Mexico. Instead, we left with the blessings of the jefe and his wife, who handed us some tamales, wrapped in corn husks, for the road.

George at one of our camps in Mexico, with Visitors. In the flora (below).

Brother George

After coming home from Mexico, life soon slid back into normal everyday routines. I resumed my job in the garage, and George went back to Toronto and his job at the CIBC bank. Life seemed prosaic. I would drive to Toronto to see George. I missed the conversations we had sitting around our desert campsites. George had a remarkable memory. He could recall entire chapters of a book he had read months before or repeat long passages from Shakespeare. To me it seemed that in his mind he had a photograph of a page from Macbeth as he spoke words and concepts new to me. "Life is but a walking shadow, a poor player that struts and frets his hour on the stage and then is heard no more." Little did I know that this was a prophetic passage for his own life.

A day with George would brighten my week and remind me that there was more to life than what I experienced in a mundane everyday workaday world. George would talk about things that were unknown to me and, always, there were stories from the history of the Netherlands told as if he had been there. I felt like I experienced the heroic deeds of Jan Van Scafelaar as he battled the Spanish invaders and leaped to his death from a castle tower rather than surrender. However, George seemed preoccupied and distant in a way I had not experienced in Mexico. It was like he had a secret. On our last visit George told me about schizophrenia. I had not heard of it. He told me it was a disease of the mind where people are afflicted with horrifying apparitions that materialise out of nowhere. They create a terrifying paranoia. No place was safe. There was no cure. In psychiatric hospitals they experimented on these people with new drugs. In the end they are no longer themselves. He told this tale like he was there. Two weeks later George came to our parents' house. He was a bit dishevelled and alluded to people that were hunting him. One Sunday afternoon while they were in church, George shot himself with the pistol we had purchased in Mexico.

Mem fell into inconsolable grief. Suicide was considered the scorning of God's ultimate gift: life itself. This was an unpardonable sin. A suicide could not enter heaven. In a not-so-distant past, a suicide could not be buried in the church graveyard. She harboured this grief in her heart for the rest of her life. Our father remained his strong stoic self, but he died a year later. “Grief that does not speak bids the o’er wrought heart to break.”

I was beside myself. My brother George, who knew everything under the sun, how could he do this? How could he be gone, forever gone. Just like that. Was all we talked about still real, still true? I was afraid, perhaps none of us were safe. George, my brilliant brother, you knew too much, you chose this end because you knew what was coming was worse. I was lost in a welter of confusion and sorrow and anger. I wept bitter tears for a brother I loved who was also a friend like no other. I was confronted with here-to unknown sorrow but, like my father, kept my grief as my own private affair.

My life appeared to go on unchanged. This habit eventually asserted itself and George slowly receded, but he never left. He remained as a private hollow place in my heart, an echo chamber for old and new grief.

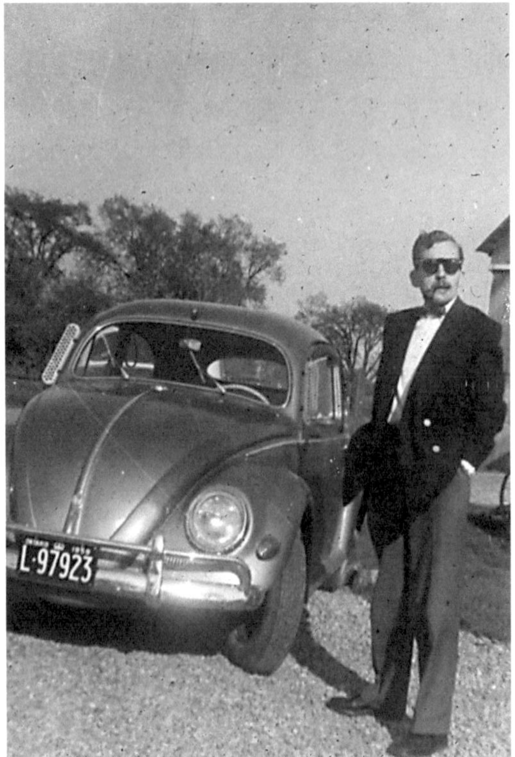

George with the Volkswagen, just before leaving for Mexico.

Opening New Doors

New Beginnings

At age twenty-six, I left working in garages for good. The under sides of cars and trucks were looking more and more alike. I had only completed grade nine. Canadian universities had all declined my applications with the curt advice to “go back to high school.” I may have only completed grade nine, but I could talk like a dominee. I drove to Grand Rapids in Michigan to talk to the dean at Calvin College, where I would be seen as one of us. I was, after all, from a Calvinist background. The dean was receptive to my spiel. I was welcome at Calvin but had to pass a probation year to prove I could do this.

Calvin was an introduction to an entirely different world. I went from garage talk of cars, women, sex, and whiskey and more sex to lectures on human achievements through the ages in art, literature and science. The richest vein for me was history. I felt I had discovered a gold mine. It was captivating to begin to understand where we came from, how our societies evolved and how all this, along with some of the accidents of history, brought us to where we are today. I fell in love with the history of ideas, which are, after all, the ultimate drivers of change. This vastly expanded world opened doors for me and would serve me well for the rest of my life. At Calvin I met Dirk Brinkman, who became a lifelong friend, and Maya Petersen, the beautiful, talented, and innocent young women who was to become my wife and the mother of my daughter Sjoukje.

Maya and John's Wedding. (Left to right: Sharon Devoss, Maya, John, Dirk Brinkman)

Summer Wages

With the summer of 1968 coming up fast, we, Dirk Brinkman, John Bosma (JT) and myself, needed to find summer jobs. All three of us were studying at Calvin College. I had heard that the communities of Inuvik and Tuktayuktuk in the Northwest Territories got their supplies during the summer by barges that were floated down the Mackenzie River all the way to the Beaufort Sea. It seemed a perfect fit with our free summer. We bought a 1962 Oldsmobile station wagon and drove to Vancouver BC, nonstop. I had an address for a company in Vancouver that handled the logistics for the barges. We took turns driving and sleeping in the back of the Detroit-built behemoth. We cut a small hole in the floor so we could put a can of pork and beans directly on the muffler to heat up our dinners. This worked like a damn. Driving up the mountain passes the can would boil in minutes. We arrived in Vancouver unwashed and a bit bedraggled but eager to get on with it. Whatever "it" was!

We went to the logistics place to check out working on the supply barges. We were much too late. This was the pre-internet world. You had to show up in person. Next day we went to the docks in Steveston and asked about working the fishing boats. We were told that we would have to join the Fisherman's Union before we could work on a fishing boat. At the Fisherman's Union office on East Hastings we were told, "can't join the Fisherman's Union until you have a job on a fishing boat." We had all read *Catch 22* and knew when to walk away.

We heard that they were looking for workers in Mackenzie where they were building a dam. The biggest, most audacious infrastructure project ever undertaken in BC needed more men. However, by now we did not have the money to go all that distance. Dirk's uncle in Langley, who made Gouda cheese, offered us a timely job painting his house. We painted that house, all white, in record time and left Vancouver with $300 cash and twenty pounds of Gouda cheese. Life was good.

We marvelled at the Fraser Canyon. The North American ice pack, over a mile high, had held most of Canada in its crushing embrace for a hundred thousand years. It took a thousand years for a mile of ice to melt and for an unfathomable amount of melt water to find its way to the oceans. The inexorable rush of water wore down the very bones of the earth and left the "Roaring Fraser" rushing to the sea in the bottom of a hundred-metre (350-foot) deep canyon cut into layers of ancient lava. We felt small and insignificant looking down into this canyon, seeing the fast flow of its wild, white waters.

We drove on to Prince George (PG), the gateway to the North. Whatever you needed for working or living in the North, it could be found in PG. This was the rest and recreation hub for the men who lived and worked in the underdeveloped north country. The four blocks of downtown PG were mostly bars, cheap hotels, and brothels. We slowly walked down 4th street making our way between entrepreneurial self-employed girls sitting on their personal gold mines and staggering drunk Indians. Alcohol was to the North as gasoline was to a car. It ain't going to run without it.

In PG the Oldsmobile began to sound like a threshing machine – clack, clack, clack, very worrisome. We parked in front of an Acklands automotive parts store, took the engine apart, replaced several hydraulic valve lifters and reassembled it. It ran like a Swiss watch for the rest of its brief life. While I was busy under the hood of the Oldsmobile, Dirk met Jarl, a young Laplander wearing a cowboy hat and furs. Jarl lived in a log cabin on his trapline up the Omineca River. He told us stories about a vast, wild, unspoiled land of grizzly bears stalking moose and mountain goats fighting off cougars; of wild, glacier-fed rivers crashing through steep walled canyons where fish leaped up the waterfalls; of eagles with eight-foot wing spans soaring in the sky, taking fish from these same wild waters. We were mesmerised by these tales of wild grandeur beyond our ken. We were exhilarated and eager to launch ourselves into these wild northlands. Come what may!

Jarl knew firsthand about the BC Bennett Dam, a giant dam project being built near Hudson's Hope. He said that in Findlay Forks, 70 miles north of Mackenzie, Herb Tilsener was hiring fallers. This new dam was going to flood thousands of acres of standing forest, and all of those trees needed to be cut down before the water came up.

WAC Bennet was a visionary and populist premier of British Columbia. A man of the people he was. His intention was to take BC from a backwoods frontier province to "its rightful place" on the national stage. To this end, Bennet built highways, extended ferry services to remote communities, opened an aluminum smelter in Kitimat, and more. He was responsible for pulp mills, sawmills, and mines all over British Columbia. His crown jewel, the BC Bennet dam, would produce the power needed to build a new industrial economy. For Bennet, any natural resources not used were wasted. Like Joey Smallwood of Newfoundland, WAC Bennet was a man of his time. They were manifestations of the ideology of modernism. They were firm believers in "progress." It was a time to forge ahead and build a prosperous future, it was a time of determined optimism and can-do attitude. He took a backwoodsy, fragmented province and turned it into an industrial, $200 billion a year behemoth. But Bennet, along with the supercharged society of the time, were blinded to the more devastating consequences for the pristine ecosystems and for the native peoples who had lived in these valleys for thousands of years.

The PG Stihl chainsaw dealer told us, "you show up in Mackenzie with a chainsaw and you have a job." Since I had worked as a faller in Ontario in my teen years, I could show Dirk and JT how to do this. "You gotta have chainsaws fore you go up there." He wanted to sell three saws! The state-of-the-art saw in 1968 was the Stihl 041, and we ended up selecting three of them, along with gas cans, files, hand-axes, and wedges for each of us. The bill came to $1000, we had $145. There was zero credit in this store. What now?

The Christian Reformed minister in Prince George was our salvation. A phone call to brother Melle, now the Christian high school principal in Sarnia, Ontario, and we had the dominee's name and address. The three of us showed up at the minister's doorstep and introduced ourselves as Calvin College students on our way to work in Mackenzie. Dirk was taking courses at the seminary; JT was studying philosophy and I was freelance taking whatever interested me. For this young minister, exiled to the far reaches of Christian civilization and only five years out of the Calvin seminary himself, we were emissaries from the Christian

Reformed Jerusalem. We were ushered into the house to meet his wife. We had a great celebratory meal and animated discussions on reformed philosophy and its long history going back to Dooyeweerd and Abraham Kuyper and, of course, Dr. Evan Runner, Calvin College's eccentric and dynamic professor-apostle of Dooyeweerd. Dirk was a member of Professor Runner's philosophy club. For the reverend it was too good to be true. As indeed it was!

After dinner we laid out our problem. We had an offer of well-paying jobs for all three of us, but we did not have the money to buy the three chainsaws we need to show up with in Mackenzie. We had come all this way to earn money to pay for next year's schooling. Our continuing education now depended on having these jobs. The dominee agreed to our request, his wife was hesitant. We were invited to bed down in their basement. In the morning, after breakfast, we headed for the chainsaw dealer. With some hesitation he accepted that we had an upstanding member of the community as guarantor for our debt, a minister no less. The dominee signed on the dotted line. We agreed to send him money from our very first paycheque. However, what we did not know is that promises and paycheques in the northlands of BC were wildly uncertain. In this frontier place all of us were still innocents.

Before leaving the reverend had a stern warning for us. The temptations we would encounter in the blaspheming world of rough, hard-drinking men could easily corrode our souls. Most dangerous of all to young men like us, he insisted, were the Indian women, whom he judged as having extremely loose morals. We assured him that as serious Calvin students we were well prepared to fend off such transitory temptation. He sent us off with heartfelt handshakes and God's Blessings. We could see that he was terribly worried about sending us off into the tents of wickedness that dot the north country. He assured us his congregation would pray for us. With a dominee's blessing and our new chainsaws and gas cans strapped to the roof of the Oldsmobile, we headed north into the unknown. A promised land beckoned, one with available women no less! However, because life in the northlands was unpredictable, we did not get paid for our first job, and the dominee's life took a haywire turn. The chainsaw dealer showed up at his doorstep and, after a series of violent, blaspheming threats made in a loud voice, the dominee and his wife were afraid. He had not heard anything from us. The dominee called my brother Melle, who was prevailed upon to pay the thousand dollars. He did.

We had a summer full of adventures and misadventures and eventually got back to Calvin College with very little money to show for our efforts, but with a wealth of stories to tell – a special currency of its own that earned me a beautiful and loving wife that very same year.

Dirk and JT Bosma changing a tire on the Olds, using a log in place of a jack.

The Northlands Are Wild in Unexpected Ways

We drove north up the Hart highway and stopped at a likely stand of trees to practise the art of falling. We fired up the new saws and selected a good-sized tree. Dirk and JT stood by while I ran them through the process: Undercut; cut a notch in the direction you want the tree to fall. Back cut: stop before you reach the front cut to leave a strip of uncut wood, a hinge to prevent the tree from falling sideways. Remove the saw blade, drive in two wedges with the back of the axe, and the tree will begin to lean. The tree squealed like a stuck pig as the hinge was pulled out of the stump or was literally pulled apart. The falling tree gathered speed and hit the ground with a satisfying, earth-shaking, thunk! Bravo!

A faller was the most dangerous job in British Columbia's growing industrial world. A puny 180-pound man would approach an 8,000-pound tree. He fired up a handheld chainsaw and would proceed to cut through several hundred years of growth in minutes. If something went wrong, the tree would break bones like they were match sticks. There were terrifying 'Barber Chair' trees that split lengthways as they began to fall, pivoting on a new hinge way up high, and then crashing to earth in completely unpredictable ways. There were 'Widow Makers', trees that broke up when still upright as they were cut into, silent pieces of dead wood coming straight down, landing beside the trunk with a solid thud. Certain death when the faller was on the same side of the tree. When things went wrong they went wrong very quickly. These were ways which even the most experienced fallers had met an almost instantaneous death. Some fallers were less lucky and got pinned under a fallen tree to die a slow death of hunger and thirst or to be found by a bear, wolf or wolverine looking for a meal. There are unexpected results when things just go sideways. Every so often the tree has the last word.

We spent three hours and felled twenty-three trees. The new Stihl chainsaws worked much better than the Pioneer saw I had used in Ontario twelve years earlier. We left behind a chaotic mayhem of downed trees, drove to a lake, made camp, and cooked our pork and beans over a proper fire. Beavers floated silently by in the water. When startled, a beaver hits the water with its flat tail making a loud warning. It sounds like a giant's hand clap. The haunting cries of a loon drifted across the still water. We felt that we had arrived. In the morning we lit up three cherry bombs, legal in Michigan, and threw them into the water where they sank for about six seconds, exploded, and sent up a ten-foot-high geyser of water. Our young male yahoo tendencies satisfied, we drove on down the Hart highway.

A dead-straight, narrow dirt road hemmed in by trees on either side abruptly ended at an enormous clearcut. We had arrived in Mackenzie. The road into "town" passed by a service station and a huge trailer park set back into the trees. At the far end of the clearcut, the new Mackenzie hotel, with an attached shopping mall sitting on an enormous paved parking lot, looked wildly out of place. For the rest, the place was one huge muddy clearcut. There were some street signs marking unpaved roads going nowhere. Some of these roads were circular cul-de-sacs. This seemed so out of place. Mackenzie was a raw boom town busy getting on its feet.

We drove to Findlay Forks, where the Findlay and Parsnip rivers join to make the mighty Peace River. It was a 70-mile long, single-lane, dusty, live logging road from Mackenzie to Findlay Forks. The dust, a particularly fine clay, was lifted up into the air so thick by the passing trucks that the road was obscured for several hundred metres after a truck went by. The trucks were in contact with each other via radio. Loaded trucks going north broadcast their position: "loaded at mile 63" and the empties going south waited in a pull-off until the loaded truck thundered by. We had no radio. Coming around a bend, we saw a loaded truck barreling down the middle of the road. There was no place to go. We were warned that a loaded logging truck would not go off the road to miss us. If he were to hit a tree, the load of logs would come forward and instantly crush the cab with him in it. It was up to us in the Oldsmobile to head into the trees, no matter what. We lost a mirror to a small tree, but the Olds came thru pretty much unscathed. The first empty going south stopped to pull us back on the road. The trucks were loaded with logs picked up out of the still rising waters at Findlay Forks and taken to one of seven state-of-the-art sawmills in Mackenzie. The truckers were paid by the mile and by the size of the load. The way to make good money was to overload the truck to the max and drive like a madman. It was a Forest Service road so provincial restrictions were not in force; licence plates and insurance were not needed. We arrived in Findlay Forks with new character lines etched into our faces.

At Findlay Forks we saw a camp up on a lightly treed bench well above the rising waters. It was a collection of canvas wall tents, some spruce bow lean-tos and dozens of campfires. The people all had an unkempt, untamed look about them. Many women, and men both, had long, raven-black hair hanging loose or done up in long braids. The men wore denim or deerskin pants, all with hunting knives on their belts. Some of the men were holding rifles. The women wore long dresses and had moccasins on their feet. Dogs of all ages and raggedy-looking children chased each other through the camp yelling and barking. Most of the fires had a tripod with a blackened kettle or pot hanging over the flames. As we slowly drove by, they all looked at us with no expression on their faces. It was a primaeval scene, with the smoke and light of the fires, illuminating the mysterious people against the dark background of the forest.

Fallers for Hire

Near the water's edge we saw a group of men wearing shiny aluminum hard hats. JT asked, "where can we find Herb Tilsener?" A short little guy with a lopsided grin stepped forward. In lieu of resumes we had all donned our new hard hats for this interview. "Hear you're lookin for fallers. We have experience!" Tilsener took one look at us and laughed. "You guys have no experience, but you're hired on anyway, we leave tomorrow – first thing – upriver." Tilsener put us up in a 16 ft. × 8 ft. wooden crate. The shipping container of the day, sitting on the gravel beach. We went to sleep feeling lucky by the skin of our teeth.

Next morning, the riverboat pushed its way through the almost flat waters of Lake Williston. The Findlay Riverboat was a forty-foot shallow draft boat made of spruce planks with a slightly curved up bow. This boat was traditionally used for travelling the rivers in this roadless region and was sturdy enough to be driven, or hauled, onto the gravely shores. There were nine people along with a lot of gear, tents, chainsaws, axes, 45-gallon drums of gasoline and food in our boat. It had a big outboard motor. An Indian woman with long black braids was at the helm. She wore moccasins on her feet and a ten-inch sheath knife on her belt. We pushed along at a good clip. Two older veteran fallers had moved the gear around to make nests for themselves towards the front of the boat and lay back to watch. Vince, a stocky, muscular man in his early fifties, proudly bragged how his enormously heavy, ancient, McCullough chainsaw could outperform our shiny new "toy saws." Vince had forearms like Popeye after having finished off a tub of spinach. The two fallers commented on how the rising water had changed the landscape. The lake was slowly filling. The water had come up about a hundred feet. It had almost 500 feet to go, drowning everything in its unstoppable path.

We boated through miles of submerged trees. The tops of the trees came straight up out of the water. The boat wound its way through with branches occasionally sweeping across the bow. It was a surreal sense of boating through a forest canopy in the throes of its living death. After hours on the water, we ran the boat onto a flat, gravelly beach. The other two boats in our convoy pulled in beside us. Instantly the sound of five chainsaws, at full throttle, shattered the pristine quiet of this wilderness. Within moments, two guys had poured gasoline on a heaped mound of newly cut wood and lit a match. Voila! There was an instant roaring fire with flames shooting thirty feet into the air. We had left the Boy Scouts in the dust. These were twentieth-century Indians. The few Indian women on the other boat took some of the burning sticks and made a much smaller fire to prepare coffee and food for twenty-five people.

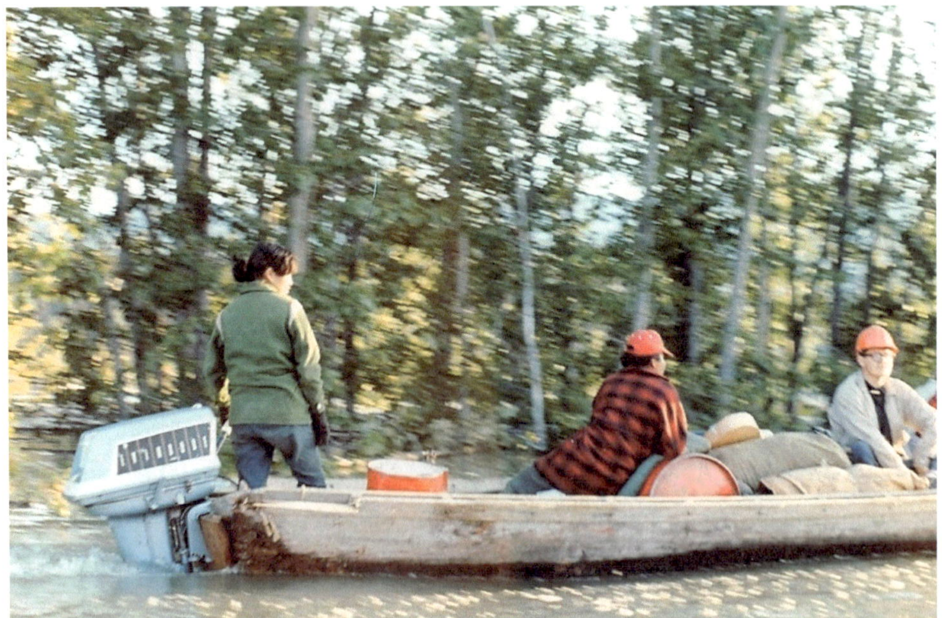

Boating upriver

JT was worried about bears. The Old Testament story of two she-bears coming out of the forest to rend and devour a group of children had created in us youngsters a primal fear of bears. This was God's punishment for a group of boys taunting the prophet Elisha for his bald head. We could only imagine what forbidden act of our own could trigger this kind of punishment. Perhaps JT felt uneasy with our dangerously backsliding ways. Then he came into our tent with good news. Vince had solved his fear of bears by suggesting that JT wear a quart container filled with gasoline on his belt. "If you see a bear immediately climb a tree, if the bear climbs up the tree after you pour gasoline in his head. Throw a match and watch the bear go up in flames." Dirk was amused. He pointed out that this would set your own tree, and your own self, on fire.

After a breakfast of coffee and bannock we were back on the water heading north. We encountered a huge raft of floating forest debris. We tried to pole our way forward, pushing floating trees aside, but made no headway. Vince and the other faller went to the front of the boat, one on either side, fired up their chainsaws and began to cut their way through the floating log jam. Vince asked to use one of our new "toy saws." He eventually admitted that it worked much better, for this kind of work, than his weighty McCullough behemoth. It was slow going, but we eventually cut our way through, and we were back in open water.

This was one of the unintended consequences of the building of the Bennet dam. The engineers and planners at BC Hydro had decided to cut all the trees about to be flooded out in order to make the lake safe for navigation. A tree under 500 feet of water, once its roots loosened, could one day shoot straight up as an 8000-pound missile that would destroy any unfortunate boat passing over it. In order to profit from the vast bonanza of lumber, the timber mills in Mackenzie let out contracts to fell the trees before the water came up. These fallen trees were to be limbed, the top cut off, and salvaged as saw logs when they floated to the surface. It did not work out this way. Hundreds of square miles of forest did eventually float to the surface, creating a massive raft of trees along with all the loose branches and tree tops. Debris would pile on debris, causing the saw logs to become waterlogged. Over 90% of these logs eventually sank. The powerful winds sweeping across 300 miles of open water would take these massive rafts of debris, eventually miles across, and push them wherever the winds wanted. Any boat on the water was in danger of being caught on the lee side of a floating mass of debris and driven towards the shore. With no possible escape, the boat would be crushed between the wind, driven debris, and the shore. The people on the boat would be marooned in a remote wilderness, possibly a hundred miles from the nearest help. Strong, unprecedented winds whipped across the new lake making big waves that could reach 40 feet that were dangerous in their own right. The winds were always moving the debris "rafts" along in unpredictable ways. The years-long project of falling 680 square miles of forest did eliminate the hazard of trees shooting up under a boat. However, this was traded off for the more predictable danger of a boat driven to shore and crushed by a raft of debris.

The log salvage did not go well either. The logs were so thoroughly mixed into, and often under, enormous masses of debris that only a few logs at the edges could be salvaged. BC Hydro attempted to remove the debris in the lake by burning it. Tree branches and other debris were piled high on enormous, flat-deck, steel barges and set on fire using diesel fuel. The waterlogged debris did not always want to burn and when it did it left a layer of ash on the water. The water was now truly contaminated with the sheen of diesel fuel floating on the water under a layer of ash. Grey ash-covered areas dotted the new lake. We went upriver when it was still early on and manageable. We were on our way to add to this man-made mayhem.

The river becoming a lake, clogged with fallen trees.

Findlay river boat, heading up river.

Working on the Move

At the day's end we pulled up to a makeshift dock. This was Tilsener's camp. A flat bench above the river with some big stumps. A canvas cook tent stood close to the river with some wooden benches, a wood stove and a huge double sink that drained directly into the river. There were a dozen faded white wall tents at the back of the bench placed up against, and into, the trees. A normal bush camp of the time. Dirk, JT and I shared a wall tent.

That first night swarms of voracious mosquitoes invaded our tent. The high-pitched piercing whines were the signal that we were about to be bitten, punctured, pierced, stung by a thousand flying nightmares. Pulling a blanket over your head would buy a momentary reprieve, but the need to breathe overpowered the fear of dreaded mosquitoes hovering, waiting, ready to drive their needle-like proboscis into your face to suck up your blood. Soon, our faces and hands were a mass of itchy bites that, when scratched, turned into angry red welts that kept itching. As time went on it only got worse. There is something about the whine of a mosquito that triggers a primal reaction. We came to hate that incessant whine, hate the piercing bite, hate the intense itch that must not be scratched, hate the scratchy wool blanket over your itchy face, hate being suffocated by breathing in warm, stale, ten-times-used air, hate the wall tent that could not be sealed up, hate Herb Tilsener, hate ourselves for being here in the first place. The moans and groans and angry swats went on all night.

In the morning Tilsener laughed when he saw our red, swollen, bitten-up faces. "Rough night boys?" He had slept slathered in mosquito repellent. He showed us where he kept boxes of green mosquito coils and a crate of mosquito repellant. The repellent with the highest amount of *deet* worked best. This repellant will melt rain gear, but the whine of a mosquito drove out any thoughts we had about what deet may do to human skin. Theresa, the native woman who was at the helm of the boat steering us through the drowned trees, was now the camp cook. She laughed at our misery and gave us a self-made ointment to put on our ravaged faces.

We were each shown an area to work in. We would be paid 50 cents for each felled and limbed tree. The three areas were contiguous so that we would be working within shouting distance of each other. In reality we could only ever hear the other guy's chainsaw. We each had a chainsaw, a red plastic can of gasoline, a quart of chain oil, an axe and three wedges. Before leaving we three stood in a huddle, wished each other good luck, shook hands all around, and then each walked away to our own piece of forest. It was a solemn, ceremonial start of our first day. We felt that life-threatening injuries could be visited on any of us, but we did not talk about this. The trees, for the most part, were not very big, and the area we worked was mostly flat forest floor covered in moss. In some hollows the moss was more than two feet thick. Laying down in these hollows, one completely sank into a green, living mattress that would form itself to hug your shape. It is to experience a kind of perfection, to be in a living bed that wraps itself around your body and holds you in its natural embrace.

Both Dirk and JT had a close call on day one. Close calls, for fallers, are the times when they feel the grim reaper's light touch, but he passes by for a later visit. The first tree that Dirk felled was a big one. He made a notch and during the back cut the tree leaned back and pinched his saw. It was stuck. Not knowing what to do, he attacked the tree with his axe to free the saw. Suddenly the tree began to fall with a change in the direction of the breeze. The trunk split with a horrendous loud tearing sound. The butt of the tree was thrown thirty or more feet straight up, then the tree briefly pivoted on the 30-foot sliver of wood extending up from the stump to come crashing down to earth with a ground-shaking thump. By some miracle, the tree landed just behind Dirk. He survived by sheer chance. The Gods were holding his hand.

JT felled a tree that hung up in a standing tree nearby. In order to get credit for the tree, he had to cut off the top. So, JT walked up the now angled tree till he got to where it needed to be bucked off, at 10 inches diameter. He was now twenty feet above the ground. He proceeded to cut the tree whilst standing above his cut, not aware of the immense pressure the tree was under from holding itself up on two points, spanned across open air The tree, part way cut through, suddenly snapped. The released top swung wildly up into the air and flung JT, still holding his running chainsaw, away. It was like he had been shot out of a catapult. He later said, "I went flying, man did I go flying." He missed the now fallen log right below him and landed in a clump of deep moss a good twenty feet away. He was rudely shook up but not hurt. JT spent the next hour looking for his glasses and his saw. He said that the tree credit, another fifty cents, was not worth it.

As long as we were working, the blessed fumes from the chainsaw enveloped us and kept the mosquitoes at bay. As soon as we stopped to gas up the saw, they were back and bent on making up for lost time. When nature called, we would build a small fire and throw moss on to make smoke. Only then did we drop pants and squat over the smoky fire. Why do this? Mosquitoes go for the family jewels, conveniently hanging low. They will, I swear, even abandon a feeding on the warm blood of a freshly bared buttock and head for the promised land. Within seconds, dozens of mosquitoes are vying for a spot on a testicle. I don't know how long the proboscis is, but I swear it's long enough to go right through the thin skin of the scrotum and puncture a testicle to suck out the most vital of a man's fluids. One unlucky worker with a grotesquely swollen scrotum was sent out for medical help. Vince suggested, "just take him to a whorehouse, with balls that size they'll do him for free!" Mosquitoes were, and probably still are, the ever-present curse of the north country. In the Northwest Territories huge herds of caribou will suddenly stampede, with thousands charging at full speed across the tundra, to escape the torment of mosquitoes. We could see a lot of sense in this.

Camp life was a rough and ready affair. A canvas cook tent with some chairs, a table made of rough sawn boards, and some more of these boards nailed to tree rounds served as benches. Theresa did not talk much but welcomed the men with her shy smile. Theresa spoke in the accented English of the native peoples, distinguished, in part, by her soft flat *a* that gave English a new, softer, unhurried cadence.

Theresa knew how to work with this kind of bush camp kitchen. She split wood for the stove, cooked fish she caught in the river, gathered greens growing along the river, and managed with Tilsener's mish-mash of bulk food to conjure up tasty meals. Theresa looked like she belonged here in this thrown-together bush camp, quietly making do with what was at hand. For Theresa, JT's hearty laugh and his awkward, shy, out of place, urban demeanour in this camp of rough and plain-spoken fallers caught her in her soft spot. She would spread her ointment on his mosquito bites, tenderly bandage his bashed finger, and cut his hair, all the while asking him questions. "Where do you come from?" The romantic possibilities that hung unspoken in the air were rudely interrupted by a hurried evacuation of Tilsener's camp because of an approaching forest fire. I like to think that the dominee in PG woke up from a dangerous dream with a smile on his face.

The fallers were mostly older, single men who had worked in the bush for a lifetime. These men had survived cutting down the big old-growth trees with crosscut saws and later chainsaws. Theirs was a tough life, living in primitive bush camps that had not changed since the nineteenth century, or working alone, for weeks on end, on the steep hillsides on the coast. They cut down only the trees that could be skidded and manhandled into the water. "Hand falling" was dangerous but paid well. Vince, telling stories of his life, said, "I made a year's wages in two months once." These guys were always ready to tell stories of their haywire, nomadic lives. They were tough, independent men; barely literate. When not working, they found their solace and their fun in drinking hard liquor. They would fight at the drop of a hat, mostly for the fun of it, or the bragging rights that came with winning. However, they would stand by a friend and put their life on the line to help when the need arose. A disappearing breed of hardy, simple men, loyal and generous to the core. These old fallers were the casualties of opening and exploiting BC's immense old-growth forest. This was the wealth that built the province. Their tough nomadic lives meant they would never settle down, have families, or share in the real wealth their work created. Many of these men, when no longer able to wield a chainsaw, ended their lives living on skid row of Vancouver's East Hastings street.

Camp life had its moments. The guys, using chainsaws and rusty nails, cobbled together an outhouse proudly known as "The Shitter." It was a rickety affair but served its purpose to prevent that unpleasant squishy step in the dark. Four days later, Seymour, a huge, 240-pound Indian, sat down too hard and broke the new outhouse. The board that served as the seat broke into three pieces. He fell over backwards, landing over the pit – his bulk saving him from a soft, messy landing. The entire cobbled-together structure collapsed on top of him. The fall drove some big, jagged splinters into his arse. Seymour, with his pants still down around his knees, crawled out from under the collapsed outhouse to raucous laughter and derision. The guys were pissed about the loss of the only proper shitter for a hundred miles and refused to help pull out the splinters. Paul Buck offered to buck off the biggest splinters with his chainsaw. Theresa eventually pulled them out with a pair of vice grips and doused his bare ass with iodine to howls of laughter from his fellow fallers.

Paul Buck was a young guy of dubious parentage, part Indian, raised by whites; but he mostly grew up in Indian camps. He was a wild man who moved fast and was sometimes just outta control. He was up for anything, any time. Some called him just plain crazy.

One day, while gassing up, he spilled gasoline on the saw and himself. He then sat on the saw to have a smoke and lit a match by reaching down and striking it against the hot exhaust manifold. Buck and his saw were instantly on fire. Karl, a lumbering huge and immensely strong German guy, was walking by. Karl lifted Buck up by his collar, heaved him into the river, threw his flaming chainsaw in after him and kept on walking, hardly breaking his stride. Because of this event, a serious animosity developed between Paul Buck and Karl. We were all sitting around a small fire later when Buck said, "you ruined my saw you German, kraut, asshole," Karl said. "Shoulda left you to barbecue you Canadian dummkopf!" Buck wouldn't let up. He continued with insults that questioned Karl's parentage in ways that made even the guys in camp grimace. Karl finally had enough. He picked Buck up, and, holding him by his belt, held him over the fire, face down. Karl asked the rest of us if we would like a barbecue. When he got no answer, he walked over to the river and threw him, as far as he could, into the river. Buck planned a brutal, painful revenge for Karl, but fate intervened. A fire a ways north of us suddenly flared up. We could see flames in the distance. A helicopter landed almost on top of the cook tent. The prop wash flattened the tent. Theresa dug her way out from under the canvas and hurled a sting of Sekani invectives at the pilot. It was the only time we saw her stoic equilibrium briefly tipped over. We were all taken out in a helicopter to Fort Graham. We landed in a flat field of about six acres still a good six feet above the rising waters.

Fighting Fires

Fort Graham had been a Sekani village before all the buildings were razed and burnt by the Forest Service. The Sekani were semi-nomadic people. They moved around the Findlay Valley with the seasons between three villages: Enginka, Fort Graham and Findlay Forks. Findlay Forks was the farthest south, the winter camp. Two years earlier some native men saw a forestry crew with drip torches burning the buildings. They asked, “why are you burning our houses?” The forestry man explained that the water was going to come up and the buildings would then become a shipping hazard. The Indians replied, “that is silly, we choose to build on this high bluff because the water never comes this high.” They had not been told that a dam at Hudson Hope, 250 kilometres away, would put their Findlay Forks village under 600 feet of water. Fort Graham met the same fate.

Fort Graham, now a vacant six-acre field, was being used as a supply depot for the fires in the south end of the Valley. It was a hectic scene, helicopters coming and going delivering supplies like 45-gallon drums of fuel, water pumps, fire hose, canvas wall tents, and crates of food. Dozens of people were milling around, guys yelling over the constant sound of the helicopters, dust and debris kicked up by the powerful rotors. The dust settled down only to be kicked back up into the air when the helicopter lifted off again. Boats were pulling up with more men and more equipment all adding to the chaos. A pack of dogs, not at all accustomed to the noise and excitement, or to each other, added to the sense of chaos by tearing around like they had become unhinged. Piles of equipment were scattered around. We had to only sit back, keep an eye on our saws, and enjoy the changing scenery. The next morning some native women had campfires going. They had coffee on the go, some bannock and fried eggs for whoever was next in line. God bless these capable, selfless Indian women. By mid-morning we were dropped off on a rocky ridge of Wik Mountain, above the tree line. The ridge was about forty feet wide. The wind made for a touchy helicopter approach. If there was a wind, the chopper pilot would not land but instead hover a few feet above ground. We had to jump. The last guy would throw the gear out to those below and then make his own exit from the swaying chopper.

From our vantage point we could see the fires far below us. The fire was moving fast in the crowns of the trees; every once in a while, a sheet of flame would shoot up into the sky. A huge old tree had just ignited from the forest floor. When an open flame reached the lowest waxy needles of these huge conifers, flames would roar up the tree sounding like a jet airplane, sending flames hundred feet up into the air. Twin engine water bombers flew into the smoke and came out farther down the mountain. Water was mixed with fire retardant to make a long orange spray over the fire. This seemed to make no difference. The fire kept moving at a gallop, eager, it seemed, to meet up with a tongue of fire coming up from another draw further down the mountainside. But the bombers kept at it.

Six of us guys were picked to – do what? We were not told. We walked down the mountainside carrying our saws, axes, and small red gas cans to where it flattened out. The foreman flagged off an area for a helipad. Six chainsaws, running full out in a small space, make an incredible high-pitched noise that reverberates in your head for hours afterwards. It rattles the very bones in your body. In less than an hour we had cleared a helipad in the midst of a dense forest. Shortly afterwards a helicopter landed in it. Good feeling, that. The chopper took us and our gear back up to the ridge.

The pilot was fresh out of Vietnam and liked to show off. He would sometimes cut the engine at 8000 feet and pitch the helicopter forward, causing the now silent helicopter to fall like a stone, picking up an alarming amount of speed. The rotors would auto-rotate with the downdraft. Just before crashing, at a mere fifty feet above the ground, the pilot would change the angle of the rotors. As they bit into the air it was as if a giant hand jerked the helicopter to a halt in midair. This manoeuvre would restart the engine (just like letting up the clutch in a rolling car) and we would land light as a feather. Those on board who had pissed themselves would cover their pants with whatever was at hand.

A camp, consisting mostly of canvas wall tents and some firepits, was quickly put up. A sullen, unsmiling young guy was the camp cook. He stipulated that we each got one scoop of pork and beans from an old cast iron pot and all the bread we wanted. Coffee was not rationed. It seemed the cook really liked his coffee. We missed Theresa. The entire camp got diarrhoea. The sullen cook kept saying, “you guys shouldn’t have shit in the lake” (a small pond farther down the ridge). There was no outhouse.

Another young guy who was on crutches had convinced his Forest Service uncle to take him to our camp at Fort Graham. He was pretty useless so he was put in charge of the radio and given a list of food to order. He sat in a chair and yelled out orders at the top of his voice for hours on end. The atmosphere caused radio signals to skip and bounce. He ended up in conversations all over the Pacific with Russians, Indonesians, Singaporeans, etc., and whoever he was talking to he repeated the list. In the end our camp got the entire order duplicated how many times over? We received sixty pounds of dates, and multiple crates of steaks.

The cold wind whipping across the ridge seemed so out of touch with the forest fires raging below us. The BC Forest Service seemed to have an endless supply of thick scratchy blankets, all marked. “Property of BC Forest Service.” Tilsener’s camp, along with every bush camp, used these same Forest Service blankets. They served us well later, when we finally had our own camp and we could sleep in warm dreamy comfort under multiple layers of forestry blankets piled so thick they were almost too heavy.

We were sent to work, and we knew we were too close to the fire. We were in a bulldozed firebreak to fall any trees that caught fire on the far edge of the firebreak. “A crazy idea,” said an older faller. For us, falling a burning tree added a whole new level of excitement. A big tree candled about fifty feet away. A sheet of flame shot straight up above the treetops, reaching for the heavens. One of the older guys yelled, “head for the creek boys!” We ran, reached a steep embankment, scrambled down, and at the bottom laid down flat in the moss beside the creek. There was a roaring sound like a jet airplane passing overhead as the fire in the trees’ crowns raced over us. Once the fire was past, we climbed back up the embankment and trudged through now burnt forest to the lake at the bottom of the mountainside.

BC Forestry had set up another camp and supply depot on a grassy flat area that projected into the lake. 45-gallon drums of fuel sat in the shallow water at the lake's edge. A stick-thin, frenetic, fast-talking French Canadian was one of two people in that camp. His name was René Plourde, and he was a teller of tall tales. A thick mat of hair covered his entire body. With his black fur his fear of catching fire by walking in the woods with his shirt off seemed reasonable, so he volunteered as a cook. He had come from the Yukon and on his way down had been shanghaied by the RCMP to fight fires. "Tabarnak!" We had a coffee while René told us, "The Forest Service will kill us all. Wild bears are prowling all around the tent waiting to pounce and have some French meat! Tabarnak!" He kept a loaded gun close at hand but had only three bullets! Dieter Schmitt, the cook's helper, joined us and we discussed the fire, mosquitoes, bears, and only having three bullets. Dieter was a husky young German guy of twenty-two. He had come to Canada to experience North America. Dieter, like so many of his countrymen, got caught up the immensely popular series of books written by Karl May. German people experience the American west through the fanciful tales of "Old Shattered Hand," a frontier man who is blood brother to Winnetou, an Apache chief. These books created an intense German interest in the Wild West and its native Indians. Karl May never actually set foot in America. We read these same books, translated into Dutch, when we were young boys.

Since we had no idea what was going on, JT, Dirk and I decided to walk back up the mountain to our own camp on the ridge. Plourde pleaded with us to stay. He was panicked about bears and, "with only myself and this romantic German simpleton, the bears will devour me." Dieter nodded and smiled.

For the next few days, we were taken to different sites by helicopter. We walked all day through a burnt forest floor and a deep layer of ash to put out smouldering stumps. By the end of these endless days, we had breathed in a ton of black dust and smoke. We arrived back in camp covered in soot and ashes. It began to sprinkle rain, and we spent a lot of time hanging around camp. We watched the water bombers fly into the smoke and held our breath until the plane reappeared again over the lake. We took to going down the mountain to visit René Plourde and Deiter. Plourde had interesting stories. He had lived a scattered life ranging from teaching religion at Polytechnique Montreal to contracting a road-building project in the Yukon. Plourde was a gambler and an inveterate scammer. Deiter was a young man from Germany with one mission, to experience America. Deiter was enthusiastic and eager to have his own stories when he returned home. Stories of life in America seen from the ground. He never intended to stay. Deiter was never unhappy or disappointed with unfolding events. The stranger it was, the more difficult it got, the better the story. He was up for anything providing it was not life-threatening. "That would not be a good story," said Deiter.

The rain eventually put out the fires. We came away from the Wik Fire believing that the entire effort and all the work had been of no use. As much of a waste as the crates of dates and beef steaks left on the mountain ridge. We were helicoptered out, back to Findlay Forks.

The Findlay Forks camp of lean-tos and wall tents that we had seen four weeks earlier had grown into a collection of rickety shacks cobbled together from old wooden shipping crates. It was a sad and raggedy scene inhabited by Sekani people whose lands were now underwater. Large quantities of alcohol, mostly brought in by the truck drivers, was traded for whatever, or whoever, the truckers fancied. There was around-the-clock drunkenness, shooting guns, and careless violence. When a bullet missed a sleeping baby by a half inch, Maudy Toma picked up her twenty-two and fired into the dark, in the direction the bullet came from. She hit someone. The RCMP came out from Mackenzie to upbraid Maudy. There was nothing to do, no one had any money and there wasn't enough food to go around. It was a sad tale of poverty and degradation for these recently free and independent people.

John Bosma cut his thigh when his chainsaw kicked back while doing something around the camp. He was flown out to have his wound stitched closed. This ended JT's BC summer holiday. I was relieved. I believed that JT would end up under a falling tree or meet his end due to some other "accident" in the rugged north woods of BC. Much better to have JT back at Calvin where he entertained everyone with his frenetic nonstop talking.

Because of the recent fires, there was no work in the bush. Renee Plourde told Dirk and I that he needed two guys to help him with a project in the lower mainland. We pulled straws to decide who got to go. Dirk drew the shortest straw, so Dieter and I headed off with Plourde while Dirk and JT stayed in Findlay Forks.

Francis Isaak, the chief of the Sekani band, and his wife Jean and their kids were in Fort Graham in his riverboat. He had heard that his people in Findlay Forks were without food so decided to go hunting for meat. Dirk and a big native guy named Seymour joined Francis. Up the Enginika River they shot three moose, butchered them, prepared the meat and headed down to Findlay Forks. The people were excited and overjoyed to see moose meat. Soon there were fires with moose meat cooking in pots, moose meat hanging off the tripods over the flames, thin strips of moose meat drying on low branches and moose nose on a stick anchored in the dirt close to the fire. By morning that nose would become a rare, tender, culinary treat. Children with blood-stained faces were laughing as they tore at the still raw liver with their teeth. The excitement and the smell of blood had the dogs racing through camp, barking, yipping, and sharing in the bounty. It was a wild, primal feast, the likes of which was not seen again in Findlay Forks.

The Forest Service offered a few small reservations to the homeless Sekani, one at Tutu Creek and one at 69-mile. Francis decided to move to 69-mile. The site had a beaver pond and guaranteed swarms of mosquitoes come spring. There were thirty-five families in his band. Dirk helped with the moving, using the Oldsmobile. The Sekani did not have cars. The BC government built thirty-five plywood houses with no insulation. During the winter, the polar winds swept down from the north and came up through the spaces between the plywood flooring where the sheets did not quite meet. The people huddled around airtight tin wood stoves for warmth.

After three weeks in the lower mainland, Dieter and I came back. The time with Renee Plourde had badly strained our faith in him and his various scams. BC

Forestry had let out a whole bunch of contracts, and we heard a guy named Jerry Klaus had gotten them all.

Firefighting staging area in Fort Graham, summer 1968

Number Eleven: Falling Trees: A Dance with Death

I was running full out with my legs pumping like a runaway steam engine. A single mass of five big fir trees all bunched together was coming down fast. I was in the line of fire.

I had cut down a tree only to see it get hung up in another tree on its way down. One way to get the tree down was to fall another tree directly on the hung-up tree and dislodge it. This did not work. I felled every tree within range onto the growing mass of trees held up by a single anchor tree. This did nothing to dislodge them or break the anchor tree. Should I get under the hung-up trees, cut the tree holding them all up and scramble for safety the moment the mass began to give way? Too dangerous! I walked away. Let a windstorm do it.

Moments later I heard an ominous crack. I did not look back, I ran, throwing the still running chainsaw as far as I could. I heard the rending sound as the anchor tree broke under the weight of five hung-up trees. I instinctively hit the ground, falling flat, face down. Several earth-shaking thud immediately followed. I lay dead still for a few minutes gasping for air. Fear had taken away my breath. I reached down feeling for my arms and legs. I seemed to be in one piece. I tried to move, and I found myself between two trees, one on either side. They had both missed me by mere inches. The two large fallen trees lay in round depressions hammered into the dry packed earth. I could not move my left arm. I saw that a broken branch has gone through my coat, pinning me to the ground. I cut myself free with my knife and struggled to get out from between the two tree trunks and the mass of branches intertwined overhead.

I was completely unscathed. Not a scratch. I walked back to our camp a good ten minutes farther downhill. This was the kind of dumb luck that saw us through the summer and fall of 1968. The Gods for oblivious young men were watching over us.

Number Twelve: Rafting to Eternity

Jerry Klaus had underbid everyone, managing to make himself widely hated, and now held all the slashing contracts in the Mackenzie Forest District. So, we set out to find him. Jerry turned out to be a wiry little guy, who greeted us with a wolfish grin. I was immediately attracted to his intense steely blue stare and his devil-may-care attitude. He was an East German who had worked in the bush in Siberia, and upon coming home, had killed the man who seduced his wife during his long absence. He escaped East Germany before they could find him, which, given that he had also trained guard dogs for VOPO (East German border guards), was easy for him. Jerry Klaus was as tough as nails.

We subcontracted our first slashing job from Jerry. The contract required that we fall all trees regardless of size and then limb and buck all trees 13 inches diameter, or more, at the butt. Jerry took us down the wide expanse of the Parsnip River in his aluminum outboard and agreed to come back before we finished the job. We had food and supplies for ten days.

We worked dawn to dusk, learning as we went. It was all steep hillside bush down to the river. We sat around a campfire at night and talked of the danger trees we had survived. In one such story, Dirk was carrying a running chainsaw when he tripped and fell. His finger was still on the throttle and gripping the saw. He managed to catch himself with his bared throat inches away from a live chain running at full speed. Soft human flesh is butter to a chainsaw.

Twelve days later we were finished. No Jerry. We carefully divided the last of our food, four shrivelled potatoes and a small flat can of sardines, for our last meal. The next morning, still no sign of Jerry Klaus. We were hungry. Dirk waded buck naked into the river with the 303 to shoot a fish, no luck. To stay was to starve so we built a raft.

Eight logs were tied together with what we had: some nylon rope, some haywire, and a few nails. The last two logs were tied on with our long leather shoelaces. Like Huck Finn we would raft the river barefoot. We placed an upright pole in the centre of the raft as our mast, fastened a lumberjack shirt to it, and placed a hard hat on top as our fallers flag. At noon we launched our raft into the

Parsnip River. A bank of mist hung low over the water. We couldn't see the sky, but the long, drawn-out honks of migrating geese drifted down through the mist. We floated along in the serenity of a Chinese poem. We could identify with a scholar exiled from the emperor's court to the wastelands of the north. After a few hours of serenely floating along on the wide flat water, the current sped up. Dirk grinned at me and said, "Hang on!" Soon we were in rapids, moving fast. The raft was hitting bottom, bouncing over rocks, turning sideways. The rocks began to cut the ropes and shoelaces holding the raft together. An outer log left us and then another log began to turn sideways. Suddenly the centre logs rode up on some rocks, and the raft came to an abrupt halt. It was late afternoon, and we had no idea of where we were. Our raft was stuck, high centered, in the middle of a big fast river and was in danger of coming apart. The shore, out of reach, was dark, dense forest. It would be dark in a half hour. It did not look good.

Dirk trying to shoot fish in the river. They didn't bite.

Just then we heard the sound of a motor. Moments later, a long riverboat pulled alongside. The boat was carrying a forestry crew of eight men who were slashing up a side creek a few miles back. The young Indian guy at the tiller nodded to us, saying nothing. Dirk handed our gear, saws, axes, etc. to the guys in the forestry boat as I held the logs together while trying to rescue our shoelaces. As we climbed onto the boat, one more log floated down river as the raft continued to break up. Not a word was said. It was as if this rescue was a prearranged thing done every day.

The boat stopped at Cutthroat Creek. Wow, bunk houses, boardwalks, electric lights, and a proper kitchen. After hearing of our food deprivations, the bull cook said, “I’m going to see to it that you guys eat till you bust.” By the size of his gut, it seemed that this bull cook never saw any lack of food himself. We sat at a table, plates piled high with thick slabs of steak, mashed potatoes, and more steak. For dessert we had three kinds of pie and then staggered out of the cook shack not feeling well. It was all too much for our shrunken stomachs. We crouched behind a D9 bulldozer to spare the bull cook. We did not want him to see us throwing up his extravagant dinner. This kind of gluttony, a common feature of logging camps, was a one-time experience for us. We were grateful to be sated, alive and well and to still have our chainsaws. We slept in a dry and warm bunkhouse. We were both happy with our choice to work and live independently and well away from this rowdy, industrialised logging camp life stuffing ourselves like foie gras geese and sleeping in overheated Atco trailers. The kind of stories we wanted to tell on our return were not found here.

Our next contract was huge. Eighty acres, quite a long ways up the Nation River. Here we really honed our skills as fallers. We set up our camp, and soon snarling chainsaws turned a pristine forest wilderness into a chaotic mess of stumps, downed trees, smashed and broken undergrowth. We did incredible damage to the forest and the creatures who lived there. A squirrel frantically ran around our camp looking for her cut-down nest, or her family, or the nuts she stashed in the now unrecognisable forest floor. Winter was coming, she could not survive. Her home, her carefully stashed food, all of it was gone. She chattered at us incessantly. She knew that it was us who brought this holocaust to her clean, orderly forest.

The whisky jacks (grey jays) were one of the few animals who benefited from our presence. These birds invaded our camp looking for anything edible.

They sat and hovered and waited until the moment they saw an unprotected dish of food. One only had to turn one's back, or walk two paces away, for a grey flash to swoop in and scoop up what they could on the fly. They were fearless. They are born thieves with a knack for adaptation.

To ramp up production we came up with the idea of 'domino falling.' This saved time because we did not notch the tree but only back cut it almost, but not quite, all the way through, and then went to the next tree and did the same. This was dangerous because a gust of wind, or one tree falling meant the entire back-cut forest could all fall en masse. This was OK providing that you were well behind your pre-cut trees because the trees were all back cut to fall, more or less, in the same direction. We would cut into trees like madmen, leaping from one tree to the next, never taking our finger off the throttle. For hours we worked our way back to a giant cottonwood tree with enormous spreading branches. When we felled the cottonwood, we shut off the saws and watched in awe. This was the beginning of a chain reaction where every back-cut tree would take down the trees in front of it. A thousand trees would fall in one minute.

A Forest Service guy had walked into the undercut forest towards the noise of our saws. When he finally noticed that all the trees around him were partially cut through, he got out of there right away and circled around through uncut timber to find us. The checker was breathless with shock and indignation as he stuttered out that our domino falling violated the spirit of every Forest Service regulation he could think of. We told him people are remembered for the rules they break, not for the rules they follow.

Up the Nation River, isolated from the world of men, with no way home. We had arrived: we were living on our own in the wilderness of British Columbia. We slept in a bed of moss a foot thick in a small two-man 6 mill-plastic shelter held up by willow wands. Our shelter kept the elements out, but that was all it would keep out. Sleep is dangerous. Our animal memory knows this. Honed by a million-year evolution, our natural animal senses came back to us by living in the wild.

It was during the dark of a new moon – waking abruptly from a deep sleep I sat bolt upright, fully alert and listening. I looked over and there was Dirk also sitting bolt upright, fully alert, listening. Our innate senses were saying, wake up! Danger! Danger! We whispered, "something is out there, better go look." I went out, barefoot, with our one feeble flashlight, poking around in the dark. I saw nothing and we went back to bed saying it was probably a moose. The next morning, walking the footpath to the river carrying a coffee pot, not yet completely awake and still fuzzy with thoughts of a lingering dream, I came face to face with an enormous silver tip grizzly bear. His head was level with mine and he was on all fours. Instant clarity! He is way too big. I was rooted in place. I looked into his eyes, level with mine, and saw beady eyes that did not blink. My brain was screaming I want outta here! I walked backwards until I reached the bend in the path, turned and ran! "Get the gun! Get the gun! There's a grizzly coming into camp." Dirk grabbed the gun, a WWII Lee Enfield, and strode up the trail to the river saying, "I'm getting a bear hide for Lois" (a young man's infatuation with a college girlfriend who was three thousand miles away). By time Dirk got there, the grizzly had retreated and was in the middle of the river. Dirk shot. The bear roared and clambered up the far bank of the river. A wounded lord of the northwoods disappeared in the slash.

All day we were nervous, looking over our shoulders, half expecting an enraged grizzly to charge out of the underbrush. That evening Dirk was at the river washing the dishes when he heard an ungodly roar that vibrated his very bones. He looked up to see the grizzly bounding across the criss-crossed fallen trees with huge leaps, his mouth wide open, roaring to the skies. A frightening picture of unrestrained rage. The hairs on Dirk's neck, and on his arms, stood straight up. This was Primal Fear. The biggest, smartest predator of all BC, a grizzly bear, in pain, and he knew who did this to him. Dirk came back to camp ashen-faced and shaking. As it got dark, we could hear the bear across the river. As it got darker our imaginations took over. With every noise we heard, "it's him! Listen, there he is." There was a splash in the river. "He's coming across the river. He's coming to get us! We have to keep him from crossing the river." We had no light. We poured gasoline on our pile of firewood and had an instant fire. Flames shot up in the air, lighting up the entire camp like it was daylight. We kept heaping more wood on the fire until the flames were thirty feet high. We stood in our circle of light, one of us holding the rifle, the other an axe, ready to repel a charging grizzly out for revenge. I lit a cigarette; Dirk asked for one. I told him to inhale. He coughed till he was retching, but afterwards he said it helped to calm him. This was the first and only time in his life that Dirk smoked a cigarette. We kept hearing noises in the dark, splashes in the river, we knew he was out there, we kept adding wood to the fire, entire logs. By three o'clock in the morning we were exhausted, our fear was exhausted, our heightened imaginations were exhausted, our emotions were exhausted. We heaped more logs onto the fire and crawled into our plastic shelter to sleep with the loaded rifle between us. It was an off and on affair, alternatively we would wake with a start, add some more wood to the fire, spread dead branches all around our shelter so we would hear footsteps, and then go back to a fitful sleep. In the morning light the threat seemed less imminent, and we went to work, believing that even a grizzly would think twice before attacking someone with a running chainsaw in his hands.

We did not see the grizzly bear again, but at Jerry Klaus's slashing camp a few miles upriver, on the other side, a huge silver tip grizzly bear rampaged through their camp, his powerful forepaws flinging gas cans, pots and pans and chainsaws every which way, and tore a tent to shreds all the while roaring his protest to the heavens. On the hillside Jerry saw small trees with deep claw marks snapped off and thrown aside. This was an angry bear. It was no doubt our bear, but he may have also been fighting back at the destruction of his forests. We heard stories of moose charging bulldozers, breaking their massive antlers on the unyielding steel blade of a D9. They too were fighting back; a tragic, uneven fight it was. Our technologies have made us Gods in the natural world. But we are seriously blind-sighted Gods who unthinkingly destroy the natural world and thereby endanger our very own existence.

On some days we visited a beaver colony well outside of the area we were cutting. The beavers had transformed a flattened dip in the land into a wetland home for fifteen. They had built a few dams to direct the waters of a small creek to flood a flat bottomland. Their big dam, about 500 feet long, was curved against the flow of the water, engineered for maximum strength much like the Hoover Dam. Willows and other succulent water plants colonised the shores of the beaver lake. Beavers create conditions that favour the growth of the trees and plants they feed on. The beavers were undisturbed by the occasional moose that came along to eat underwater plants growing in the shallower waters.

Six or eight round beaver houses dotted the lake. The entrances to the beaver houses were under water, but the rounded top of the beaver houses were above the surface. Inside each of these there would be a shelf running all the way around just above the water level. Here the beavers and their young live and survive the freezing cold of winter. There are stories of people escaping from enemies by diving into the water, finding the underwater entrance and hiding in a beaver house until the danger was past. The houses, made of interwoven sticks and mud, are solidly built and once frozen are impenetrable to all predators who, in winter, can get to the house by walking on the ice.

A beaver felled a large poplar tree two feet in diameter. The beaver, standing on its hind legs, walked round and round the tree all the while chewing into the wood. Eventually, what was left was a smaller and smaller point of wood at the centre of the tree holding it up. At some point the tree had fallen in no predictable direction. There was no undercut to guide the direction of the fall. It is not uncommon for a beaver to be killed by a falling tree. In order to get this bonanza of food to the lake, two beavers were digging a canal. Over two weeks they dug it, and during the process of floating the large tree they enlarged the canal as needed, straightening any curves that restricted the movement of the tree and chewing off any branches that held it back. Eventually the two-foot poplar tree floated into the lake. By spring new willow shoots would be growing along the new canal.

Beavers use their tails as rudders. A single twist of the tail is enough to change course by ninety degrees. With a clap of our hands all work came to an immediate halt. The beavers would respond with their own multiple claps as their flat tails hit the water. An early-warning system par-excellence.

During the cold clear nights of late October, in the light of a full moon, the night came alive. Wolves would howl. It would begin with a lone wolf howling a long, drawn-out howl. When this howling ended another wolf would answer with a long, drawn-out howl coming from a completely different direction. One by one a half-dozen wolves would howl their lonesome call to the full moon, penetrating the solitude of the vast north country to proclaim, I exist. I am a part of us all. At some mysterious breakaway point wolves from all points of the compass would howl all at once. This wild chorus, coming equally from all directions, would completely fill our senses, banishing all thoughts of self. After this coming together, the night would revert to one lone wolf howling, and then another and another to end with a new crescendo. The chorus was in perfect harmony. No conductor needed.

Wolves are social animals. Like us, they live and survive within a close family group. Wolves howling raises the hair on our necks. There exists a deep recognition that we, at one time, in a far and distant past, were brother to the wolf. It came naturally to domesticate wolves, who eventually became man's best friend. Then we domesticated ourselves! Wolves however stayed wild. To hear wolves howling is to remember that we were once wild and free. We, in that far and distant past, unequivocally, belonged to our group, our tribe, our clan. Life outside of these bonds was not life. In the Old Testament the most feared punishment was banishment. To be expelled from your family and your tribe was worse than death. The wolves howling at the full moon made us feel lonely. It triggered deeply buried memories, stored in our genes, that we too once belonged.

We stayed at this camp for over a month and left it as veteran fallers. We left a half acre of trees around our camp standing until the last day. For whisky jacks, squirrels and other wild critters, our camp was a deceptive bonanza of food and warmth. We learned to recognize individual birds and other creatures. We learned to boat the wild waters of the canyon of the Nation River by moonlight. We howled at the moon and, occasionally, a wolf would answer. This we considered a gift like no other. We left a huge, tall tree standing for a bald eagle. This was his perch from where he could survey his airy realm. On the last day we cut this tree and the half acre of trees around our campsite. It felt like a betrayal.

Our camp on the Nation River (both images) Top: John.
Bottom: Jerry Klaus, John and Dirk

Number Thirteen: A Cannibal Sees Only Meat

Dirk and I, both university students on a very extended summer vacation, were experienced at falling trees, an occupation so dangerous that it occupied its own special place in the annals of the British Columbia Workers' Compensation Board. However, we were to find out that there were other, unanticipated hazards lurking in the great north woods.

Dirk, as a 23-year-old philosophy student, felled trees to thoughts of Kant and Heidegger. Myself, as a 28-year-old history student, tended to live in the past. We both shared in a youthful illusion that we were invincible and therefore could not be killed by a mere falling tree. The newly completed BC Bennett Dam, 600 feet high, was flooding an enormous untouched wilderness in order to generate electricity to power the city of Vancouver, a thousand kilometres away. We were on our way to clear cut another eighty acres of forest that would be under water once the water came up to its final height. The site, accessible only by boat, was up the Nation River, later to become the Nation arm of Williston Lake.

To complete this last contract before winter set in we hired Ted Gorensef, a 32-year-old refugee from Bulgaria we had met in the Mackenzie bar. Ted was a stocky, barrel-chested guy with no visible neck. His short legs bowed out at the knees. This gave him a rolling kind of walk. Coming towards you he looked to be a human tank. Gorensef had escaped from a prison in Bulgaria, killing a guard en route, and then had taken a long walk to freedom. He survived by breaking into summer cabins, stealing what he needed, eating anything he could lay his hands on. "Raw or cooked – all the same," he said. "When I saw something moving, I only saw meat." We did not ask too many questions. He survived four months of winter, walking the wind swept, icy, ridges of the Carpathian Mountains to reach Austria. A tough, determined survivor, this guy.

It was late October when we motored up the Nation River in our little outboard, loaded to the gunnels with supplies and gear. We figured we could finish the contract before the river froze up. Once on site we set up an extravagantly large clear plastic tent so we could stand upright. We used up a whole roll of 6-

mill plastic sheeting for this extravagance. The tent had a tin "airtight" stove in one corner. We collected enough green moss for a deluxe, foot-thick mattress. Then it was off to work.

On the second day, Dirk cut through his heavy leather boot into his big toe. His toe was split in two all the way to his foot, with the pieces dangling from the bottom of his foot by a wide piece of skin. Lotsa blood. This needed a doctor. We bandaged and duct-taped Dirk's foot up until he was deemed good to go. We jury-rigged a long, straight branch from a tree onto the tiller, using hose clamps and duct tape so Dirk could steer the boat kneeling on a pile of forestry blankets at the bow. We figured that this would work to get him through the fast waters of the canyon with its whirlpools and sharp protruding rocks. The three of us shook hands and Gorensef and I bid Dirk a safe journey. It was a solemn parting. I experienced butterflies of apprehension when I saw my best friend, Dirk, and the boat, our only way out of there, disappear around the bend in the river. Dirk was strong, and immensely capable in most any situation. Underneath a deeply poetic nature he was a tough Ontario farm boy. Shivers ran up my back at the thought that this wild dangerous country could overwhelm Dirk, or perhaps overwhelm us all.

We, along with hundreds of other men, were living in remote worksites scattered all over an enormous wilderness area, falling trees ahead of the rising water, using wickedly dangerous chainsaws. It was extremely hazardous work. There were no first-aid attendants, no radios, nor any communications with the outside world. It could take days for an injured person to get medical help. There were enormous masses of logs and debris floating in Williston Lake. We ourselves contributed to this every working day. The winds drove this mass of logs, whole trees, branches, and debris into a chaotic floating mass. It was unpredictable as to where these "rafts" were going to be. A boat heading for Mackenzie could be trapped for days trying to chainsaw their way through.

Alarm bells finally began to go off when the doctors in the PG hospital began to see gangrene in men who had suffered deep raggedy saw cuts. For an injured man it could take as much as a week to reach medical attention, if he could reach it at all. The doctors had not seen gangrene since WWII. Work-safe BC stepped in, but whatever new regulations they came up with never reached us. We just carried on.

Three days later Gorensef and I stood on the banks of the river looking at the fast-moving water, a turbulent flow that seemed to have no beginning, no end. As the sun sank behind the mountains, the clear night sky turned an eerie green. The stars appeared as bright shimmering diamonds that seemed to shiver against the fabric of a surreal green sky. We had never seen anything like this. It was getting cold, so we turned in to sleep.

Three hours later we woke up freezing cold. It seemed that the very marrow in our bones was turning to ice. We filled the airtight to the brim, gave it a good shot of gasoline, put a heavy weight on the lid, held a lit match to the air vent at the bottom of the stove, and with a mighty whoomp, it was lit. We waited until the airtight was red hot and moved our moss beds and our piles of blankets as close as we could without setting the blankets on fire. We went to sleep in a cocoon of warmth, but every three hours a bone-chilling cold woke us up and we would repeat the cycle. It was a long night. We had been told as children to never ever go to sleep in the cold; you would never wake up! This is a folk myth – the cold wakes you up shivering like an advanced stage of malaria well before you freeze to death. Thank God we had a huge number of forestry blankets "borrowed" from the forestry camp at Tutu Creek. My personal pile was eight blankets thick with a paper-thin Space Blanket laid on top for good luck.

The next morning, we stood on the banks of the river. The speed of the flowing water was undiminished, but the fast-moving water was now carrying a chaotic mass of chunks of ice hurtling past our feet. Even with a boat, the way back to civilization was now clearly impossible.

A bag of oatmeal, several dozen eggs frozen solid, five loaves of frozen bread, some pieces of meat from a moose shot a month earlier, and frozen cans with the labels rubbed off was what we had left for food. Walking out was not possible. We were on the wrong side of the Parsnip River as well as the Nation River, with no way across either one. We were stuck there! I looked at Gorensef thinking, “when the last of the food is gone, Gorensef will survive.” Underneath these layers of winter clothing, he sees me as meat. I was reminded of a story Jerry Klaus told about two prisoners planning an escape from a Siberian gulag. A younger man was invited to join them. He was, unknowingly, their self-propelled, self-preserved food, to be butchered and eaten when needed. This arrangement did not turn out well for any of them.

Francis Isaac had told us it was too late in the year to make a camp that far up the Nation. We replied, “no problem, we have a boat. When the water begins to freeze up, we'll leave.” “NO!” he said. “The river will freeze up and you'll be trapped.” But we, in our overeducated minds, knew that a big, fast-moving river like the Nation couldn't freeze up, just like that, in a single day. Now we stood on the banks of the Nation River as wiser, if not exactly humbler, men.

We worked the short daylight hours of the North. It was a pleasure to work in the brisk temperatures with no mosquitoes. Gorensef was a fast, determined worker, dancing from tree to tree, felling them like a demented Paul Bunyan. On day ten we were down to some cans with unidentified contents, a few frozen potatoes, a pound of butter, and a loaf of frozen bread. Gorensef wanted meat. What to do? I suggested that we walk to a camp on a small slashing contract that Dirk and I had finished a month earlier. It was located on a steep hillside above the canyon about seven miles back down the Nation River, and on our side of the river. We had left the little two-man plastic shelter standing and well as some canned food and the hind quarter of a moose. The meat was a bit ripe, green in places, when we left it, but it was probably still edible. The camp was on a ten-foot-wide bench on the steep hillside not so far above the canyon walls, sitting in the middle of a jumble of trees felled earlier by Dirk and me.

The next morning Gorensef and I set out on our salvage mission. We climbed to the top of the ridge and then walked it. The snow wasn't very deep, but it was bitterly cold. After several hours we stopped to build a small fire and warm our feet. I was wearing Dirk's fancy knee-high all-leather Mountie boots. They looked great walking down a paved city sidewalk but, here in the bush, they offered little protection from the cold. After a hot instant coffee, we continued on. After four hours of walking, we took a chance and headed downhill. Lady Luck was blowing us kisses. We hit the top corner of the clearcut. From here it was easy to find our old camp.

The shelter was still up and intact. Yeah! Gorensef went into a purple rage when he saw the food left behind. Some one-gallon cans of peaches, frozen solid. "We walked all this way, we froze our asses, we risked our lives, for what? For frozen peaches? Are you crazy! I want meat!" He levelled the 303. I saw madness in the angry dark eyes looking me over. He was seeing meat!

I talked to him. "We stashed a hind quarter of moose meat. It's under the snow. I can find it." The moose quarter was stashed a ways from camp because it would attract bears. I found it under a foot of snow. It was frozen solid with lots of long sliding tooth marks in the frozen meat. It had been gnawed on by wolves, wolverines, and other critters.

We fired up a small kerosene stove left in the shelter, which immediately filled it with smoke and the smell of kerosene. Gorensef muttered a stream of Bulgarian curses. We cut holes in the roof to let the smoke out, ate some frozen peaches and went to sleep. The moss floor and our sleeping bags kept us kinda warm. At first daylight we lit a fire, heated up the cans of peaches, drained the liquid to get rid of weight and packed it all up along with the frozen hind quarter and headed back. It was a long slog carrying heavy backpacks. We took turns carrying the moose quarter. It was an awkward load lashed to the outside of the backpack. Walking warmed us up. At dusk from the top of the ridge, we could see our camp by the river. We saw a black shape on the other side of the river moving erratically. "It's a bear" said Gorensef as he raised the 303 and fired twice. I told him to stop wasting ammunition. At best he would only kill something we could not get to. Once inside our shelter we dropped the backpacks and poured some gasoline into the loaded-up stove. With an explosive whooomp it was lit. My back and shoulders ached, and my feet felt as frozen as the moose meat. We heard a yell! What's this? There was no one within fifty miles. We rushed outside. It was Dirk standing on the other side of the river, wearing a long black coat. It was impossible. He had a snowmobile loaded with food, but there was no way to get it to us. We yelled back and forth over the noise of the ice flows. Dirk tried to throw some cans to us, but they fell into the river halfway across. One orange made it and landed at our feet. Had Gorensef been a better rifleman he would have shot Dirk. We would not have known. We would have thought that he had shot a bear. Dirk and I yelled ourselves hoarse, to no avail. Dirk eventually waved goodbye, fired up his snowmobile and disappeared in the distance. I felt incredibly sad to see my friend, so close, but so far away. There was nothing we could do. I feared that Dirk would meet his death in this vast frozen wasteland. The thought of my best friend dying out there, cold, and alone, sent a chill up my back. It seemed like the ice, the fast-flowing water, the cold, all these implacable forces of nature, could defeat us. My sense of invincibility was meeting its match.

Dirk had gotten himself to the hospital in Prince George and had his toe stitched back together. Dirk's story of his time getting to the hospital and then his impossible journey to get back upriver to bring us badly needed food was a hair-raising tale: a super-human effort that very nearly cost him his life.

Gorensef walked away, before Dirk left, muttering curses into his beard. When I saw him walking away in his rolling gait I realised that I hated him. From this point on, day or night, my eight-inch sheath knife was on my belt.

We worked for six more days. I was completely warm only when working, moving fast, enveloped in the hot exhaust gases of the chainsaw. Gorensef cut down the last stand of trees. That evening we sat by the fire. The question, "now what?" hung unspoken in the air. We heard the ice floes grinding against each other in the river. Pieces of frozen moose meat hung over the fire. Gorensef was hunched over sharpening his knife. Canada is replete with stories from the last century of mad trappers stuck in Canada's northlands with no way back to civilization. Most often one of them goes barking mad. The stories never end well. The thought, "am I living one of those frontier stories," was lodged in my mind. "Now what," still hung in the air. I said, "I'm turning in. We can talk in the morning." Gorensef only grunted. I fired up the airtight till it was cherry red, pulled the bed close and turned in. We had three more days of mostly silence. The topic of "what now?" Had a short, simple answer. "We wait." Wait for what – that elicited a shrug of the shoulders. I was more convinced with each passing day that Gorensef saw me as meat. He probably thought best not to talk too much to his future meat. The possible scenarios were a merry-go-round running round my brain. One night I had vivid dreams of the Donner Party, stranded on a mountain pass in mid-winter. They resorted to eating their own.

A forestry helicopter on its way to Mackenzie made a small detour because the pilot was curious as to how fast the water was rising this far up the Nation River. As he approached, he saw a camp and flew lower for a better look. He was astonished to see people way out here in the dead of winter. The chopper circled and landed close to camp. When the pilot saw Gorensef, a raggedy, unwashed guy with long unkempt hair and beard rushing towards his helicopter yelling like a madman, the chopper lifted off. We were dumbfounded. We both knelt on the snow, our arms raised in supplication. The helicopter circled and landed again. The pilot opened the door and said, "you guys could use a bath." We took our guns, saws, blankets and other gear. We left the plastic shelter standing. An hour later we were sitting in a warm restaurant in Mackenzie having our first real meal in weeks. Near-death stories, close calls, were a kind of currency in the Mackenzie bar, and we had stories to tell. Gorensef recovered his ability to talk, and we regaled the patrons of the Mackenzie bar with our stories.

Gorensef, in a matter of an hour, went from being a cannibal who might well have me for dinner to my adventure partner who shared in our stories of survival in the bush. Both were equally real. How quickly our perceptions change. It's the circumstances that make the difference.

Many years later, in Georgia, I met a young woman who told me how she and two women friends, caught up in a merciless drive for revenge for the deaths of two children, had lured three Abkhaz men into their house and murdered them in the most brutal way they knew how. She said, "before this I would not have hurt anything. A baby crying pained my heart. I am a mother. Now that I am safe here in Tbilisi, again I cannot hurt even a stray cat."

Human nature encompasses a vast range of buried possibilities. Our "real" self knows few boundaries.

1968 Our last camp, with a hugely expanded plastic shelter

We lived in luxury (even able to stand up inside) until the temperature dropped to minus fifty degrees

The Human Price of Progress

The Sekani people lived in the remote valleys of the Findlay rivers for many thousands of years. During the 1960s, the twentieth century dropped on them like a ton of bricks.

The building of the Wacky Bennet dam precipitated Canada's last major colonisation. A free people living their traditional hunting, fishing, gathering life saw their familiar homelands disappear under hundreds of feet of water. Gone were the always reliable fishing places, the hillsides thick with huckleberries, the beaver dams, and the rich swampy wetlands where one could always find moose grazing on succulent plants. Gone were the stands of giant trees where caribou gathered in the winter, when the temperature dropped to forty below.

The land had been their self-renewing source of simply everything. Frost-repelling wolverine fur to line the hood of a parka, soft lynx fur to make a baby blanket. A caribou coat valued for the supreme insulation afforded by its unique hollow hairs, a moose hide for making tough, durable moccasins, and abundant renewable food. Everything needed to sustain life and culture was present, here, in their homeland. The identity of the people, who they were, where they came from and what life was about all came from the land. The land was the source of everything they knew.

The Sekani peoples were completely integrated into their sub-arctic environment. Even in the dead of winter a person could decide to visit a relation in Fort Macleod, a five-day walk, at 30 below. Using their ancient trails, people could walk as far as Alaska. They were not an isolated band but a secure, self-sufficient people who were connected to faraway peoples by a vast network of trails. This came to an abrupt end in 1968, with the completion of the dam. The land, now under as much as 500 feet of water, was only a memory. With it went their trails, their homes, their livelihood, their identity as the People of the Beaver and the very purpose of their lives. Now the world was an uncertain, dangerous, and foreign place for the Sekani.

The people were moved onto a 32-acre reservation on the Findlay road at mile 69. Logging trucks roared by day and night. Truck drivers, hungry for some diversion, were a ready source of alcohol for the people. For many, alcohol filled a haunting emptiness. Hunger stalked the plywood cabins at 69 mile. The moose, always plentiful, were now scarce. Jarl, a trapper living up the Omineca River and on his way to Findlay Forks by boat, encountered a stranded moose. The moose had, as always, proceeded to swim across what he knew to be a river. Partway across the new lake his front feet got straddled around a floating log. He could not free himself and was stuck, slowly starving to death. Jarl shot the moose to end its suffering. By the time he reached Findlay Forks he had used up the whole box of fifteen 303 cartridges, and meanwhile, the people at 69 mile felt the pangs of hunger and wept as children cried themselves to sleep.

Six years on, the people decided to leave 69 mile and move back to the Ingenika camp at the very head of the lake to escape the ravages of the dissolute life fuelled by emptiness and endless supplies of alcohol. They were motivated by the belief that the Sekani band would perish if they remained at 69 mile. Beyond Inginika the Findlay River still ran free.

But even here, beyond the flood waters, life in their homelands had changed. The fish had gotten much bigger. The flooded forest floor was rich in nutrients. However, the flesh of these fine-looking fish was a pale white. The flooded soil and the sunken trees released mercury into the water that became concentrated in the beautiful big fish, now unfit for even their dogs. The fluctuating water levels seasonally exposed wide shorelines with no vegetation. During the spring, sandstorms, driven by the newly powerful winds, darkened the noonday sun. Sand was driven into every crevice, into sleeve ends and parka hoods, into the houses, the beds, the food. Airplanes flying over Lake Williston stayed above 10,000 feet to avoid the fine clay dust that shortened the life of the engines. It took another twelve years for the logging road to reach Enginika and close the circle. For the Sekani people there was no escape.

Jean Toma and her government build plywood house. Winter is coming.

Below: Francis, his cousins, and Dirk bringing back moose meat

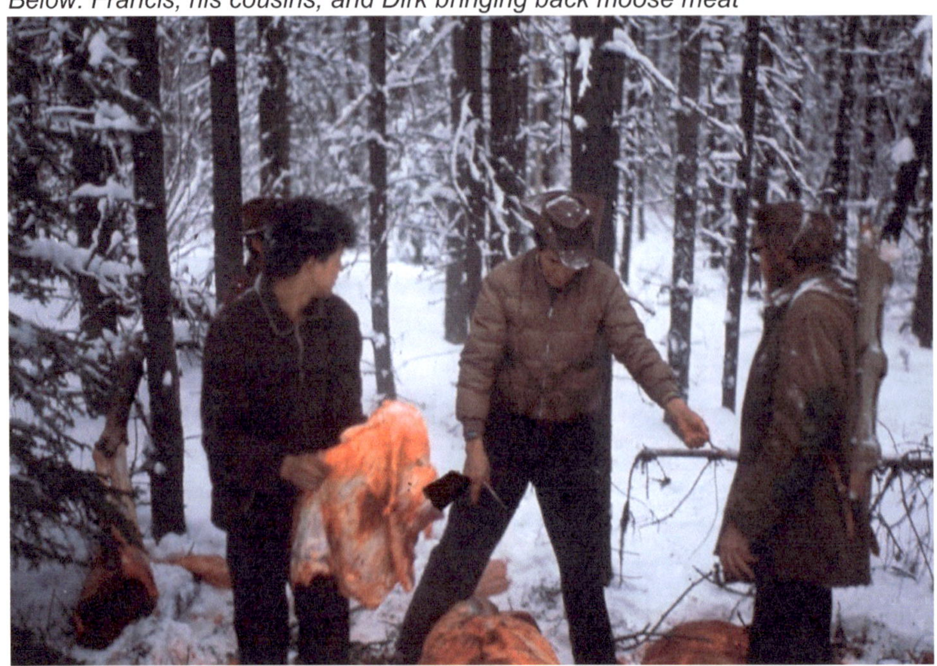

Number Fourteen: The Fire and the Phoenix

We were out of work. Dirk, myself and Ted Gorensef had hunkered down in an abandoned storage and repair depot for logging trucks. The five-acre clearcut, a few miles south of Mackenzie, contained a three-room shack with a propane-fired kitchen stove and an old, carbureted oil stove for heat. It was late November, and cold. Most nights it hovered around 20 below, on the Fahrenheit scale. We still slept under a six-or seven-thick pile of forestry blankets. Our frozen breath hung in the air. We were never really warm. I had wired a car radio to a spare car battery. Sometimes when the aurora borealis was just right Dirk could tune into faint rifts of Vivaldi or Mozart. A huge repair shop next door, with a cement floor and massive double doors which were permanently jammed open, dwarfed the shack. Inside was a chaotic mess of discarded truck parts and broken equipment. The shop had the unhappy look of a place hastily abandoned. Around the edge of the landing, up against the trees, half a dozen random vehicles were completely covered over by a massive snow drift.

We were preparing to leave for Ontario. Dirk found two 45-gallon barrels full of gasoline where a fuel truck had rolled off the road. He managed to get the abandoned barrels onto the 1962 Chevy pickup truck we had gotten after the Oldsmobile met an ignominious death that had almost killed Dirk. He set the barrels vertically against the back of the cab under a self-made plywood canopy. We loaded our chainsaws and the rest of our gear into the back of the pickup, and we were ready to roll. But our preparations needed one more last-minute tweak.

I wanted to run a gas line, salvaged from one of the buried vehicles, directly to the 45-gallon drums. With a siphon between the two barrels, we would be able to drive halfway home in one go, without stopping for gas. We drove the truck into the shop. It was quite dark in there, so we brought in a Coleman lantern. I crawled under the truck and disconnected the line from the truck's own gas tank, which was behind the seat, and began to attach this to the line coming from the two barrels. Gasoline ran out onto the cement floor and onto my bulky canvas coat as my clumsy frozen fingers fumbled with the connection. I could not see well in the darkened shop. Suddenly, with a mighty whooomp, the Coleman lantern ignited the gas fumes. In an instant there was fire everywhere. Dirk, who was sitting in the truck to turn the key to begin to pump gas from the barrels, felt the truck lift. I rolled out from under the truck, a mass of flames. Dirk grabbed me by the collar and ran me headfirst into a snow drift. A few armloads of snow smothered the fire, and I was out. But not so our truck. We yelled for Gorensef as acrid black smoke filled the shop. The three of us ran into the murky, smoke-filled shop. Hacking and coughing, with tears in our eyes, we pushed against that truck like it was Sisyphus' boulder. Thoughts of two drums full of gasoline gave us the indomitable strength of truly desperate men. As the truck began to move, the fire followed it as gasoline continued to run out of the still-disconnected gas line. Once outside, flames played up the sides of the truck. I rolled back under the truck through the flames to pinch off the leaking gas line with a pair of vice grips. With the fuel for the fire cut off, the flames slowly died out. Dirk helped me dive back into the extinguishing snow drift. With the gasoline flow cut off and a few thrown armloads of snow, the fire under the truck was out. However, the fire under the hood, fuelled by burning wires and hoses, was still burning. Gorensef muttered a string of Bulgarian curses while keeping a considerable distance from an imminent explosion. I jimmied the jammed hood open. More armloads of snow put the fire under the hood out as well as one inside the cab. In one incredible burst of energy, the truck, our gear, the drums of gasoline, and the repair shop; all of it was saved. But our truck had suffered grievously from the flames of our ambition to drive nonstop to Winnipeg.

Our Chevy truck had melted wiring, burnt spark plug wires, a distorted, twisted distributor cap, a burnt fan belt, burnt brake hoses, a burnt hydraulic clutch hose, and collapsed radiator hoses. The front seat upholstery was gone. Gorensef's pronouncement, "this truck is not going anywhere," seemed only too true.

But we went to work. My experience as a mechanic came into play. For the next week we kept going back to our midden, tunnelling through five feet of snow to scrounge essential parts off the buried vehicle wrecks – brake fluid, antifreeze, high tension wires, heater hoses, brake hoses, fan belts, a coil, a distributor cap, all scavenged by twentieth-century hunter gatherers. With frozen fingers, using duct tape, electric tape, and scrounged lengths of wire, we taped up and replaced burnt wires, and left some burnt wires be. Who needs dash lights? We modified the brake and clutch hoses from an old International truck. Using haywire and judicious applications of epoxy, found in the glove box of one of the buried trucks, and solder, scraped and carefully collected from old wire connections, we made it all work! It took a week but in the end we revived the burned pickup truck. There was a mighty cheer when the Chevy truck coughed, sputtered and with a cloud of black smoke roared back to life. Gorensef anointed the Phoenix with a few drops of whiskey. Dirk and I drove off, leaving Mackenzie and what seemed like a lifetime of northern memories behind.

Number Fifteen: An Accident Makes Our Fortune

Once back at Calvin College, Dirk and I would hold court in the commons and tell our tales of exciting lives lived in the wilds of northern British Columbia. Maya, a beautiful, bright, and talented actress, was enchanted with our stories. We fell in love to images of fast-running rivers, mysterious, wild animals and endless forest too vast and too green to be real. Perfect timing. We were married six weeks after we met on the Calvin seminary campus, in the spring. We lived in a low stone room building set a foot or so into the ground, almost hidden from view by the lilac bushes and ivy growing up against its walls. This was an old farm milk house which we converted into our snug, hidden-away home. It was our most romantic hideaway. It was an idyllic time of life. She was a gentle, loving addition to my life, the likes of which I had not known was possible.

A few weeks earlier, during a visit to my mother in Sarnia, Ontario, my brother-in-law, Martin, sold us his immaculate, not even a scratch on it, Vespa scooter for $100. We loaded it into the trunk of our 1960 Valiant and took it home. On a hot summer evening we decided to go to the quarry for a swim. The quarry was only three miles down a country road, so we took the Vespa. About halfway there we passed a car driving slow. Just as we were beside the car, it turned left into a driveway. In order to avoid a collision, we took to the ditch. The Vespa tipped over, and we skidded along in tall grass with the scooter on its side. We came to an abrupt halt when the front wheel hit a rock. A little dazed, we stood up and took stock. I was not hurt. The skin on Maya's forearm was cut and partly abraded. She had hit her head, and it was bleeding. The scooter still ran, but it was almost a foot shorter. Maya had a concussion. I thought she was the picture of courage and bravery as she later sat up in our bed, her arm and head swathed in white bandages, with a big smile on her face. She was our wounded warrior when the insurance adjuster showed up. The accident was clearly not our fault. We ended up getting $3,600 and negotiated to keep the Vespa.

While attending Calvin College, I had been working part-time at South Eastern Garage, in East Grand Rapids. I took the Vespa to the shop where we tied one end of the scooter to a tree and the other to the winch on the tow truck. The powerful hydraulics then stretched the scooter back to pre-collision length. Done! I immediately took the Vespa on a test drive down the four-lane Twenty-Eighth Street at full throttle, fifty miles an hour. It seemed as good as new right up until I was going through a green light where a two-seater sports car, coming the other way, turned left in front of me. There was no warning. The Vespa hit the right front wheel of the car and I went sailing into the air. I landed on the hood of the car with a great thump, bounced, and kept on going. I landed on my feet on the other side of the street, running full out to keep my balance, reached the sidewalk, and sat down. I heard loud, enthusiastic applause behind me. Three guys in the corner car lot had seen my double flip. "Worthy of a Hollywood stuntman" they said. The driver of the sports car, a sixteen-year-old, was in tears. She was so excited to be driving her very first car and had gotten only two blocks before she made the fateful left turn. I was not hurt except for a sore thumb. "Sore thumb, not worth much," the insurance adjuster said. But in the end, I received $1,300 and got to keep the Vespa. Back at the shop, after some wry comments on the continually shrinking scooter, we stretched her out again.

Maya said that Martin's scooter was bad luck and refused to ride on it again. Maya was kindness incarnate. She never said that her aversion to the scooter might have had more to do with how I drove it. I sold the now battle-scarred, but still low-mileage, Vespa for $100. Our scooter-created good fortune provided the means to finance many of our next ventures.

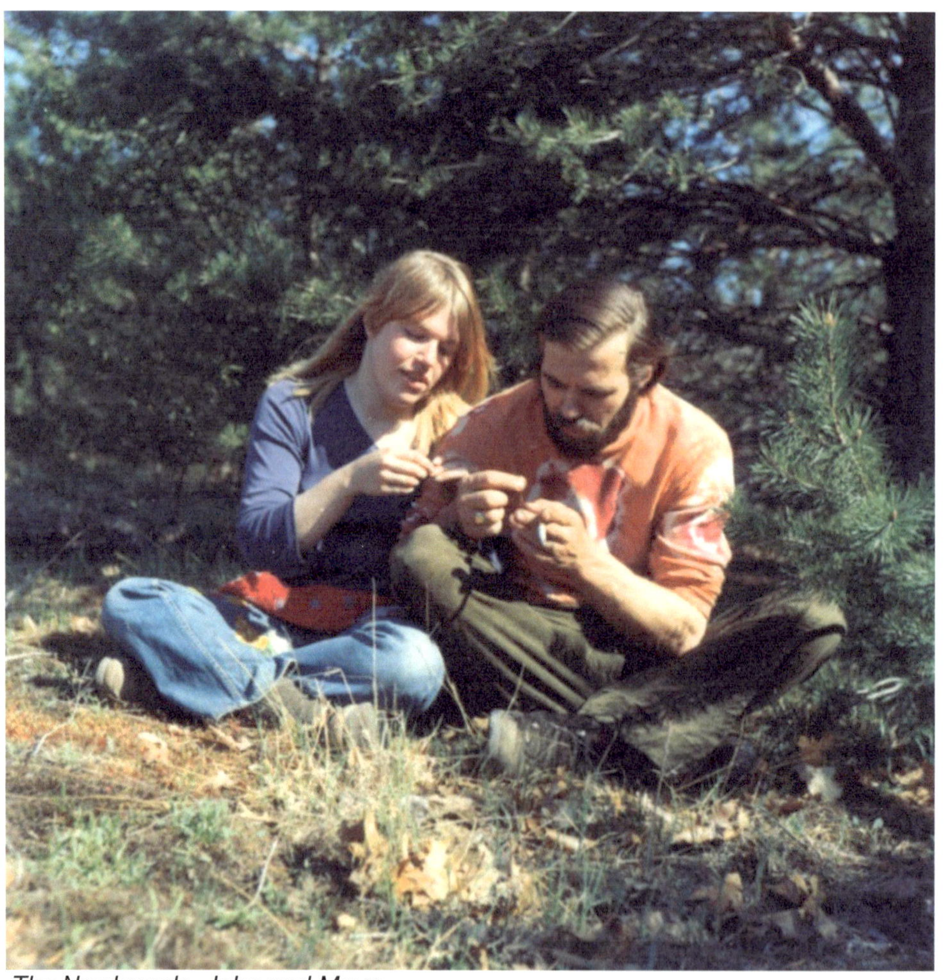

The Newlyweds, John and Maya.

Number Sixteen: Witness to an Execution

It was dead dark. We were driving a narrow, winding road on a moonless night, somewhere in the vast emptiness of the highlands of Chihuahua, having spent time on an extended newlywed road trip through Mexico. The gas gauge was bouncing off empty. Time to stop. We turned onto a little one-lane road to the right, circled around to the backside of a hill, and clambered up to a level hilltop, our Corvair van making like a 4 × 4. We turned off the engine. It was completely still. There were no stars out – must be overcast. The deep darkness enveloped us. We felt invisible. The only sound we heard was the chirp of a single cricket. Eighteen hours of potholed back roads across Chihuahua had us so tired. Once stopped, neither of us could keep our eyes open. It was as if our eyelids weighed a pound apiece. In mere minutes we were fast asleep in the back of the Corvair.

We sat up with a start, wide awake, listening as loud voices and staccato Spanish commands rang out in the night air. We hastily dressed and climbed into the front seat. We sat anxiously peering into the dark, seeing nothing. We heard men's voices at the bottom of the hill, angry voices, other voices, talking fast. There was an urgency in their tone. A single voice with a clear high pitch, it sounded like a woman's voice. We did not understand the Spanish but could make out some words. "Por favor, por Dios," a voice begins to plead. A gunshot rends the night air, a soft thud, then silence, anxious moments. I was holding Maya's hand. Her touch helped keep my fear at bay. I had no recollection of taking her hand, or did she take my hand? We waited, only silence. They did not know we were here, on this hilltop, maybe forty feet away. We had both front windows open, straining to hear something, to see something. A soft breeze whispered in the shrub beside the driver's side door. We sat ever so still to wait out the silence, holding our breath, long minutes passed, an eternity, then a scrape of a boot scuffing the flinty dirt of the desert floor. Is someone coming up our hill? Maya whispered, "let's go." I whispered back "yes, let's go." I pushed in the clutch, and the van began to roll down the hill. Halfway down the hill I let up the clutch, the engine came to life. I floored the gas pedal. The dirt road we came in on was directly below us at the bottom of the hill. We careened down the hillside, hit the dirt road at an angle with a wicked thud, swung hard left. The Corvair was momentarily airborne and then we were on the pavement, pedal to the metal, going full out in second gear. Gunshots echoed through the night air, but we were gone. Moving at 60 mph, drifting through the curves, the Corvair driven right to its limit. The gas gauge was still on empty. We can make it, make what? ..... ten miles maybe. All eyes were peeled for a place to take us off this road. Coming round a corner we saw a light on the left, it was a tienda with a single gas pump. They were just turning off the lights. We both let out a pent-up breath we didn't know we were holding and pulled up to the pump. *Lleno* (full). A bent-over old man, Hollywood's dream cast for Methuselah, turned the pump back on and filled the tank. As we went to leave, he pointed to a back tire and said "Esta plano." The right rear tire was flat. A quick tire change and we were back on the road. In Mazatlán, when I picked up the repaired tire, the guy who fixed the flat handed me a grey lump of lead. He said *quarenta y cinco, esta muy peligroso señor.*

John and Maya somewhere in Mexico.

The Kootenays

Sjoukje – Magical Realism

We left Grand Rapids and moved to Toronto. Maya and I enrolled in Ryerson Polytechnic, Maya to study theatre and me for a photography programme. Not surprisingly, Maya became more pregnant as the summer rolled on.

Finally, I was sitting in a chair in the waiting room in the Women's Hospital in Toronto. This birth was taking a very long time. In 1974 the father was not allowed in the delivery room. I was quite ambivalent about this imminent baby but resigned to what was happening.

A doctor in a white coat walked into the waiting room. He said, "there are complications with the birth, and we have to do a Caesarian." I nodded and settled back in my chair for what I assumed would be a long wait. Not a good beginning to our new venture, I thought to myself. Within mere minutes a nurse came in and said "would you like to see your daughter?" "My what? So quick?" She took me over to an incubator on wheels and I looked into the glass box to see a tiny red-faced baby fast asleep with a tiny thumb in her mouth. I felt a jolt that caused my body to shiver as if I had been doused with cold water. I knew this baby! I immediately recognized her. She was someone who had been very important to me. Someone who really mattered had somehow returned.

For the next three days I was intoxicated with a pure joy. I could think of little else. The most precious gift in the entire universe, one I did not even know I had, had been returned to me. The powerful certainty of what I had seen was unlike anything I had experienced. It was a "Road to Damascus" experience. It was a miracle. It was pure magic. That afternoon I gathered up an enormous bundle of flowers and covered the new mother in a blanket of living colour. Three days later the new baby came home. Eventually she became her own little person with a loud infectious laugh, solidly fixed in reality.

We named her Sharon Marie Elizabeth. When she was a year and half old we moved to the West Kootenay Valley in British Columbia. We bought an old farmhouse on ten acres in Queens Bay, a bench overlooking Kootenay Lake. The Kootenays were (and still are) one of the most beautiful mountain regions of BC and land was “dirt” cheap. Having grown up on a farm, it felt like coming home. At that time the Kootenays saw an invasion of hippies, American draft dodgers and back-to-the-landers, coming from everywhere to realise a dream of living on the land, building their own house, and living the simple life.

Treeplanting was the way we all made the money to build our handmade houses and generally finance our mostly self-sufficient lives. In spite of a back-to-the-land ethos, everyone still needed some money. It was all somewhat messy but I loved the glorious revolt against control and order. A true revolution was asking for too much from a new hippie culture that was, to the core, individualistic and selfish. For Maya it was not her home. She saw more clearly than I that the hippies, in spite of it being in revolt against 1950s conformity, demanded conformity to their own ill-defined ways. How to dress, to talk, to be OK with the fuzzy thinking and fuzzy use of language. The second year in Queens Bay our second baby came but she only lived a few days. Little Anneke was born with physical and mental disabilities that were caused by rh factor and other blood incompatibilities, things that may have led to a different outcome decades later but were either not detectable, or not found, in 1977. After this sad event our marriage slowly foundered. Maya’s crushing grief and my lack of skill to navigate through the experience, coupled with discovering that we were incompatible on such a basic level, proved too much.

Maya and Sjoukje, 1974.

The old farmhouse in Queen's Bay with Sjoukje in the window, 1978.

Toad Rock

Dedicated to JD Cooper

When you drive six kilometres past the Balfour ferry landing, just before the road dips down into Coffee Creek, you pass by a ten-foot-high rock beside the road. It has an odd, irregular shape with patches of moss making it look alive. We all drove by this rock countless times but it was John Cooper, with his unique artist's view of the world, who saw the rock for what it really is. It's a petrified toad. Toad Rock was one of the things he liked to paint, over and over, and so it became a well-known local landmark. The Toad Rock motorcycle campground is blessed with its proximity. Motorcyclists from all over Canada and the USA have spread the name Toad Rock across the entire continent. I recorded this story some time ago, to go along with a John Cooper painting of Toad Rock for a story and art festival in Proctor, BC.

In the beginning God created the heavens and the earth. On the first day God sai", "let there be light." And there was light. And God saw the light that it was good. For the next six days God laboured mightily and created all that we know and love.

On the evening of the sixth day God looked out over his creation and saw a beautiful green earth teeming with an amazing variety of swimming, crawling, flying, leaping and walking creatures. God saw that his creation was good, proclaimed it finished and commanded its living creatures to sing his praises. But, unbeknownst to even God, there was a glitch.

One small narrow strip of earth, wedged between two mountain ranges, had been overlooked. There was a raw ugly scar of primaeval rock, mud, and ooze across the face of God's new green earth. Loki, the imperfect angel left over from another creation, the sly one, the trickster, was the cause of this oversight. Loki had drawn a veil of mist over a steep valley lying at the foot of a tall pyramid-shaped mountain which he had chosen as his own. Thus it was that the fallen angel Loki caused God to miss this small piece of earth in his flurry of creation.

Many aeons later an exceedingly large, and grumpy, toad with leathery warty skin was thinking that his home had become much too crowded. One morning, bright and early, he left the sunny valley of the Slocan and made his way, one hop at a time, across the low Fish Lake pass and descended into a thick veil of mist. Since toads are quite given to dank wet places, this was OK with the toad. When the toad finally broke through the veil of mist, he saw a scene of utter desolation. Below lay an absolutely bleak landscape with no trees, no flowers, no birdsong, no life of any kind. There was only a great grey silence. However, since aesthetic was not a big part of his toady nature, this was just fine with the travelling toad too. He merely looked at the lifeless emptiness of the valley below him and croaked "mine all mine!" He was after all quite a grumpy, greedy old toad.

Weeks later a gloomy, footsore, and very hungry toad decided he had gone far enough. He took his last creaky hop, stopped, and just sat. His warty skin hung loosely over his emaciated body. He had not seen, let alone eaten, a single living bug in weeks. He longed for a single ray of sunshine (a most un-toad like impulse). The toad looked out over the bleak and empty landscape with new eyes and saw only a great sameness of rock and mud. Below him the mud merged into a large flat body of thick wet ooze. As far as the eye could see nothing moved in this sunless, colourless landscape. The toad uttered a great croaking harumph that broke the eternal silence of the place and gave voice to his deep despair.

"Who is this God who proclaimed his creation beautiful and good and complete and would have us sing his praises forever. I live and starve in this desolation, this vale of death. I will sing no such praises to a God who cannot finish what he started."

High in the heavens God heard a solitary voice rise against him and said, "who dares to utter such unseemly words! Who dares to speak against God!"

He searched his creation, moving clouds here and misty veils there until he saw a most miserable, thin and warty toad sitting in the mud in the midst of the unfinished valley. God gathered his energies, leaned forward, his right arm extended down from the heavens, his index finger pointing to the very middle of the valley, a bolt of lightning flashed. In an instant the entire valley turned green with trees and grass and flowers and birds. The flat grey mass of mud and ooze turned into a crystal clear, Kootenay Lake. The sounds of creation filled the air as legions of animals, birds and insects swarmed over the land. The sun burst through the gloom and flooded the newly created valley with a radiant and golden light. And this valley was complete and beautiful beyond all his other creations. God had learned a thing or two about creating since his last efforts.

The toad sat in the green grass dumbstruck. God moved his finger ever so slowly until it pointed directly at the toad. The toad gulped once before a jagged bolt of light shot from the end of that pointing finger and the bug-eyed toad turned instantly to hard grey granite. God was still sort of a youthful god and not very good with criticism yet.

To this day the outspoken toad sits in stony silence looking out over Kootenay Lake and Mt Loki, a lasting tribute to the creation of the Kootenays and a monument to those who speak out against overbearing authority.

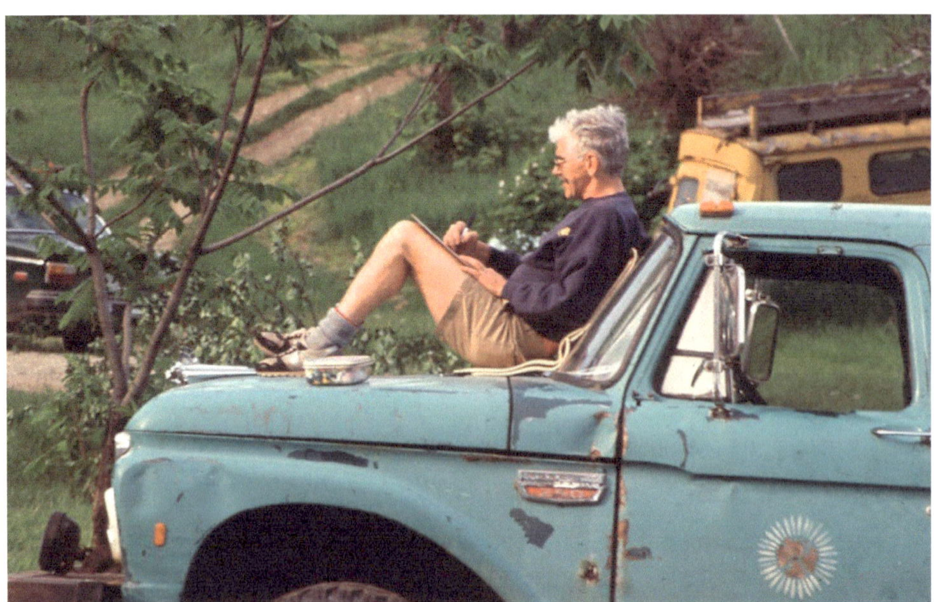

John Cooper painting on the hood of the old farm truck.

Magical Realism Becomes Reality

Maya left one cold November day. It felt lonely and empty rambling around that old ramshackle farmhouse, but I was not alone! I was a single dad with a little four-year-old girl. It was November 22nd, her fourth birthday. Sharon Marie Elizabeth had become Sjoukje in the years since her birth. We had lived with Maya's friend Sharon for a time. Having two Sharons in the house was confusing so our small Sharon became Sjoukje, a good Frisian name.

Sjoukje was one frightened little girl. She had never liked sleeping in her own room and now she was terrified to be alone anywhere for any amount of time. There were horrifying monsters in the closet and under her bed that came out as soon as she fell asleep. "Sometimes even before I sleep." I slept in a room connected to the front room, not far from the wood stove, with a circular stairway in one corner. I made a small and enclosed bed for Sjoukje under the stairs. We hung a Chinese paper lantern in her new "bedroom" and pasted colourful pictures on the bottoms of the steps above her bed. There was a small shelf for her beloved animals to guard her while she slept. "They never sleep." There was a gauze curtain she could open or close. My bed was only ten feet away. It tore at my heart to see her so small, so innocent, so young, and so frightened. I dropped everything for that entire winter. I had a mission, to take care of Sjoukje, to see that this little child was warm and happy and never needed to be afraid.

The first thing was to get the house warm. The turn-of-the-century farmhouse was not insulated. The 20 below (F°) cold seeped in through every crack and crevice. We stoppered the cracks and crevices with cloth and cotton wool. Sjoukje, all bundled up in coats and sweaters, helped to find cracks and used a small opinel knife to jam bits of cotton into a crevice, both of us chattering all the while. "We are keeping winter out of our house." At day's end she was so proud. We were winning. But in the end, we could not win. It was all one big open space with the kitchen half again as big again as the front room and the bedroom alcove combined. The wood stove, our only source of heat, was in the front room. So we hung sheets of 6-mill plastic from the ceiling to the floor, thus isolating the entire kitchen. A heavy blanket that could be pushed aside served as a door. The kitchen was a frozen wasteland; any water left in the sink would freeze solid. The front room became our winter refuge. It had a large bay window with a sweeping view of Kootenay Lake and the towering snow mountains of the Selkirk range across the water. The floor was covered with rugs and carpets. The wood stove kept us as warm and cozy as any house in town.

Sjoukje was so afraid to be alone. When I needed to go into the kitchen she had to come along. I had made a solemn promise to never leave her by herself. I would bundle her up for our expeditions to prepare food. The kitchen had a large gas cook stove. We also cooked on the wood stove, which had a bucket of warm water sitting on it at all times. The same routine was followed when I went out to get firewood from under the front porch.

We had an enormous green pillow chair, four feet across and over three feet high, stuffed with cotton batting. We would sink into it and be enveloped in the soft green fabric to read books. *Green Eggs and Ham*, *Winnie the Pooh*, fairy tales retold where little girls could do everything, and *Bambi*, the first book I had ever read in English. Her favourite was the Narnia Chronicles. We would make up stories. Sjoukje could choose an ending. We would make up local legends about Kootenay Lake, the snow mountains, Coffee Creek, Toad Rock and the magic that lived in the Kootenays. We played fun games; the favourite was to fluff up the big green pillow and then throw her across the room backwards into it. She would completely disappear. The big green pillow folded up around her, and eventually she made her way to the surface with her great full body laugh. When my friend Andy came to visit we would play catch with her, a live screeching ball catapulting across the room. We never missed! When she was a baby I would whirl Sjoukje round and round over my head in a pillowcase. Maya double stitched all the pillowcases before she left. Sjoukje loved this game, but at four she was too heavy.

As the wintery weeks went by we made an agreement that I could go into the kitchen by myself, leaving her in the front room by herself, as long as I kept talking. While I was in the kitchen she couldn't see me, but if she could hear my voice it was OK. Going outside by myself for firewood had to wait. We were making progress.

The bay window, the green pillow and (below) a country visitor

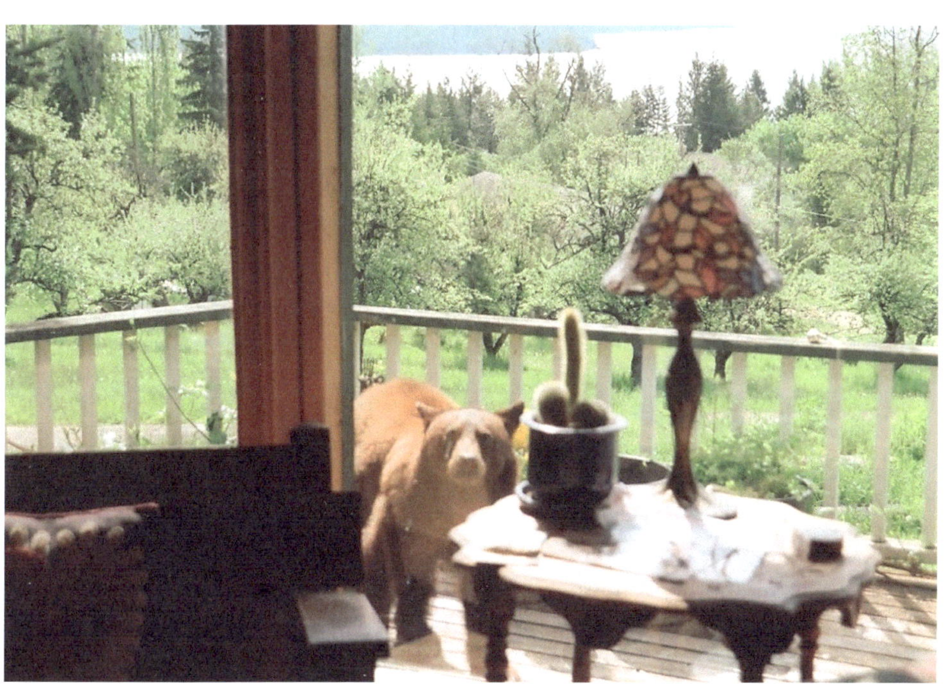

I developed a mother's ear. The slightest whimper from the staircase and I was instantly awake and totally alert, listening for what was coming. Now that I am in my eighties I could sure could use something to wake me up like that. When she had a dream that frightened her she would sleep for the rest of the night on my big bed. She would have scary dreams where monsters appeared out of the dark. We talked about dream friends. She could call on a dream friend when a monster appeared. The dream friend could be anything she wanted, a ferocious tiger or a fiery dragon who would burn the monster to a small pile of wood ashes, or Andy, our bearded, bushman friend, with his chainsaw to cut the monster into little pieces.

Spring sun on the bay window warmed the room and encouraged blue crocus flowers to emerge outside. The end of winter was in sight. It was the time of rebirth and the promise of new growth. We made a brave new agreement. I was going to walk all the way to the shop. Sjoukje could stand in the bay window, from where she could watch me walk down the driveway as it skirted the apple orchard to where it met the one-lane Queens Bay Road. The shop, an old apple-packing shed, was on the road where it met the driveway, a three-minute walk from the house. I explained that I would go into the shop only to get a key-hole saw and then come right back out. I would be out of her sight for less than one minute. On my return, we celebrated her brave vigilance with special store-bought cookies. Sjoukje was a brave little soldier. Maya once said, “it's not the ones who are seldom afraid but people like me who are easily frightened but go ahead anyway who are the really brave ones.” She was right.

As winter waned everyone came out of hibernation. The community of Queens Bay was located on a bench overlooking Kootenay Lake. The original English settlers who came here in 1908 had cleared the trees, planted apple orchards and built their wooden houses as well as the exquisite St. Francis of the Woods Anglican church. We arrived in Queens Bay just as the generation of the first settlers was passing on. As properties, mostly 10-acre lots, came up for sale we notified friends from the treeplanting community. In a matter of a few years

Queens Bay went from quite a proper British settlement to an alternative back-to-the-land, treeplanters' community. Empires come and go.

As Sjoukje became more independent we visited back and forth with the other families with small children in Queens Bay. The house came alive, ringing with the voices of a half a dozen children. They played games and liked to scare themselves silly looking for the ghost that was reputed to live in the dark, unfinished attic. Soon there were sleepovers. Sjoukje and Kendra liked to sleep in the huge, six-foot-long cast iron bathtub we had in the corner of our enormous kitchen, filled with foamies, blankets and pillows.

We organised a kids' swap meet where the children would gather up the toys and things they no longer wanted as contributions to the swap meet. The individual kids could then take what they wanted, change their mind, trade their newfound treasure for other claimed items. A dozen kids played and bartered the afternoon away.

The Queen's Bay kids with assorted ponies and horses at the farmhouse porch.

I learned that the women in the community were an active support network for each other. They baby-sat each other's kids, they traded expertise and information, and generally were there to look after each other. The women would get together for afternoons of canning fruit, making jam, baking bread and so on. As a single dad I was invited to join, to trade work and pass on valuable information (gossip), which I did with the best of them. I learned, firsthand, that it takes the presence of women to make a community.

Come September we enrolled Sjoukje in kindergarten. After the first week she came home and said she didn't want to go to kindergarten anymore. "Why?" "Today I asked the teacher when we were going to learn to read." She said, "we don't teach you to read here. That happens next year in grade one. I don't want to go anymore." We agreed, never mind the kindergarten teacher, that I would teach her to read. She was a quick learner. When Sjoukje got to grade one she was the only kid who could read on day one. Even though she could then read her stories herself, she still wanted story time with me reading to her. However, she would now correct me if I missed a word or skipped a boring part. Sjoukje remembered every word read to her.

Sjouk (a more grownup version of Sjoukje) would go with me wherever I went. Going to town, visiting friends, or trips to Vancouver, or to a treeplanting camp. As a treeplanting supervisor (project manager) I would look to hire planters that had small children. In a treeplanting camp with children present, one of the women would invariably set up a daycare system for the children rather than plant trees, leaving myself, and other planters with children, free to work during the day.

Sjouk became adaptable to changing circumstances. Wherever we were, she would come to me at eight o'clock sharp, carrying a book and saying "it's story time" (she had an internal clock set at eight). I would read her a story and put her to bed in some place where she was safe, i.e. where she wouldn't be stepped on. She didn't care where she slept, as long as she had her own personal blanket and I was there should she wake up. We had guy friends, like Andy, come and stay at the house to visit and help with the ongoing renovations. Sjouk picked up bits and pieces of salty language. One winter evening I was carrying her up a snowy driveway. I thought she was asleep. When I slipped and momentarily stumbled, a little six-year-old voice in my ear said "drop me and you're dead meat."

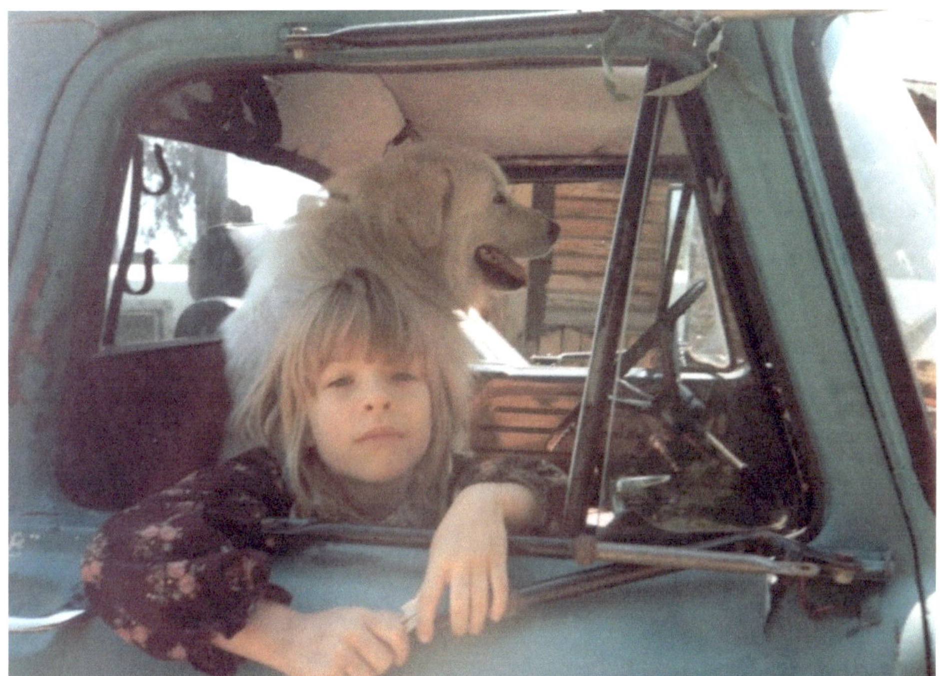

Sjoukje and a neighbour dog in the old ford 4x4. Queen's Bay 1981

For the next four years she was always by my side. She was my little sidekick. A disapproving school principal informed me that my daughter had the worst attendance record of the entire school.

Maya would spend a week or so with Sjoukje in the summers, sometimes in Vancouver, sometimes coming to Queens Bay to see her daughter. Later on, Maya moved to Laramie, Wyoming, and Sjoukje would spend part of her summers with her mom in Laramie. However, for those four years it was pretty much Sjoukje and I against the world.

Two months before her eighth birthday, I took Sjoukje to Laramie and left her there. Maya had fallen in love with Phil, a gentle, educated and responsible man. He was a better husband for Maya than I. Maya moved into Phil's house and now wanted her daughter to live with them. I would not refuse Maya her daughter or refuse Sjoukje a time to live with her mother. As well, I would now be able to live my own life although I was unsure if I could remember how and what that was exactly.

The hardest thing I have ever done was to drive away leaving my little sidekick standing on Maya's doorstep. I felt I had betrayed my daughter, my best little friend. I got home and wandered an empty Queens Bay house for two days. The cedar boards in the front room must be imbedded with her voice, her one-of-a-kind laughter, but the house was as silent as the grave. I felt hollowed out.

Two days later I fled the house and drove all night to reach the West Coast where I bought a used kayak and launched myself into the Pacific Ocean. Kayaking was new to me. From Tofino I kayaked to Meares Island and back to practise paddling and balancing this precarious craft. I loaded the boat up with food, fish line, camping gear and a BC road map that showed the coastline and its bays and inlets. I secured the spray skirt and headed north towards Hot Springs Cove. I was out there for six weeks and, with an exception at Hot Springs Cove, saw not one other person. There was an abundance of mussels, clams, and rock cod. A wild west coast storm drove me off the water. I survived the wild October waters. In six weeks I had become expert at paddling this most remarkable craft, that one actually wears, so that I felt as one with the water. I didn't want to go home to Queens Bay so I drove to Victoria and stayed there with friends until spring. When I walked back into my house in mid-April it felt a little less empty. Time is indeed the great healer.

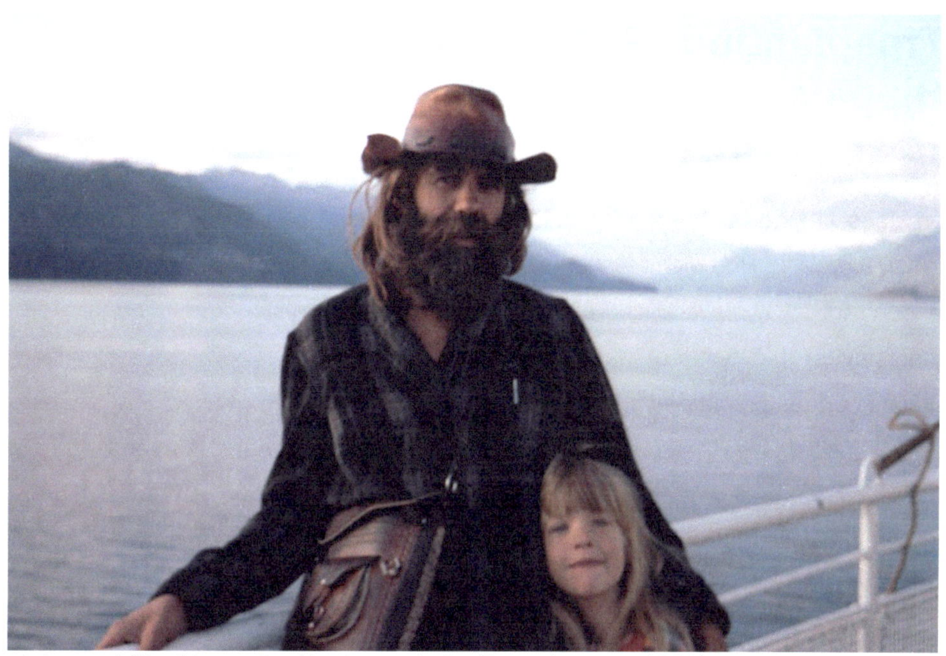

John and Sjoukje on the Kootenay Lake Ferry (approx 1979)

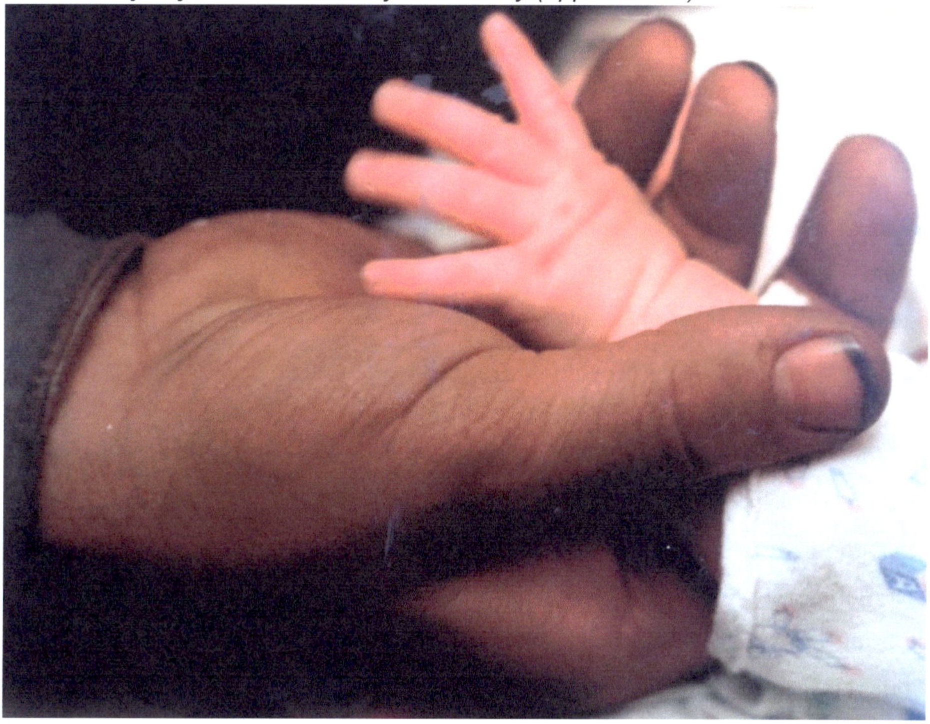

Hand in hand sometime in 1974

Treeplanting: God's Timely Gift to BC Hippies

Millions of trees a year are planted all across British Columbia on previously logged or burned forest lands. Treeplanting as we know it today started in 1972 up Wild Horse Creek, with Dirk and a friend named Ted Davis bidding on a contract to replant a cut block. They camped on site and did the work themselves. It expanded wildly from there. Within a few years, several dozen private contractors fielded treeplanting crews of anywhere from ten to fifty planters each season. Over the course of a season, thousands of young men and women from a mix of backgrounds and experiences would leave their homes to take up the nomadic life intrinsic to treeplanting. They would travel the length and width of British Columbia, live in a series of temporary bush camps, endure difficult conditions, and fully experience the pain and exhilaration of hard physical work.

A miraculous transformation would take place over a season. The crew, mostly young people, were working and living together in remote bush camps, isolated from society. They reverted to a more ancient form of social cohesion. A crew became a tribe with a strong sense that they all belonged to this small group. It was a primal experience, harking back to our ancient roots of nomadic hunter-gatherer bands who saw themselves as "The People." To experience this primal sense of togetherness was deeply satisfying. Many lifelong friendships had their beginnings in a season of treeplanting. Trees are planted in the rest of Canada as well but in my telling I will write only about BC.

The planting season began as early as February, in the frost-free regions of BC. The first treeplanting projects of the year were on the rugged West Coast of Vancouver Island and on the Queen Charlotte Islands (Haida Gwaii), planting the logged-over sites of the once towering rainforests of the West Coast. It was a reverse migration, chasing the last remnants of winter. Just as the new swelling buds on trees were about to reveal the pale green leaves of spring, the crews would take down the camp, load all the gear into trucks and migrate back into the end of winter. From the West Coast we moved into the interior highlands of

Vancouver Island and up the fjords and inlets of the mainland coast. Kincome, Bute, Jervis, Knight Inlet and then onto the river valleys of the Homathco, Bella Coola, the Nass, and the Dean. Just as new leaves of spring began to appear there, the camps moved onto the uplands of the Chilcotin plateau and the vast boreal forests of the north. The towns and hamlets of interior BC were our pit stops for supplies, essential laundromats, a meal in a restaurant, an evening in a bar, a night's sleep in a motel. Terrace, Fort St. James, Mackenzie, Prince George, McBride, Blue River, Fort St. John, Lillooet, Boston Bar, Valemount, Cache Creek; these names resonated with the migrations of a planting season. In July, the slow march of spring moved us home to plant onto the high elevation sites in the Kootenays, the high mountain valleys of the Selkirks, the Monashees, the Purcells and the Rockies. We came home to finish the season.

During a season a treeplanting crew could have as many as six moves. These could be anywhere from an hour's drive to a thousand kilometres. To get to the remote sites, treeplanting crews would travel on highways and logging roads. The crews and camps would move in convoys of trucks and personal vehicles, or on the coast it was hundred-foot barges towed by a tugboat up the secluded inlets. We got around in the bush, or on roadless logging sites, with 4-wheel drive pickup trucks, tracked all-terrain vehicles, and 4-wheel drive "boonie bikes." For inaccessible sites we used float planes or helicopters.

Treeplanting gave a ramshackle group of Dutch immigrants, draft dodgers, back-to-the-landers, poets, hippies, and magicians a way to make some money to pay for the things they could not grow or make. Dirk and I got to be there, and participate in, the very beginning of this creative and primal way of making a living. For three or four months we travelled the length and breadth of BC in Gypsy caravans along with our wives, girlfriends, children, dogs, cats, and the proverbial kitchen sink. We lived in self-sufficient bush camps and planted trees for 6 to 10 cents a tree. Maya worked as the camp cook in many of the early contracts. She excelled at making everyone feel welcome and was a really good cook to boot. For Dirk and myself, we were working off our faller's karma. In the end we planted far more trees than we had cut down. Our debt was paid. We worked and lived in some of the most remote areas of BC. Travelling by barge, loaded with an entire camp and crew, pulled by a tugboat, we went up the coastal inlets. We drove logging roads to their very end points into the highest mountains of the interior of BC and always found a place for 30–40 people to camp and stay for up to a month. We built camps that would have been familiar to the Sekani people we'd met in Finlay Forks. We had learned from them how to temporarily house and provide for groups of people in the bush. If anything went awry – broken-down trucks, flat tires, cook stove quit, marauding bears in camp, a wild windstorm taking down the cook tent, an injured planter, a wife or girlfriend having a baby, whatever it was – we were on our own and we dealt with it.

Canadian society has seen huge changes in the last fifty years. How treeplanting is done is no exception. Our early, primitive, built-on-site camps and the dilapidated vehicles have been replaced with prefabricated camps featuring hot showers, kitchen trailers, new 4 × 4 trucks, new safety procedures and communication devices that link a treeplanting camp to the outside world. The unique sense of rediscovering a more primal tribal cohesion gave way to planters communing with their devices. The sense that after surviving the challenges and hardships of a season's treeplanting a person could survive anything, do anything, gave way to living in safe, efficient camps where individual planters are not called on to improvise, to make it work, or to discover a surprising inner resilience. "Progress" has its costs.

Maya Huizinga, intrepid treeplanting cook. Unknown contract around 1972

Treeplanting camp life. We were young with energy to burn!

1976, north of Mackenzie, near the Parsip River. Original Treeplanting camp, showing a homemade plastic cook tent which was later much improved upon (hot!), also showing the Corvair van that had driven us to Mexico (on the left)

On the way to work (1976, Mackenzie)

The communal cook tent

Bottom Left: Treeplanting kids, dirty and happy as heck. (Sjouk is on the right)
Bottom Right: Self portrait in a truck mirror circa 1976

Number Seventeen: An Industrial Flogging

By June the treeplanting camps would migrate to northern Alberta where we used winter roads to access the blocks. Frozen solid when it's cold, these winter roads turn into deep sticky mud roads in the summer. The infamous Alberta gumbo was impossible even for our four-wheel drive trucks. We had the use of a skidder, a huge diesel-driven machine used to drag logs out of the slash to a landing. It had four articulated wheels, each one five feet high. In the summer of 1983 we used the skidder to pull a stone boat made of two large logs decked over with some old bridge planks. (By the end of the project, the huge round logs had worn down to a mere sliver of wood and the stone boat had come apart). With bales of straw for seats, this was how we transported trees and a crew of planters.

The skidder had a huge winch on the back with a main-line cable that had six, or more, smaller choker cables spliced into it at staggered intervals. Each choker cable could be attached to a log. A steel "bell" at the end of each choker cable allowed a worker to secure a log to the cable using a choke hold. A skidder can drag as many logs as there are choker cables. The main line is wrapped around the drum of the huge winch. This was an old, retired skidder used mostly to pull out stuck trucks. The main-line cable was still on the winch along with its six rusted and frayed choker cables. All the choker bells were gone, or so I thought.

We were on our way to pull out a tree delivery truck that was stuck in the mud – virtually buried, it was. Ted Davis, a mountaineer of some repute, was driving the skidder. Ted had never driven a skidder, but he was game. We had two miles to go on a dry sandy road to get to the mud. Ted was driving along at a good clip (30 mph), I was sitting in the back, on the winch. The winch was up against a heavy wire mesh, there to protect the driver in case a cable snapped and whipped forward. Suddenly the winch came alive. Ted had accidentally hit a long lever beside the steering wheel. I immediately stood up and clutched the steel mesh. The choker cables began to whip around the drum, flaying me with each pass. This was a diesel-driven cat of nine tails. I wound my fingers into the mesh as the choker cables, one after another, hit my back. To fall was to land between two spinning five-foot-high tires two feet apart. It would be instant death to fall. I yelled, I bellowed, I screamed. The diesel engine completely drowned me out. The loose ends of the six choker cables came around again and again, lashing my back. Thank God I was wearing a heavy canvas coat and my ancient aluminum hard hat. I felt a tremendous thump on my lower back. Oh! Oh! One of the cables still had its choker bell. I reeled with pain. The next time the bell came around it hit the wire mesh with a clang beside my head. I waited for the next hit; I knew this was the end. With no warning the skidder slowed and stopped. It had run out of fuel.

My coat was in shreds. My back looked like that of a sailor tied to the mast and flogged. In the Grand Prairie hospital I was told I had a fractured vertebra, fifth lumbar. There was one positive unintended consequence, a full year on Workman's Compensation at 80% of my wages. During that year I thought some about unsafe practices and for ways to make for safer working conditions. However, it took ten years and an eventual back surgery to get to where I was no longer plagued with debilitating sciatica. This accident was a small step in the long slow realisation that I could be injured or even killed, just like that. I was growing up.

Famed Alberta Gumbo

A Wider World of Hardships

Médecins Sans Frontières

Two French doctors, during the civil war in Biafra (1971), were shocked by what they saw. Civilians caught up in the war, their livelihoods destroyed, their homes burnt to the ground, entire families sick and people suffering shortages of everything. The militaries of the world tend to look after their own, but the civilians are outta luck and on their own. The two doctors went back to France and started an NGO (non-governmental organisation). This was the beginning of Médecins Sans Frontières (MSF). MSF declared that access to medical aid is a human right that supersedes the rights of national governments' desire to keep outsiders out. MSF goes anywhere in the world to bring disaster relief to people in need. Unlike the Red Cross, MSF does not wait for a government invitation to send teams into war zones and conflict areas. In such cases, they have well-established procedures to operate based out of neighbouring countries in what are known as cross-border operations. MSF projects bring worldwide relief to natural disasters, famines and the world's endless war zones. To the displeasure of many governments, MSF teams are also there to witness what goes on in the forgotten corners of the world.

Driving to Vancouver in the spring of 1991, listening to CBC radio, a Dutch accent perked up my ears. It was the voice of Jos Nelle, a recruiter for MSF. The various positions he described included that of a logistician, essentially a project manager who looks after housing for the team, deals with the national staff, communications, vehicles (Toyota Land Cruisers or pickup trucks), security and anything else that comes up. It sounded like a perfect compliment to the job of a tree planting supervisor.

The next morning, I went for an interview in Vancouver, where I met Jos Nelle in person. He later because a good friend. He agreed that running a remote treeplanting camp seemed a good fit for an MSF logistician. Three months later I drove Sjoukje to Montreal to begin her first year at McGill University. I went to

Amsterdam and then on to the Ogaden desert region of Ethiopia to begin my first assignment with MSF

Above: Medieval Ethiopian Christian paintings

Below: To get to Bareh (where my first project was located) from Dolo Odo (where the road ended) improvisation ruled the day. A haywired together raft of logs and a few small boats was winched across the river by a stationary military tank set into a cement pad.

Life, Death and Food

For mediaeval Europeans, Ethiopia was the mysterious Christian kingdom in the heart of Africa. Ethiopia's dynasty has a mystical origin story. The oldest dynasty in the world, it reached back to King Solomon and the Queen of Sheba. The Solomonic dynasty came to an abrupt end with the 1974 murder of Haili Selassie, by then an old man. The dictator, Mengistu Haile Mariam, is said to have personally smothered the emperor with his own pillow. Haile Selassie was a man who had once moved his fellow members of the League of Nations with an eloquent plea for justice in the face of Italy invading Ethiopia. The fact that the League of Nations ultimately did nothing about Mussolini's brutal invasion of Ethiopia encouraged Hitler to invade neighbouring countries and thereby launch the Second World War.

Following Haili Selassi's murder, there were seventeen years of a brutal Soviet-sponsored dictatorship, referred to as the Derg in Ethiopia. When I arrived in Addis Ababa, Mengistu had just been overthrown a few months earlier. The city still had armed soldiers posted on street corners. It felt unsafe.

We were on our way to a famine relief project in the Ogaden desert, fifteen kilometres north of the Somali border (although in fact, the Ogaden is one huge desert, encompassing vast expanses on both sides of the man-made line in the sand). Ten thousand refugees were camped on a barren hillside a half kilometre from the town of Bareh, a small trading village of some 500 people. The refugees were Somali nomads who had fled the chaos in their homelands. Somalia was a violent, lawless, and dangerous place. Bands of armed men driving stolen and modified Toyota pickup trucks known as Technicals terrorised Somalia. Fifteen or more men, or boys, all armed with AK-47s, along with a 50-calibre machine gun mounted on the roof of the truck, were a law only unto themselves. These marauding bands would come out of the desert, a frightening, fast-moving nightmare, to invade a camp or village. They took what they wanted: camels, goats, cooking pots, girls. They would kill anyone who stood in their way.

This violence sometimes spilled over into the Ethiopian side of the Ogaden. The chaos in Somalia did not, however, reach Bareh. A small Ethiopian army base, half a kilometre away, had a contingent of soldiers from Tigray. These young soldiers were battle-hardened men and women, the victors of the seventeen-year long struggle to defeat the Soviet-backed dictatorship of Mengistu. The army base ensured that the chaos stopped at the border, some fifteen kilometres to the south. These soldiers had stopped an invasion from Somalia, headed right for Bareh, just two weeks before we arrived.

The MSF team was made up of three expats: a tall, aristocratic British doctor, a plump American nurse and a long-haired Canadian logistician, along with a national staff of six Ethiopians. We all lived in a compound fenced off by impenetrable thorn bushes. The six Ethiopians, who all spoke English, were four nurses, a driver, and a nutritionist. We were a small community of outsiders, living in a sea of Somali people.

Fitsum, the nutritionist, was a young woman of twenty-three from Addis Abada. She was as beautiful and bright as the morning sun. She had the long legs of a Somali and was the only team member who spoke the Somali language. They call her Firtum (ostrich). She was my buddy and mentor for understanding the seemingly unpredictable Somali nomads and for everything Ethiopian. I soon learned that the Somalis were not unpredictable. They just moved to a different drumbeat. A local staff of 100 Somali men and women, cooks, guards, registrars, and construction team, helped to organise the activities of the famine relief project.

The project was to deliver famine relief to the ten thousand Somali nomads, now refugees. They came to Bareh, where there was water, no food, but life-sustaining water. The refugees put up houses by bending flexible willow poles anchored in a circle in the dirt. The poles made a dome which was then covered with sun bleached hides or cloth. A Somali house looked, for all the world, like an upside-down bird nest. There were several thousand of these bird nest huts scattered over the hillside just south of our compound.

Somalis are tall, thin, graceful people with golden brown skin the colour of honey. They are said to be the most handsome people in the world with their aquiline noses, slightly slanted eyes and high pronounced cheekbones. So many of the faces looked as if they had walked straight off the pages of *The Arabian*

Nights. There were simply stunning refugee women, barefoot and dressed in rags, who would have been sought-after international models had a capricious fate been kinder to them.

The Somali nomads were pre-agricultural people who lived in small family groups of up to thirty-five people. They moved constantly to find sparse grazing for their flock of goats and to harvest frankincense, both to use and to sell. It is their one source of cash money. Life was hard and uncertain. A Somali's first loyalty is to their family and then to their clan. Those who are not of their clan are, at best, expendable. Droughts like this one were normally survivable for a clan. During a severe drought they could lose up to one third of their family, mostly children. But the life of the clan went on. However, this time the Technicals had swooped down on their camps and villages and taken whatever they wanted to take. The nomads were left with nothing. Even when the rains came back, they no longer had the means to survive their harsh desert life.

The local people of Bareh were Somalis as well. They spoke the same language, they shared the same culture and five times a day they all knelt, touching their head to the ground and bowing towards Mecca. The people of Bareh had given up their nomadic life to live in more permanent mud-and-wattle houses with four walls. They understood the newcomers, but they were wary. Their small trading settlement could be overrun.

The project fed three thousand children twice a day. A long line of always dusty children walked by the cooks, who spooned porridge into a blue plastic bowl held out at arm's length. The children then moved farther into the feeding centre and sat on the ground where they ate the porridge. After two months the children looked happy and healthy. Some of them still had traces of orange hair caused by severe malnutrition (kwasiorkora). Adults can survive for many weeks with no food or on found food, insects, scorpions, snakes, tubers, and some kinds of tree roots. Small children without food die in a matter of days. Hundreds of small mounds on the bluff along the dry riverbed attested to the ravages of a famine amongst the very young.

At first, I was taken aback by seeing malnourished children with extended bellies walking on stick-thin legs and thousands of thin, raggedy, adult people slowly starving to death. As we focused on our work, Bareh and the multitude of refugees and their marginal lives became "normal." Years later, working as security advisor, I saw how MSF teams could, over time, become inured to danger by thinking of their dangerous situations as normal, and not recognizing that they also were at risk. What stays with me is the calm, matter-of-fact attitude of people facing their death and the death of their children. Would my own people back in Canada, accustomed to a life of extravagant plenty, react with the same courage as these Somali nomads if faced with this kind of disaster?

How the beliefs and expectations of a people are shaped by living hard nomadic lives was made clear to me one day by the head cook. At the feeding centre, an extremely thin, barefoot old woman, dressed in stitched-together rags, held out a tin can with a wire handle and gestured for me to fill it. She was a living picture of a starved survivor from Auschwitz. I walked over to where the cooks were heating a 45-gallon drum of porridge for the children, asked them to fill the tin and gave it to the old woman. The next day the head cook accosted me to say, "that was a bad thing you did yesterday!" "Why was that a bad thing? She was hungry." The cook replied, "the woman is here all by herself. There is no one else from her clan here, so it is not possible for her to stay alive. She knows this! You just threw away food for children." This seems harsh to us, but in her world it had its own irrefutable logic.

Inside the feeding center. Twice a day, 3000 children were fed.

Above: Two of the seven cooks in Bareh, outside of the feeding center.
Below: Somali mothers with their children waiting in line.

Above: Woman who had just arrived in Bareh as a refugee.
Below: Somali woman and children outside of their houses, easily deconstructed, transported (by camel) and reconstructed to suit the nomad life. They resembled upside down bird's nests.

Life, Death and Water

The temperature was 104° Fahrenheit and rising. The sun was a blazing inferno that washed all colour out of the desert landscape. I had only walked forty paces and could already feel the sweat seeping into my shirt. It would be another hot day in Bareh.

Just outside the gate of the MSF compound), a woman was sitting on the ground in sackcloth and ash, the ancient biblical expression of inconsolable sorrow and grief. She was a small Somali woman with her head draped in a coarse, black cloth of woven goat hair, with a mound of ashes placed on top. The old woman was as a statue, her shoulders hunched forward, her head bowed, looking down at the ground. She was a picture of complete, final dejection; a meditation on suffering. For me this was a picture from our old, illustrated family bible come to life. Months of living in an isolated, famine-stricken desert had inured me to the everyday suffering I saw. It had become normal life. But, seeing this woman in sackcloth and ash I experienced a hollow, nauseous feeling in my gut. It was only a few steps back into the compound to get Fitsum. She was our soft spoken Ethiopian nutritionist who also spoke Somali. Fitsum was my mentor for understanding the Somali nomads and their mysterious nomad culture. She would know what this was about.

Fitsum asked, “why do you mourn, mother?” The woman kept her head down as she whispered, in a barely audible voice, “I mourn because my son Effi, the water for my soul, is dead.”

I was taken aback. Effi was one of my twenty-five construction workers. They had just excavated and walled off sixty latrines to replace the defecation field. The occasional strong winds had been creating stinging dust storms that blocked out the noonday sun. Along with sand and dust, the dried out leavings in the deification field would become airborne, creating a toxic mix of dust, sand and human waste. For the few days following a dust storm, children, already weakened by malnutrition, would be brought to our field hospital where they would be taken care of until they died of their respiratory illnesses. After the latrines had been completed, I experienced an unexpected result. A delegation of Somali women came to the MSF compound to present me with a square piece of precious translucent amber. This, they said, was in gratitude for no longer having to wait until dark before they could relieve themselves.

Fitsum said, "I saw Effi an hour ago. He is digging a well with two other workers. He is alive and well. He is our best worker" The old woman, her head bowed, continued looking down at the ground, saying nothing. Fitsum said, "She may stay here, like this, until she is dead. I will ask the cooks what's going on" she said.

Seven Somali women cooked the CSB (corn, soy, butter oil) mix over open fires in 45-gallon drums. The tops of fuel drums were cut back with the sharp edges turned over and hammered flat. The women put a measured amount of ground corn, soy and butter oil in 45-gallons of water. Then they constantly stirred the thickening broth until it was thoroughly cooked. This was hard, heavy, and very hot work. The seven cooks ruled the feeding centre. They were also the local gossip central. There was not a loose word floating by that escaped their net.

While Fitsum was off information gathering, I went on my daily rounds to check on things around the sprawling refugee camp, starting with the construction crew repairing the endlessly collapsing feeding centre. Voracious insects chewed the wood in the poles leaving only sawdust inside normal-looking, intact yellow bark. A pole could collapse at any time, with no warning.

A week earlier we had begun to dig a new well by the feeding centre. During a public meeting with the elders of Bareh, held shortly after starting that well, a most unusual response had slipped past me. After discussing how to deal with the week's issues, we offered to dig more wells to help with the shortage of clean water for the refugees. This announcement was met by a pronounced and curious silence. There were no comments from people who normally discussed, at length, everything we said. Water is central to the people of the Ogaden. Water determines where they live, where they travel, which animals to keep. Water is life itself; the absence of water is death. A new well was a desert treasure. The town of Bareh had one well that they all drew their water from. The refugees were not allowed to use this well. The MSF team got their water from a drilled well on the nearby military compound. The refugees dug shallow pits in the black sand of the dry riverbed which filled overnight with silty, brackish water.

Traditionally the Somalis dug wells at a diameter that allowed a person's legs to simultaneously reach both walls. Footholds were made into the wall so that a person could spread their legs wide and climb up or down the vertical walls with amazing ease and speed. One person down in the well dug into the flinty desert soil. He shoveled dirt into a leather bag attached to a rope, which was hoisted up by those on top, emptied, and thrown back down. It took about three weeks to dig a well. The men were paid fifty cents a day.

When I came by on my rounds, Effi was at the bottom of the new feeding centre well. They had reached water at a depth of sixty feet, good news. The water was fresh and sweet. Each new well was a gamble. One never knew if the water would be brackish or sweet. In spite of the good news, the two men at the top of the well seemed uneasy. They had shovels at hand even though they had no need of them. Effi was in the well sixty feet down, alive and well. He needed to dig down another five slushy feet to call it done.

I walked down the dusty road and felt a tension in the air. There was always an underlying tension between the people of Bareh and the refugees. The people of Bareh were, after all, hugely outnumbered. But this felt different. The tension was palpable. Many of the men were carrying heavy wooden sticks or short sturdy clubs. The carrying of clubs was new. Bareh suddenly felt dangerous.

Back the compound, Effi's mother was still sitting by the gate, hunched over, concealed under her black head covering, sitting in the sweltering heat of the mid-day sun waiting for her death. At day's end Fitsum and I went for our daily run, first crossing through the random collection of refugee huts. Somali nomads all understood the human impulse to run for the sheer pleasure of it. Farther up the hillside, by a dry creek bed, we stopped at a three-foot-high, large, flat rock. "Made for us," we said. Here we would sit to rest, to talk over the events of the day and to answer my endless questions. When the sun dropped below the horizon it immediately cooled off. The desert does not retain the heat of the day. Fitsum had a tale to tell.

It seemed that some of the people of Bareh wanted Effi dead. They believed that the new wells would encourage the refugees to stay. Already, some women had been seen preparing the ground to plant cassava, thinking that they could soon irrigate their small plot using water from the new well. To stop the digging of more wells Effi had to be killed. The head cook whispered to Fitsum that Sheik Hassan was behind this.

"Why Effi?" I asked. "He is a giant. He had the body of a Mongolian wrestler, the biggest, most muscular guy in the entire construction gang. Probably in the whole refugee population, for that matter."

Fitsum explained, "Effi and his mother are the only ones in Bareh from the Fasahaale clan. Effi can be killed with impunity. With Effi's death there will be no retribution, no clan feud. It would be safe and easy. After Effi's death, your workers will refuse to dig more wells. It is a good solution for Sheik Hassan."

Being well versed in the Old Testament, the Somali Muslims understood the ancient tradition of a scapegoat, a sacrificial goat killed to pay for the misdeeds of the people. Over three thousand years ago, the wandering Jewish peoples took the story of Abraham sacrificing a ram, in place of his son Isaac, as a lesson from God. Killing a ram was a symbolic way to pay for the people's sins. This was the radical new idea that ended the need to sacrifice a human being. Facing hard times and extraordinary circumstances the men of Bareh were rewinding history. Effi was to be the living human sacrifice that paid for the survival of their small desert settlement.

Early the next morning, the entire construction crew was waiting at the gate of the compound, at my request. Twenty-five all white t-shirts with the letters MSF and the crossed bars of our logo emblazoned in bright red, were handed out, one for each man. The guys joked, laughed, preened and traded t- shirts back and forth for better fits. Wearing our new, distinctive, "uniforms" we all shouldered a shovel and walked in unison to the market in Bareh. Fitsum, wearing an MSF t-shirt, was waiting for us along with all seven feeding center cooks. A curious crowd quickly gathered around us. I saw Sheik Hassan at the edge of the crowd with his steely grey eyes watching intently. Fitsum and the seven Somali cooks stepped into the centre. The head cook raised her right hand, a signal that a meeting was taking place. A hush fell over the crowd. There was not a sound, it seemed that even the whispering sound of the breeze had stopped. Fitsum and the head cook, speaking Somali in loud clear voices, conducted a ceremony to induct the twenty-five men into the clan of MSF. At the conclusion I walked into the center, took each man's hand in turn and said "nabadeey dhamaanteen" (peace for all). As I shook the last hand the seven Cooks broke the stillness with ululations, the wild human equivalent of wolves howling. that raised the hairs in my neck This was immediately picked up by the other women in the crowd . This joyful, high pitched, trilling sound, heard all over Bareh, filled the morning air. Sheik Hassan's was standing at the edge of the crowd looking at me. When our eyes met I nodded my head. He stood there for a long moment, nodded in return, turned 180, and slowly walked away.

We walked through Bareh as a group, all shouldering long handled shovels. In a matter of minutes twenty-five shovels filled in the new well. An MSF flag was planted on the mound of dirt. The clubs disappeared. Two weeks later the clan of MSF began to dig a new well. We rotated who dug so that, when the well was finished, twenty-five men of the construction crew and the MSF logistician had all participated in the work. The new well water was as sweet as a fresh plucked fig. The clubs remained stashed. Effi's mother put away her sackcloth and ash, and walked the dusty street of Bareh as another anonymous refugee women. When I saw her in the market my mouth went dry and the hollow feeling in my gut dissolved. On my rounds the hard daily life I saw around me was once again normal Bareh life.

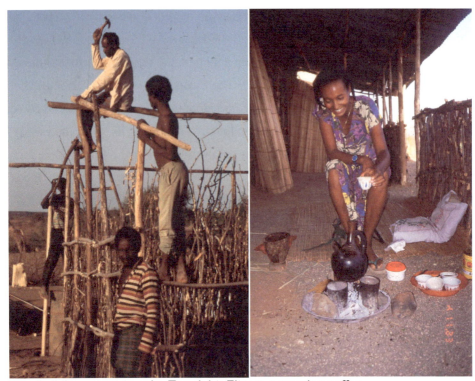

The Building crew at work. Top right: Fitsum preparing coffee.

With Dr. John Harley (our doctor) in front of our Trigano tent field hospital (prior to building a more permanent hospital).

An innovative break time solution to the stifling Ogaden heat, upwards of 40 degrees Celsius on most days.

A hospital that we built during this MFS mission, to provide more shade and protection from the rain than the trigano tents had done.

The inside of one wing of the hospital on the day we moved the patients from the tents.

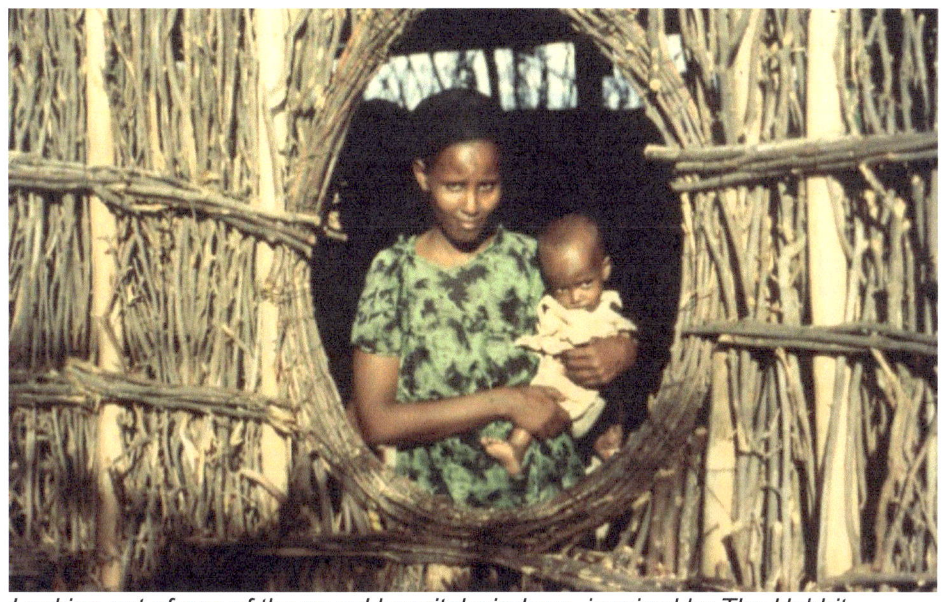

Looking out of one of the round hospital windows, inspired by The Hobbit

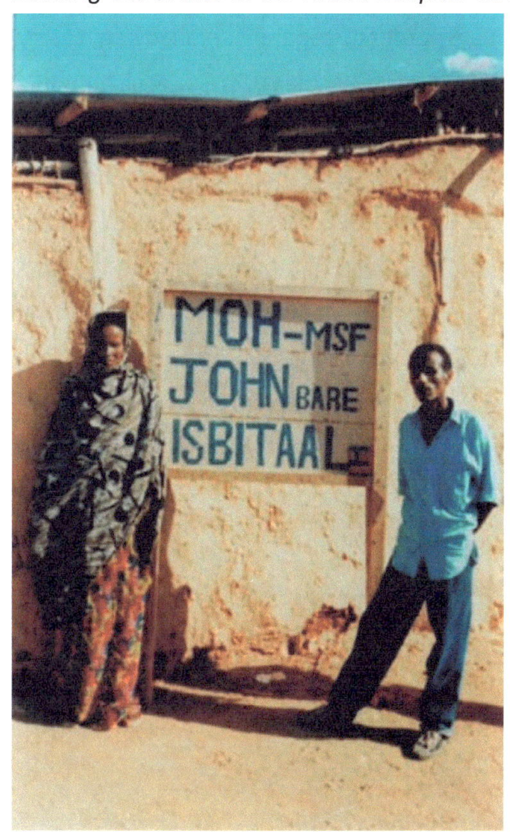

*A photo sent from MSF staff some months after I left with a sign denoting this as MOH (ministry of health)-
MSF (medecins sans frontiers) John Hospital in Bare.*

Number Eighteen: Child Soldiers

I was driving the Land Cruiser to a dry riverbed ten kilometres away to collect willow wands for the new mud-and-wattle hospital. I saw a group of stick-thin boys a short distance away. I drove over to see if they needed help. As I pulled up, a boy of twelve or so stepped forward. He had an AK-47. He pointed the gun at my head and demanded.... I had no idea what? His high-pitched, asthmatic voice wheezed as he talked. His eyes were dilated, sharp black points rimmed in red. He was high as a kite. The boy was trembling. His hand shaking and his finger on the trigger, shaking. This kid was frightened. This was more dangerous than being held up by a Shifta (Somali bandit). An adult knows what he wants. How can you know what a stoned twelve-year-old wants. We always carried a looting bag in the truck in case we got held up, containing a carton of cigarettes, several lighters, a bag of candies, a flashlight, a two-litre bottle of water, some Ethiopian money in small bills and, most important – a pound of sugar in a plastic bag. Sugar was white gold to the Somali nomads. They could kill for white sugar. You could generally drive off while someone was looking through the looting bag.

I did not have a looting bag in the vehicle, thus breaking my own rule. But there was ten pounds of sugar in a brown paper bag on the passenger side floor. A gold mine. As I handed the bag over to the kid with the gun, it slipped from my fingers and broke open when it hit the ground. There was an instant swarm of small boys scooping up the spilled sugar. The kid with the gun, unsure what to do next, momentarily looked down. I hit the gas and took off. One gun shot, a bullet nicked the roof rack of the Land Cruiser, and then I was out of range. Back at our compound we celebrated my good luck with an Ethiopian beer. The Ogaden temperatures made Ethiopian beer the best in the world. A week later, one of our drivers was shot by a child soldier, a ten-year-old boy.

I was distraught with our driver's unexpected death, but a mother showed me another way to think about this. A Somali woman was in our field hospital with her severely malnourished child for over two weeks before her child died. Children in this state usually died in a matter of days. Two days later I saw her, with two other women, walking past the feeding centre and went over to say that I was sorry to learn of the death of her child. She seemed confused and did not understand what I was saying. When I rephrased my condolences, she looked me straight in the eye and said, “Why do you bring this up? This already happened.” Given the circumstances of these people, they simply could not afford to stop and grieve whatever disasters came their way. Doing so would jeopardise the survival of their family and their clan. This reaction made me see how much grief and mourning is a luxury that we take for granted in Canada.

Fleeing War

MSF was in Azerbaijan to assist refugees fleeing the war with Armenia. It was 1993 and we could hear the big guns on the front, a mere 20 km away. Stalin had moved people and borders as it suited his paranoid fantasies. Russia gave Azerbaijan the Nagorno-Karabakh, a high mountain region containing a lake sacred to the Armenians. The end of the Soviet Union spawned wars all over the collapsed empire, many to address these kinds of arbitrary partitions. The Armenians launched a military attack and took back their traditional territory. Seven hundred thousand Azeris fled the Nagorno-Karabakh, creating three quarters of a million instant refugees. MSF was there to bring medical aid to this population of refugees. Our project was based in Barda, a town close to the mostly inactive front.

Everyone was in a tizzy because the Armenians had launched a new assault. Thousands of people were on the roads, some walking, herding their cows, pigs, flocks of noisy protesting geese, some with tractors or horses pulling a wagon loaded with their possessions. It was a scene reminiscent of WWII. We drove out to see what we could do. We handed out hundreds of blue plastic tarps and loads of blankets and treated half a dozen injured people and eight frightened children. But it was like having a hand towel to wipe up a flood. We felt helpless. A woman at a roadside camp stopped our vehicle to ask for matches. Their wagon served as a windbreak. She had her wood stove set up on the roadside to cook a meal for her family. She pointed to a column of black smoke in the distance and said, “That is my town. The Armenians have my house, but I have my life.” She placed her hand on her chest and laughter bubbled up from the depth of her being – she had put one over on the Armenians. To this day thinking of this Azeri woman gives me courage.

Above: refugee women from Azerbaijan

Below: Fleeing the Armenian invasion.

Getting a Feeling for the Soviet Union

Living in the ex-Soviet Union, shortly after its collapse, was a brutal eye opener. It was a society where the state owned everything and initiative was disincentivized, so no one took responsibility for anything. I saw many apartment lobbies, stairways, sidewalks and other public places that were uncared for and strewn with garbage. I remember seeing a gas pump that was broken open, dribbling a steady stream of fuel onto the street and into a sewer grate for weeks on end. I asked my Azeri national staff why no one was fixing it, or at least shutting it off, and they just shrugged. There would only be trouble for someone who got involved. Once inside and behind locked doors, however, I would be in an immaculate home. A proud tour of the apartment usually followed. I would be shown the family photos on the walls and brought to admire the fine china kept in a glass-fronted case. Inside their home people were wonderfully warm, welcoming and incredibly hospitable. But pride of place and ownership did not exist on the other side of the door.

There was only one method to build, decreed by Moscow. All apartment buildings in the Soviet empire looked exactly the same. Blocks of grey cement with rows of steel balconies fixed to the sides. Streaks of rust, embedded in the raw cement, highlighted the buildings. Once Moscow had decided on a design it did not change. How hard a person worked or how good a person became at their job was irrelevant. What mattered was to curry favour with someone in the hierarchy who could get you into a better position.

The trick in this life was to not stand out, to not be noticed. Getting noticed could get you in trouble with the authorities. Consequently, the men all wore the same long grey or black coats and the same hats. I could wander the streets of Baku or Tbilisi and with the right coat easily blend in. It was a grey, cement-encased world that many survived by drinking truly incredible amounts of alcohol.

Very soon after my arrival in Azerbaijan, the MSF national staff invited me out for a traditional Azeri breakfast. They wanted me to experience the national dish of Khash. At 7:00 the next morning, we entered a cement block building and sat down at a long cement table covered with a brightly printed plastic tablecloth.

I was introduced to a man wearing a greasy, food-stained, once-white apron. This was the chef. He set five large drinking glasses, filled to the brim with vodka, on the table. One for each of us. I was encouraged to drink up and finish the vodka before breakfast came. I tried one sip and realised that finishing the whole glass could kill me. My compatriots happily finished my glass for me.

Breakfast came in a large, steaming, cast iron cauldron. It contained an oily broth with unidentifiable pieces of meat and at least two eyeballs floating on the surface. The guys, for this was a completely male environment, slugged back the remainder of their vodka and complimented the chef on how good it smelled. We dug in. The guys fished for the meat and pieces of a gelatinous white substance that turned out to be sheep's brain.

I gingerly filled my bowl, taking great care to avoid the eyeballs and anything that could be boiled brain. I was chided for avoiding the sheep brain. This, after all, was what made the Khash a special treat. I was told that the Khash had cooked for several hours, and I therefore figured that it was safe to eat and dished myself a less picky bowl. The Khash tasted like a salty broth with an odd sweet flavour that reminded me of horsemeat. After several hours, and several more full glasses of vodka of which I continued to take only one careful sip of before filling my neighbour's glass, I came away wondering if the Khash made the vodka drinkable, or if the vodka made the Khash edible. Later I would tell people that I'd made a vow to God not to drink, which seemed acceptable and let me avoid the impossible situation of trying to pretend to keep up with Azeri men.

To shop in a Soviet grocery store was to go back a hundred years (or more). The store consisted of a series of glass-covered counters with six or eight people behind each counter. You pointed to what you wanted to buy and received a receipt for that item. After going to all the counters, each devoted to different foods, you stood in a long line for the cash register. At the cash register your receipts were stamped as proof that you had paid. You then went back to each counter you had previously visited, handed over your stamped receipts and received your food. Well over half the time was taken up by standing in line. To add insult to injury you left the store, carrying all your bags, by squeezing through a 36-inch door. No matter where you looked, the top-down rigid system ensured that almost nothing worked well.

Some months into the Azeri mission, I developed a toothache. For several days I could only think about my throbbing toothache. I needed to get to a dentist, now! My Azeri translator Sahil, an enormously strong young man of twenty-three with a single black eyebrow over both eyes, guided me. I could barely see it hurt so bad. My vision came and went in the 60-cycle rhythm of my heartbeat. As we walked up the steps of a big cement building, we met a man coming down the stairs holding his head, spitting blood. The front of his shirt was stained with blood. I said, "that don't look so good." Sahil shrugged his shoulders. The crowded dentist office was filled with unhappy-looking people. Sahil saw to it that I was placed at the head of the line. In the Soviet Union you get what you want by bullying. Sahil had learned to use his muscular bulk and a very loud voice to get his way. I was ushered into a dentist's chair that looked like it was left over from the Russian revolution. The dentist, with a pockmarked face, was wearing a white smock with splotches of blood on it. He too looked like he had survived the Russian revolution. One look in my mouth and he said, "pull tooth." I said, "no way." A weary shrug of his shoulders and he said, "I fix, first drill out." Sounded ominous. He stabbed a needle into my gums and injected something. Next, he tapped my sore tooth and asked if I felt anything. "Yes, that hurts." He shrugged his shoulders and explained that this would have to do because they were short on anaesthetic. He had a clunky drill that was powered by compressed air. I kept my mouth open as far as possible to allow the constant stream of air to get out. The rush of air on exposed nerves was excruciating. My entire body shivered. Boyhood stories of Nazi torture to make Resistance fighters talk came to mind. I was ready to say anything, answer any question, but no one asked. The drill slowed down, but he kept grinding. A high-speed drill cuts through tooth enamel with ease. A slow drill grinds at the enamel with jolting starts and stops. It's like doing dentistry with a file or corundum stone. The dentist pushed down harder. This slowed down the drill even more. The dentist said I wasn't keeping my head still, so he instructed Sahil to hold my head between his two huge hands. The dentist continued to drill. With my head in a human vice, I could only endure.

Finally, he said, "good enough," and filled my hollowed-out tooth with a pink paste and blew with compressed air to dry it. This lifted me right out of the chair. He told us that he would drill out the hardened pink paste next time when the gold cap was ready. None of this was making sense to me. I staggered out of the building spitting blood and cursing Azeri dentists to hell and back. My head still throbbed at 60 beats a minute. It could explode. Had I just "survived" a Russian torture session? Too early to tell.

I was not going back. We called the MSF office in Moscow, and they arranged for me to see a dentist there, in two day's time. Two sleepless nights and a day of agony followed. I had a new understanding of how people in mediaeval Europe could go stark raving mad from an infected tooth. A flight to Moscow, a session with a "normal" dentist who told me that they had anaesthetic to spare. This experience, though not life-threatening, deepened my perspective of everyday life in the Soviet empire in a direct and unforgettable manner. Sahil went back and got the gold tooth the dentist had made for me. It sits in a matchbox as a reminder that our Canadian experiences of everyday life cannot be taken for granted.

Dentistry was not the only example of a backwards and inefficient way to do things. The Soviet system was designed to kill all personal initiative. The government decided everything, and the people simply forgot that an individual could do things for, or by, themselves. A Polish engineer I had hired to rebuild old Soviet medical equipment for hospitals told me a story that illustrates the degree to how the system suppressed individual initiative. When the assembly line in a factory he worked in broke down, the normal procedure was to notify Moscow and they would decide how to deal with it, and send the parts to fix it. This engineer and his team instead redesigned the thirty-year-old assembly line to work better and dealt with the problem themselves. He was fired. Moscow was furious. How could he, one puny individual, think he knew better than the almighty Soviet state. The state had suppressed the natural human desire to experiment, to explore, to just try things out.

Our Azeri staff's general approach to problems was to declare that any proffered solution was not possible. My response was the same every time: "nothing is impossible." The slowly changing post-Soviet mindset was like watching a glacier move, but at least it was moving.

Abkhazia: A gas station which has seen better days.
Below: John in front of the MFS Azerbaijan garage

Georgia on my Mind

Georgia's civil war began in 1991, with the Soviet Union's collapse. The far western province of Abkhazia broke away and declared its independence. A brutal ethnic and religious cleansing followed. Georgia is Christian, Abkhazia is Muslim. All Georgians living in Abkhazia fled, often in the dead of night, or were killed. Abkhazia became a dangerous lawless place ruled by Jihadist militias. The militias were free to do, and take, whatever they wanted. Fighters from Chechnya, Mujahideen from Afghanistan and some so-called soldiers of fortune from North America came to Abkhazia to join in the free for all. It was a dangerous black hole of extreme violence and intimidation.

MSF had a project in the city of Zugdidi a few miles from the border with Abkhazia. We were there to assist three hundred thousand refugees that had fled for their lives from Abkhazia. By the terms of the peace treaty of 1994, MSF had the right to cross the Ruggi River bridge into Abkhazia. We would cross to supply a few of the still open hospitals with medical supplies. Given that our Georgian translator, if discovered, would be taken away to suffer an uncertain future, we went alone. Without a translator we were more vulnerable. Heavily armed militia men cruised around in stolen Lada cars. The Abkhaz militia were always armed and most often drunk.

On days when there was little to do, I would cross the Ruggi Bridge and drive to the first town about 15 km into Abkhazia. In the rush to get out of Abkhazia many old Georgian grandmothers had been left behind, very often left with grandchildren or an ailing spouse. These women would walk to the Ruggi Bridge to meet relatives, who would have some food and other necessities for them to take back. Old babushkas would walk up to ten miles or more, sometimes with blood in their shoes, pulling a child's wagon or pushing a baby buggy, to carry back the food for hungry grandchildren or medicines for elderly loved ones. They were trapped on the wrong side of this civil war. I was there as a taxi service for these women. The women would, tentatively at first, get into the Land Cruiser and then be driven, each one, to their own doorstep and given two dollars' worth of Russian Rubles. Tears of gratitude would trickle down their wrinkled cheeks. I would shuttle back and forth all afternoon, offering rides going both ways. It now seems that driving these old women was the most rewarding thing I did during my time with MSF. In a refugee camp, where thousands of people are in need, helping individual people is not possible or effective.

Tibilisi- With very little gasoline and no public transport, people mostly walked
Below: Life went on in spite of the war. Renowned Georgian artists selling their paintings for pennies in the park

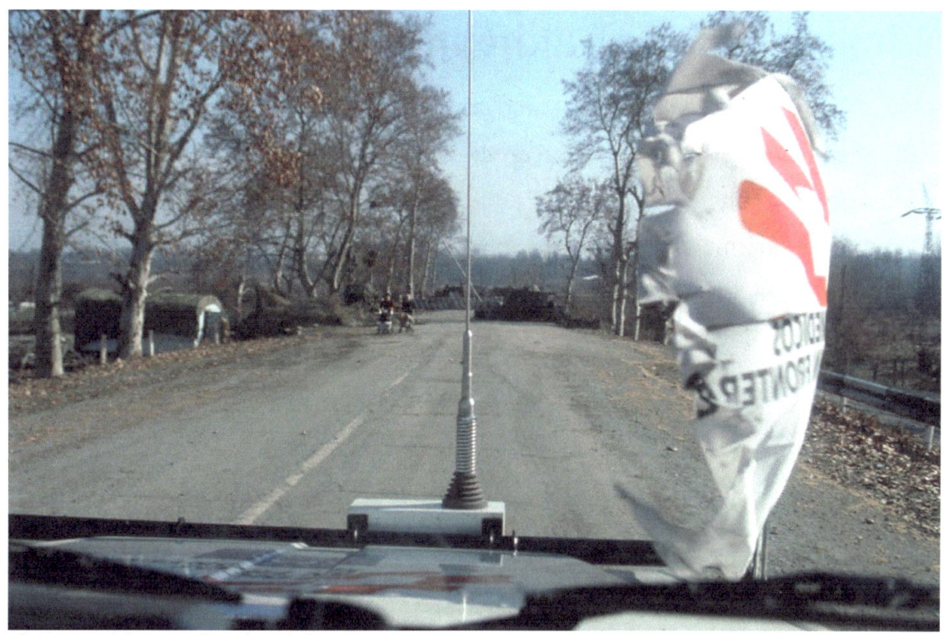

Approaching a checkpoint

Below: With our 4 wheel drive Land Cruiser, high up in the Caucus mountains, to bring badly needed medical supplies to an inaccessible region of Mestia

Number Nineteen: Life in a Lawless Land

Carmen, the MSF doctor and myself were driving back from bringing medical supplies to a small hospital on the shores of the Black Sea. Carmen was a courageous twenty-eight-year-old doctor from Barcelona. She had previously worked in the infamous orphanages in Romania and had seen the brutalities of war in Chechnya. In spite of these experiences, Carmen was the most gentle and upbeat person I have ever met.

Carmen on a trip to the Caucuses

I loved this feisty young woman. I would have risked death to protect her. Fortunately, this was never put to the test. The Toyota Land Cruiser was recognizable with MSF logos on the doors and a Red Cross painted on the roof. A woman wearing one shoe stepped out onto the road gesturing for us to stop. She was so distraught. With tears and frantic gestures and our few Georgian words we understood that she wanted us to go to her house. A short distance on we stopped by a wooden gate leading to a house set back from the road. The gate was off its hinges, and a dead dog lay by the side of the path. Inside the house we were hit with a strong smell, like someone had burned a roast. In a half-lit room, we could see several women hunched over a bed by the far wall. A soft, low moaning came from the bed. By the light of a flashlight, we saw three older women sitting on chairs by the bed, softly keening in sorrow, and a young man on the bed covered with a sheet. Carmen pulled back the sheet. A handsome young man, perhaps 19 years old, had a cross burned into his bare chest. A militia had found him, a Georgian man, on their turf. They told him, "we make you a good Georgian Christian." They wired two pieces of rebar together in the shape of a cross, heated it in the family stove until it was red hot and pressed it onto his bare chest until they hit bone. I was nauseous at the sight of his charred black ribs. The militia men had left, laughing uproariously and saying, "we come back." We laid the young man down in the back of the Land Cruiser. Carmen sat with him. She held his hand and did what she could do to ease his pain as we drove back to the Ruggi Bridge, a distance of some twenty kilometres.

At the intersection with the main road to the border, two Ladas, parked sideways, blocked the road. I stopped with my front bumper inches from one of the Ladas. A half-dozen men, brandishing Kalashnikov assault guns, greeted us with menacing laughter and hilarity. They were all drunk. When one of them saw the man in the back of the Land Cruiser he shouted out, and they all began to yell and dance and clap each other on the back. One guy stepped up to the driver's door, pointed at the young man and said to me in broken English. "Mine! You thief! Out!'" as he thumped himself on the chest with his gun dangling on his back. I nodded and mumbled "OK" as I carefully shifted into second gear. He grinned and stepped back as I made to open the driver's door. The door was half open when I hit the gas. The Lada blocking our way was pushed sideways and careened off our front bumper into the four men standing beside it. There was a scramble to get out of the way. We heard gunshots. They were too drunk to shoot straight, but not too drunk to fire up the other Lada and give chase, emptying their guns as they drove. A Kalashnikov has a range of 600 feet, two city blocks. We were soon out of range. The Ruggi Bridge and the two Russian tanks guarding the way onto the bridge were ten kilometres away. We would make it. For the Russian soldiers, an opportunity to obliterate these yahoos would make their day. Knowing this, the militia car dropped back well before the border.

We took the young Georgian boy to the hospital in Zugdidi. Carmen stayed with him all night. In the morning I went to pick her up. She had tears in her eyes. It was the only time I saw her cry. The Georgian boy had died, holding her hand, just as the sun came up.

The cruelty, the hatred and the killing in Georgia went on and on with no end in sight. In Georgia I experienced the utter brutality, and cruelty of an all-out civil war. We saw the timeless violence that is a part of us, part of the human species. It was there when I was a child in occupied Holland, when our entire family was in peril. The well of violence that it took to survive a long, tough, human evolution surfaces during the extremes of war.

Roads Less Travelled

Into the Copper Canyons

Mexico 1997. I wanted away from MSF and the cruelty and chaos of war zones. I had invested some money in a cattle ranch owned by Mexican friends close to Alamos, in the state of Sonora. I decided to drive to Alamos and check up on things there. We toured the 2,500-acre ranch on horseback. The 300 cattle (about a quarter of which were mine) looked to be in good condition and would be ready to ship in a month. I had some time and decided to drive from Alamos to the town of Creel. Creel is on the Chihuahua uplift plateau several 100 kilometres east and about 6,000 feet higher. Creel is the staging place for exploring the Barrancas del Cobre. (Copper Canyons). I set out to drive a network of seldom-travelled back roads. Friends in Alamos advised me to be very careful. This is a wild, lawless region of Mexico. The deep canyons and rugged terrain are a refuge for "narcos" and growers of marijuana and opium poppies. The steep, seldom-maintained mountain roads made the entire region barely accessible. Better to take the Copper Canyon train to Creel, they told me. However, I had a 4 × 4 Toyota pickup, years of driving mountain back roads in BC, and sixty spare litres of gasoline. I assured my friends, "no problema."

A few hours out of Alamos I was flagged down by a man at a crossroads. He appeared to be a peasant farmer and wanted a ride to Milpillas. A village two and a half hours farther on. He took his time climbing into the back of the pickup. In minutes there were a dozen people standing around the truck. After some discussion seven adults, two children, along with several boxes and two burlap bags filled the back of the truck. An old stout woman, dressed all in black, got into the front seat. The road was rough and rocky with some very steep places. We seldom got over twenty kilometres an hour. The crone did not speak, but she occasionally crossed herself.

For three hours we climbed, grinding up badly eroded portions of the road, straddling deep ruts and carefully manoeuvring around hairpin turns with thousand-foot drops a few feet away. Just before Milpillas we saw the first vehicle, a Dodge Ram pickup (the Mexican Macho favourite) parked at the side of the road. Three armed men ordered us to stop.

Everybody out. After a very minimal search of the truck, they accepted that I was *turista*. However, it took another twenty minutes of posturing, arguing and looking at a long list of names before they cleared all my passengers. As we drove off, I asked the old woman "son policia?" She shrugged her shoulders. "Que quieren? What do they want?" For the first time she looked directly at me, placed one hand over her heart and made a slow back and forth motion with the other hand all the while shaking her head. I think it meant, "don't ask."

In Milpillas they all got off and set me up with a new passenger. He was a wiry, dark-skinned mestizo man with a creased face the colour of well-worn leather and tufts of grey and white hair on his chin. One tough old guy.

His name was Jesus and, unlike the crone, he wanted to talk. His rural Spanish was hard to understand so I said, "mande?" or "como?" a lot. Jesus, in turn, began to speak louder, no doubt assuming that my deficiency in Spanish could be overcome by yelling. For the next two hours the road continued to climb ever higher. The rocky thorn scrub desert slowly gave way to a pine forest with scatterings of small oak trees. The truck bounced and jostled us in our seats as it scrambled up the steep, eroded parts of the narrowing single-lane road. Jesus continued to talk, or yell. He told me that he was a miner. That he was going to Chinipas to work in a mine. That he was also a vaquero, and that the policia without their guns are cabrones sin huevos. This declaration was followed by emphatically spitting out the window. Nice gesture!

After some time, I stopped the truck and put on a set of foam ear plugs I kept handy. I explained that I have sensitive ears. He liked this and told me how the loud noises in the mine were *muy malo* for his ears. But his stentorian voice did not flag.

The road finally levelled off. We drove across sunlit uplands at 8,000 feet. The air was fresh and crisp. There was a constant steady breeze. The road wound through an open, park-like pine forest. There was very little underbrush. The forest floor was a cover of pine needles and oak leaves. Scattered throughout were stubby, eight-foot-high palm trees with large green fronds. They looked like giant ferns and gave everything a strange, exotic feel. Here and there were enormous vertical rocks standing like great grey sentinels amongst the trees. They looked like they had been there since time began, mysterious monoliths that looked like something out of a more ancient age.

We stopped by a small creek. My MSR stove boiled a pan of water in minutes. Jesus said, "muy rapido. Como un gringo." He had some chewy corn paste that he shared. He told me that bad men (*hombres muy malos*) live in these mountains. The peasants grew poppies in steep rocky fields, others refined the poppy paste, the labs for refining were hidden away in the canyons below us, still others move the finished product to the coasts. Everyone there was armed. He pulled a handgun out of his pack. "It's loaded, a .45 calibre automatic, could kill an elephant at close range."

"Shoot them here!" with his index finger on his stomach. "In the gut. It stops a man dead in his tracks, and he gets to feel his body before he croaks," Jesus said with a toothy grin. After this explanation, Jesus inexplicably began to talk at a normal volume. I took out the ear plugs.

When we passed a cross at the roadside, marking someone's death, my mestizo friend took off his hat. I wondered if this was in deference to the dead guy or if it was in deference to death itself. The crone had ignored the roadside crosses but made a quick, well-practised sign of the cross with her right hand each time we passed by a roadside shrine (always to the Virgin of Guadalupe). Perhaps when one is under the protection of the Virgin there is no need to pay tribute to the grim reaper.

The edge of the uplands was abrupt. We made our way down through switch backs and hairpin turns. Chinipas lay far below, in the centre of a large valley nestled in the bend of a wide, winding river. The all-white buildings of the town shone in the afternoon sun. There was no bridge. I took off the fan belt to prevent the cooling fan from throwing water onto the ignition and drove across the river, the truck slithering on wet slippery rocks. In the July rain it would not be possible to cross. This day the water was only three feet deep. I was grateful for a high-centred four-wheel drive.

Chinipas began as a remote settlement set up by the Jesuits from which to convert the Indians of the Copper Canyons. Later, large deposits of silver were found, and Chinipas became prosperous for a time. In the town centre stood a very pretty plaza fringed with tall, stately palm trees. In the centre of the plaza an ancient, rusty steam engine sat on pieces of railroad track embedded in concrete. Going nowhere. A tarnished monument to better times. Along one side of the plaza was a simple stone church, tucked away in a grove of trees. Most unusual. In Mexico the church usually dominates the plaza. Perhaps the lure of silver displaced God for a time.

A massive wooden door studded with large square-headed nails stood partway open. Inside it was cool, dark, and hushed. On the wall, at one side of the door hung a life-sized, bearded Christ covered in a black robe with his feet and hands showing. The crown of thorns sat lightly on his brow. An intricately woven headband held his long, jet black hair in place. His arms were spread out along a wooden beam in benediction. The Christ was a noble, serene figure radiating a quiet dignity.

On the other side of the door a life-size radiant Virgin Mary stood looking down on a simple wooden crate with rough boards on top and wooden slats as sides so one could see inside. An almost naked, chalk-white Jesus with blood encrusted hands and feet was visible through the cracks. He appeared to be oozing blood from a ragged hole in his side. The crown of thorns was gone, and blood red tears ran down a gaunt, lifeless face. A dark-skinned mestizo woman was there holding a small child. She looked up at the Virgin, made a sign of the cross, then reached between the slats to touch her bruised and beaten Lord. This was holy ground, a place of contact with the eternal, a place of solace and comfort, to help alleviate the hardscrabble life of impoverished rural Mexico.

I sat down for a meal in a restaurant on the plaza. A sloppily dressed Mexican man with a great protruding belly and a gun stuck in his belt sat down at my table. He looked me over. Local policia? I soon tired of my silent, self-invited guest and told him, “I am from Canada, I am travelling the barrancas on back roads, I am going to Temoris." No reply. I proceeded to eat my enchiladas made by two giggly young girls who watched my every move. The policia left, not having said a word. Once outside I was approached by a man who asked for a ride to Temoris. "Sí. No problema. Get in." No, no the ride was not for him, it was for.... He pointed to a tall young man walking towards us. The young man looked a bit of a dandy. He wore white jeans, an embroidered shirt and a white, brand-new hat that still had its plastic wrapper. A pair of chrome cufflinks dangled from his belt. We shook hands. His name was Rafael. "Sí bueno. Meet me here in half an hour." I wanted to walk around some. As Rafael turned to go I saw that he had a gun stuck, mid-back, in his belt.

Half an hour later I found Rafael in the pool room along with the pot-bellied "policia" and three other guys. They all had guns in their belts. It was exactly how the young Georgian mafioso men liked to wear their guns, for all to see, while they danced with their made-up molls at the swanky bar-hotel in Tbilisi.

On our way out of town we saw a cluster of mostly women and children and one very old leathery-faced man in baggy white pants and a wool poncho. A picture of the Mexican peasant farmer from the long ago past. I stopped the truck. They all immediately clambered into the back of the truck, hefting up boxes and burlap bags and two chickens. Not a word was said. When someone wanted off, they thumped the roof of the truck.

Rafael was not much of a talker, mostly we rode in silence. Rafael took his gun out of his belt, removed a loaded clip, checked and rechecked the mechanism and then forcefully thrusted the clip back into the gun with a sharp double click. He said, "bueno."

Rafael liked my driving. "Como un caballo," he said as the pickup, in four-wheel low, scrambled up a steep rocky pitch. "Sí, como un Semental!" I replied and forcefully spat out the window, a visceral macho punctuation I had learned from my last passenger. Coming around a sharp uphill bend I cranked the wheel to miss hitting a pickup going the other way. The truck skidded sideways on the dirt and stopped just short of the drop-off. It was two guys in uniform, driving fast in a Dodge Ram truck with a tiny flashing red light fixed to the roof. Rafael snatched up his gun and then they were gone. I turned to look at him. He threw me a huge grin, held up the gun and said “listo.” I was relieved that they were going the other way.

We stopped at a flat bench beside the road. The railroad tracks of the fabled Copper Canyon train were below us at the bottom of a deep canyon. The ramshackle village of Temoris hugged the hillside above the tracks. The passengers in the back dug out packed lunches, tortillas and tamales, and shared these with Rafael and myself. Some of the women looked over the edge and crossed themselves as many as five times. Rafael took out his gun, removed the clip and handed it to me. It was a .45 calibre. Seemed that hombres in the barrancas looked to firepower as their saviour. “Señor, even a .45 calibre gun without a clip is of no use.” I held out my hand for the clip. Rafael gave me a sly smile, shook his head, and took his gun back.

We rolled into Temoris, a single-lane street a block long with a decrepit “Hotel de Barrancas” advertising Cervesa Frio. Across the street was a small tienda selling liquor and gasoline in glass bottles and four ramshackle houses. The left-over passengers departed with a chorus of “muchas gracias” and “buen suerte.” The street ended at a railroad station with no one home. Strung along the tracks were more buildings, some old houses and a century’s collection of scrap iron, old locomotives going back to the steam age and rusted or bent steel tracks and other industrial detritus. Rafael took me down the one side street and pointed out two houses, whorehouses both, the only houses in Temoris that were painted. He explained that the yellow house was no good, dangerous, they will kidnap you, (something lost in translation). The house on the right was the place to go, “tiene mujeres muy simpáticas.”

We went into the hotel for a beer. Outside was a hand-painted sign, “no minors, no guns, no men in uniform allowed.” Bars, the men’s clubs of Mexico, are sacrosanct. Policemen in uniform are not allowed. This ideal, left over from the revolution, is alive and well in rural small-town Mexico. Inside, a long-curved bar of two-inch solid mahogany was fronted by three-legged bar stools. The hotel was from 1880. This bar was built before the revolution. Rafael showed me two bullet holes, one in the front of the two-inch-thick slab of wood and one in a wooden pillar at the far end of the bar. Looked like they used 45s even way back then. A copper foot rail ran the length of the bar, and the original brass spittoons were strategically placed close by.

A half-dozen men, workers for the railroad, sat at a corner table. They ignored us. At another table farther back in the gloom there was a card game going on. These guys greeted Rafael with loud enthusiastic laughter. We walked over. In spite of the sign these guys all had guns. There were lots of jokes and slang that I couldn't follow. One guy asked Rafael, "you travel with a gringo?" And placed his gun on the table. Another guy made obscene gestures with a pool stick. After a few more exchanges, Rafael said, "let's go." Back at the truck I asked if there was a place for me to stay in Temoris for the night. Rafael immediately said, "es peligro." It is not safe for a gringo to stay here."

I bought 40 litres of gasoline in glass bottles and drove back up to where the pine forest began. I camped well out of sight of the road. The next day I drove east. Temoris was a dead end. No maps and with only the directions of an occasional person to guide me, I often ended up at a dead end or simply lost.

I was deep in the Barrancas del Cobre. The landscape was a chaotic maze, a seemingly random jumble of rivers, ridges, canyons and valleys with jagged peaks crowning the chaotic scenery. The country is enormous. The three main canyons are each the size of the Grand Canyon. The road was often just a track with dirt scraped away to bedrock. I was driving up 45-degree mountainsides and then descending into high hidden valleys, only to climb up the other side, crest a ridge, to descend again into another valley or to the bottom of a narrow, rock-walled canyon.

In the valleys I found small settlements, ranchitos. These consisted of clusters of small adobe houses with rusting tin roofs. The people of the barrancas were mestizo farmers with dark inscrutable faces. They wore white, dirt-stained clothing made from homespun cotton or hemp, straw hats, and tire-tread sandals and carried broad-bladed machetes. These were the Indio farmers who wrested an impoverished living from the stony earth of these canyons.

I also met larger men on horseback with slivered saddles, thick leather chaps and always a rifle stuck in a leather scabbard. They were not friendly, reticent to talk beyond simple directions that would lead me out of their neighbourhood. The road eventually took me up to a high plateau of large, widely spaced pines.

I met two young women wearing jodhpurs, leather riding boots, black riding helmets and riding well-groomed horses with silver bridles. The girls were in their early twenties, light-skinned with long, raven-black hair. Definitely not local peasant girls. They were friendly and eager to talk. They spoke some English and would correct each other and laugh as they talked to me. They both had a gun in a leather holster attached to their belts, albeit a much smaller one than the 45-calibre horse pistols I had seen so far. We talked of horses, mountains, barrancas and Canada. I offered to make them a coffee and showed them my camp stove. They both giggled. “No gracias!” I asked, “which way to Creel?” They shrugged their shoulders and muttered, “no sé.” “Where does this other road go? The one you came from. Can I go that way?” “No! No!” “Why not?” “Es muy peligro!” “Por que?” They giggled some more, turned their horses, and trotted back up the forbidden road. I went the other way.

Away from the valleys, in the high country at the canyon rim there was no water, no people, no houses. I saw only trees, rocks, ravens, and eagles soaring over the deep canyon below me. It was truly a wild, untamed land that still belonged only to itself. It is the kind of place I cherish, the kind of landscape that with every passing year becomes more of a rarity on this increasingly crowded earth. This was a place that had escaped Loren Eiseley’s world eaters.

I camped at the rim of a canyon under a gnarled twisted tree with red peeling bark. In BC we would say it’s a type of Arbutus. Here it was called the bleeding Judas tree. The Urique River was 5,000 feet below, a thin green line winding along the canyon floor until it disappeared into a narrow, rock-walled gorge. The train tracks of the Chihuahua al Pacifico, a mere pencil line following the sinuous green line, disappeared into the black mouth of a tunnel at the point where the river disappeared into the gorge. It is one of 86 tunnels blasted through solid rock. The Chihuahua al Pacifico railroad was completed in 1961, a full century after it was begun. The Copper Canyons did not easily surrender their wild solitude.

The sun set and stars slowly appeared. Darkness settled over my camp; a deep silence settled over the canyon. A full moon rose over the far canyon wall. The landscape became dim black shapes and deep dark shadows. The canyon was an immense black bottomless chasm, the mountain wall on the other side, dimly illuminated by the stars and the ghostly light of the moon, which loomed huge in the night sky. A slow steady breeze came up, bringing with it a sighing sound that broke the silence. The sound of the wind whispering through the pine needles filled the night air, there was no other sound. To speak aloud would be a sacrilege. A primal sense of mystery rose up out of the canyon. It permeated the night air and prowled in long-forgotten caverns of my mind. I was so very alone. I could vanish into the vast mystery of this wild land. No one would ever know.

In Creel I read a newspaper. It told me that the World Bank had offered to allocate 45 million US dollars to help develop an efficient lumber industry for the region. The Copper Canyons contain more species of pine trees than anywhere else in North America. This could jump start the economy of Northern Mexico. They do not understand, they do not care, they do not think about the irreversible evil this would visit this great wild region.

In Creel I was told about a lost town at the bottom of a canyon. A steep winding dirt road plunged from the top of the uplift deep into the earth. The truck skittered down the steepest pitches in low gear. The road was lined with vertical rock walls over a thousand feet high. Millions of years of geological time were etched into the rocks as layers of limestone, sandstone, granite and black basalt. I looked for the fine line of iridium that marks the end of the Cretaceous, the end of the dinosaurs, but did not see it.

Batopilas was at the end of a three-hour drive. The town was at the bottom of the 6,000-foot-deep canyon of the Batopilas River. The town was strung out along the fast-moving river. Looking up from anywhere in town, no matter which direction one faced, you would see steep mountain walls. In Creel, on the plateau, it was cold, near freezing. Here in the canyon it was tropical with banana and mango trees all loaded with fruit.

The Spaniards first came here in 1610. They found great slabs of silver on the river bottom polished by the flowing waters of the Batopilas River. Spanish lust for wealth made them stay. For 300 years the seemingly inexhaustible mines of Batopilas financed wars, supported empires and created vast fortunes. A small portion of this wealth was used to build this exquisite colonial town and some extravagant haciendas. In 1910, the mine owners, who by this time were American, fled for their lives. The revolution was in full swing. The wealthy landowners, ruling over the vast territories, the Catholic Church, the owners of the mines, they were all despised by the revolutionaries and were often killed on sight. There are intriguing stories of treasures hurriedly hidden away in caves. The mines and the great haciendas fell into ruin. Mexico fell into a violent chaos for the next 30 years. The population of Batopilas fell from 20,000 to 600 people living a marginal hardscrabble life at the bottom of a canyon lost to the world. 85 years on, the sign coming into town read "Batopilas población 1035."

However, international tourism has discovered the Barrancas del Cobre. In Creel, glossy brochures features Batopilas, "The Jewel of the Barrancas." The more adventurous sorts brave the hairpin turns and 2,000-foot-drops and stay in an upscale, family-run hotel, a renovated hacienda, for up to $200 a day. The hotel makes a daily run to Creel in a huge GMC 4 × 4 with leather seats bolted to the roof. Once again there is money to be made in Batopilas.

The Monse House faced the plaza in Batopilas. On the sidewalk, balanced on three legs, was a hand-painted sign that read, "Monse House, Lodging and Artifacts. Welcome." Señora Monse was part Tarahumara Indian. She was a stocky, broad-faced woman who had a look of one about to break into a smile. Her husband Carlos Luis Acosta was a small, dapper Spanish gentleman in his early sixties from Mexico City. They both spoke English. One entered the Monsa House by a small yellow door set into an adobe wall. A short passageway opened into a shaded courtyard with huge old mango trees, green bushy lime trees and some tall vertical palm trees. Flowering bougainvillaea vines climbed the walls of the courtyard. Señora Monse's yard was a cool oasis, a tranquil refuge from the heat of the plaza.

Scattered around the perimeter of the courtyard were a few small, whitewashed adobe rooms for guests. This arrangement gave the courtyard a maze-like quality. The room I slept in was up against the outside wall. I could hear the Batopilas River just on the other side of the wall. I had my own little grove of lime trees with a table and chair sitting in their shade.

Señora Monse's garden was a refuge, a place to stay for the Tarahumara Indians coming in from the canyons. Here they could cook their food over an open fire and wash up. The Tarahumara were small, dark-skinned and shy. They came to town dressed in their traditional clothing: a white cotton skirt that is longer at the front and an embroidered shirt for the men, bright-coloured long skirts and blouses for the women. The Tarahumara guests preferred to sleep and cook out in the open in the back courtyard.

Señora Monse was a widow until Carlos came as a guest, two years prior to my visit. He never left. "This man," she told me, "mi esposo, he is very old and he still has so much to learn in how to live with me." She laughed and fondly ruffled his hair. "Es verdad, no?" Carlos laughed and said, "women, they want their men to be children and their children to be men, es verdad."

Several Canadian mining companies were active in the barrancas. There was a base camp with a helipad 10 km down the road. One early morning a helicopter clattered over Batopilas. It belonged to Francisco, an exploration company whose spectacular finds had rocked the Vancouver stock exchange six months earlier. Carlos was vehement in his condemnation. "They are international pirates, come to corrupt our leaders and rob us of what we have left." Señora Monse said "it is very bad what they plan to do. It will become difficult for the earth to breathe."

What they planned to do was to have a mine on the top of the ridge above Batopilas. The tailings would cascade down the mountainside, the cyanide would leach into the ground. The plans for this mine collapsed after a feeding frenzy of speculation and stock manipulation in Vancouver. A good ending, this.

The Copper Canyons looking down at a typical road.

Below: giving rides in the back of the 4x4

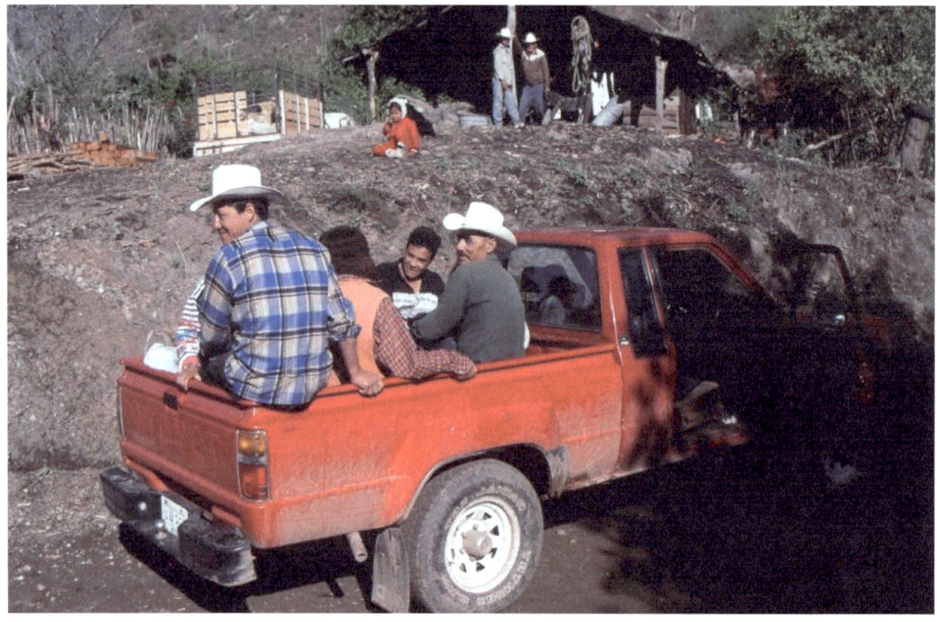

Global Witness

In 1998, I joined a Global Witness project spanning Vietnam and Cambodia. Global Witness is an NGO that investigates situations where violations of human rights and ecological degradation come together. Their work includes investigating blood diamonds in Africa and the violent expulsion of indigenous people out of their homelands in the Amazon forests.

They knew that remnants of the Khmer Rouge and post-Khmer Rouge warlords were logging the old-growth teak forests of Cambodia and were either enslaving the tribal peoples living in these forests or killing them outright when they resisted. The four years of the Khmer Rouge reign of terror left a shattered Cambodian society. One third of its population was dead and the remaining people were trying to put their lives back together. The international community and the UN came to Cambodia's aid to help reconstruct a civil society and create an accountable government. The destruction of the forest that was financing the warlords threatened to undo their efforts. Global Witness was there to investigate and document the logging and find out how the Cambodian teak got to the international market.

The year with MSF in Georgia had left me shaken. I wanted no more of the implacable hatred and brutality, the murky militias and buried landmines. I went to work for Global Witness thinking that merely recording violations would be less traumatic than living and working in war zones. This was not exactly how it worked out.

Spying Out the Far East: Vietnam

We were a team of two, working undercover in Vietnam. We passed ourselves off as representatives of a European garden-furniture consortium looking for factories that had secure sources of teak furniture. We were working as spies. At the Global Witness headquarters in London colleagues had already researched the bigger teak garden furniture factories in Vietnam, and we arrived with a list of names and locations.

The bait we dangled for garden furniture factories was the promise of long-term contracts with fictional European companies. Everyone we talked to was interested to seal the deal, however, they had to demonstrate that they could actually supply us with a guaranteed stream of teak furniture. A condition of our contract was that they show us their secure, ongoing, source of teak in person. We were pretty sure that this would mean taking us to the Cambodia–Vietnam border. The second factory we talked to agreed to show us their source of teak. Two friendly men and a woman (who seemed to be the person in charge) showed up at our hotel with a car, and we drove for an hour and a half into the bush.

When we stopped, we saw six captured American army trucks from the 1970s loaded with huge teak logs. The trucks were six-wheel drive GMCs with a PTO winch mounted on the front bumper (a power take off winch). These aren't so common anymore. They run off of the vehicle engine instead of electricity. Nothing is too heavy for these winches, until the cable breaks). The Vietnamese had welded a huge steel tripod (with a pulley on top) to the front bumper. This converted the old army vehicles into self-loading logging trucks. These massive six-wheel-drive trucks, still bearing American insignias on the doors, were all left behind during the chaotic departure of the US military from Vietnam in 1975.

Our hosts told us that we were now in Cambodia. They told us that these trucks, loaded up with teak logs, were then driven to the Vietnamese port city of Nha Trang. From there the logs went by ship to Singapore, from where the teak was dispersed into the world.

We had with us one of the bulky video camera bags of the time. We asked if we could take a video of the loaded trucks. Our smiling guides said, "No! No!"

We smiled too and closed the bag back up. All the while, however, we were secretly filming with a pin-hole camera that was hidden in the camera bag's false bottom.

We left our visits expressing that we were satisfied but needed to confer with our company and would return in a few weeks' time with the contracts

The video evidence we collected clearly showed that.

Vietnam's hands were dirty when it came to the illegal teak trade. They had signed international agreements to not buy, sell, or move illegal Cambodian timber. The evidence from Global Witness allowed the UN and other international agencies to pressure the Vietnamese government. They could shut down development money if Vietnam didn't get their act together.

Getting busted in Vietnam would have been a bad experience for us. I was nervous the whole time and happy to get out of there.

Number Twenty: On the run in Cambodia

I was in Cambodia on my own. My colleague from Global Witness had gone back to London and I had a new mission: to buy a concession to log a given area in Cambodia. Part of our work here was to find evidence of who in the new Cambodian government was in collusion with the illegal logging, and who was making money from it in Cambodia. With a logging concession contract from the Cambodian government in hand, Global Witness could go to the UN, which had helped set up the post-Khmer Rouge government and which had the power to root out this kind of corruption.

I was posing this time as a representative for a Canadian timber company, a so-called division of Brinkman Forests. Since I didn't know London at all, the Global Witness handler in London had decided it was better to have the mythical timber company based in Vancouver and to use the Brinkman Forests offices as our address. My old buddy Dirk Brinkman, now the president of Brinkman Forests, was on board to help with the ruse. My daughter Sjoukje had made fake company stationery and would send me the necessary replies answering any questions that I needed to "check with the office in Vancouver" about. I would email her the questions and the answers I wanted, and she would send me a fax on company stationery that I could show if need be.

I spent a month speaking to various people in the Cambodian forestry department. They all said, "we are no longer selling these concessions." I eventually got an appointment to see the Minister of Forests himself. The minister was sitting behind an enormous desk, wearing a striped suit, a white shirt and a red tie. He looked like a B-grade movie depiction of a mafia don. Sometimes life holds hands with art. There were half a dozen armed thugs hanging around wearing an assortment of army pants, camouflage shirts and the ever-present Kalashnikovs loaded with their distinctive banana-shaped clips. It felt like I was back in Georgia. The minister stood to greet me and offered me a seat.

I sat, carefully placing my briefcase so that the hidden mic would pick up our conversation, and explained that we dealt in teak at a wholesale level in Vancouver, Canada. There was a huge demand for teak, but our teak supply in Brazil had dried up. Environmentalists had buggered things up. They had pressured the Brazilian government to stop logging the forests in the Amazon. We had heard that Cambodia was a good place to do business. There was a lot of money to be made. We needed two million board feet a week, almost 5,000 cubic metres.

We talked for a half hour. The sums involved were in the range of a million dollars a week. The minister was interested. He said he had other business partners from the West, but could probably add one more. As I left, I could see a shiny new Mercedes reflected in his opaque black eyes.

I was handed over to a guy named Kosal who spoke suspiciously good English. We met three times to discuss the details of a timber concession. When we would pay, money transfers, how we measured lumber board feet, using the metric system, etc. He had some odd questions about Vancouver, street names, and restaurants on Commercial Drive. It seemed odd until he let slip that he had lived in Vancouver during the Khmer Rouge years. He was checking me out. The last time we met, I slipped up. I made a very basic error about cubic meter measurements. He immediately caught that. He followed up with more questions about Brinkman Forestry, where were we located, and how long had I done this job. Kosal appeared to be satisfied with my answers, but I left with an uneasy feeling.

I was staying in an out-of-the-way place at the end of a long, winding, sandy path on Boeing Kak Lake. The lake was located in a run-down part of Phnom Peng. Keith, a Scottish scam artist, and his tattooed-all-over Thai wife had built the place. It consisted of a bar featuring a dance floor and a thirty-foot-long slab of polished teak as a counter. A 100-foot-long dock ran out into the lake and had eight separate little cabins resting on stilts made of bamboo along one side of the dock. It is common in Cambodia to have houses over the water on stilts. His Thai wife would dance to entertain us, or herself, not sure which, while a six-foot-long snake slid and glided over every part of her body. It was the most sensuous dance I have ever seen. She had a very well-trained snake. Keith was one of many foreigners living in Cambodia. His business card read: "Scam Asia." Since there were no extradition treaties with anywhere in the world, Cambodia was a safe haven for Keith and others who were living on the margins of the law. Keith's open-air bar was a great place for stories of expat lives, lived on the edge in Asia. This place suited me to a tee.

One afternoon, two days after seeing Kosal, I rode my borrowed scooter up to the bar. It was early evening, Keith looked frightened. "You gotta go man! You can't say here. The police, the really evil ones, came looking for you. You gotta go, now! I can't have you here, you're dangerous!" His Thai wife smiled at me and stroked her snake.

I went to see my translator, Bora. He understood immediately. The visitors were the private government police. Very bad. No one survives. He told me, "you stay here, you leave in the morning. Cambodian Police, army, will watch the southern road to the coast, to Sihanoukville. They will watch boats going to Sim Riep and Angkor Wat. The road east to Vietnam is dangerous for you also. You can maybe take the train. They will not watch because foreign people are strictly forbidden to get on this train. The train goes to Sihanoukville on the coast. From there the Thai border is 200 kilometres away. Very bad road for car, good road for you. I go check."

Boran came back in an hour and handed me a train ticket. The train left at eight. "I know how to get you on train. I stay with you till Sihanoukville." The next morning, well away from the ticket office, Boran pried a board off a wood fence. I squeezed through, saw a train car with the door open and sat down on a straight-backed wooden seat. Three people were already seated. A half hour later, Boran found me. He had gone through the ticket booth and had a stamped ticket for me.

The train moved slow, stopping to let people off or on. It seemed that the people took this train to take produce and animals to markets along the route. Seats were piled high with produce, in some cars there were cows and pigs. On the roof of each car, living feathered rings of panting chickens with their feet tied together at the centre and their heads at the outside of the circle lay in the sun. The owner would take a mouthful of water and place a chicken beak in his mouth to give each panting hen a drink of water. He did this, going around the circle of chickens again and again, for the entire trip. The few times the train stopped at an actual train station, Boran would send me up to the roof of the car to hang out with the chicken guys.

On the rails in Cambodia

I sat for a while next to a woman who, to my great surprise, spoke some English. She said, “you are on the wrong train, it is forbidden to foreigners.” “Why? I do not hurt anyone.” She replied, “this law it is for your protection.” She continued, “I was on this train one year ago. We were one hour farther on from here when I heard a loud explosion. Khmer Rouge soldiers fired an RPG (rocket-propelled grenade) through the front of the locomotive to stop the train. Men with guns came on the train and took all the food people were taking to markets. In my car were four foreigners, three young men from Europe and one from America. The soldiers got very excited when they saw the foreigners. They yelled and screamed at them, poked them with their guns and took everything they had. Books, pens, wallets with money, two small knives, passports, their hats and even their shoes. Everything! The young men’s eyes were big like this egg.” She took out a small banty egg from a woven basket on her lap. “Their faces were white like this egg. Those young men were very afraid. They walked out of the train car each one with a gun barrel held against his back. One boy stumbled and fell. His soldier yelled and kicked him five times before he got up. They tied the four young men to a tree with a long rope that went round and round them and the tree many times. Two Khmer Rouge men sat on the ground pointing their guns at prisoners. I show you the tree when we go past.”

She continued, “They made us all get off the train. The soldiers had unloaded many piles of produce and rice along with hundreds of chickens, some pigs, several cows and a single Water Buffalo alongside the railroad track. The individual owners of the various foodstuffs had to stand beside their property and then help to transport it. They rounded up as many more passengers as were needed to carry, or herd, everything. I was given a bag of rice to carry. A long train of people, goods, and animals, guarded by armed men, walked off into the jungle. The four prisoners, tied together with a long rope, walked at the back with one soldier, carrying a Kalashnikov, for each foreigner. It took two days to reach the Khmer Rouge camp.”

She told how several months of frantic negotiation followed and finally a ransom of ten million dollars was paid. A few days later a wicker basket with four decaying heads arrived at the UN peacekeeping office in Phnom Penh. It was apparent that the four hostages were already dead while the negotiations were in progress. This brutal killing really shook the UN and the fledgling Cambodian government. For the international agencies that were making huge efforts to put Cambodia back on its feet, this horrific event called into question the progress they were making. Their first step was to no longer allow foreigners on this train. The story ratcheted up feelings of vulnerability that were kind of dormant, but I was much more afraid of the private political police who were actively looking for me than the somewhat more abstract Khmer threat. Regardless, I had no real choice other than to stay sitting on the train.

At dusk we pulled into Sihanoukville. As a safety precaution, we jumped off the slow-moving train before it arrived at the station. Where to stay? Boran said, "stay in whorehouse. Safer than hotel." He walked me through backstreets to a three-story, nice-looking house. He knocked and the door was opened by a stout 50-year-old Thai woman with glossy black hair that fell almost to her knees. They obviously knew each other and had a hurried conversation in Cambodian. She then turned to me and said, "Hi I am Chastrea. You call me Mom." She spoke quite good English. Her wide flat face broke into the biggest smile I had seen in all Cambodia. Boran left and I blurted out, "I need to get to the Thai border." She already knew my story. She said, "we find someone. You are safe here. We take care for you." I was in the company of the right segment of society – outsiders who have no truck with the police or their agendas.

The next day, Chastrea put on a dinner for me along with six house girls. They were all quite young and giggled at everything I said. They were like teenagers and seemed so innocent. The girls were shy and demure, so out of character with their profession. Chastrea said, "these are like my daughters." I could not knit these threads into a fabric I understood. I felt completely out of my element.

Three days later a muscular young guy driving a motorcycle pulled up to the house. He spoke almost no English and said, "hung on" as we roared off. The road was not paved, it was mostly sand. The motorcycle could easily go around some big holes that looked like bomb craters. He drove insanely fast for the entire distance. He really knew how to handle his bike. We didn't meet a single vehicle. Suddenly he turned onto a one-lane road to the right. After a few minutes, he stopped and pointed to a game trail on the left. "Thailand" grinning all the while. I paid him thirty Yankee dollars. He gave me another wide grin and took off. I was left standing by the roadside, unsure, wondering if I had been taken for a ride. I set off down the path. Within ten minutes' walking it intersected another sandy path that veered left. A short while later I stood on a paved road a few hundred yards past the border, safely in Thailand. I could see the border post and a Cambodian exit check in the distance. My shoulders dropped six inches. For the first time in eight weeks, I felt safe. At that moment I decided that this cloak and dagger stuff was not for me. For eight weeks I had constantly told lies, thought lies, even dreamt lies. It had been a life of deception, continually waiting for the other shoe to drop.

Touching the Void

Number Twenty-One: Life is Breath

I was meeting my niece Karen and her husband Philippe in Ladakh for a Himalayan trek. Karen was a Rhodes Scholar and had a tenured, well-paying job at the University of British Columbia. Philippe was a Frenchman, a sadly out of place guy in English British Columbia. He travels all the time hoping to find what he left behind. I liked Philippe right away. He inspired me to consider why we constantly move on, leaving behind people we love and situations that fit our natures. Always, we think we can do better than this, but in the end "better" was in our grasp all along. Our nature propels us along so that we never get to savour what we build, or what we could have built. Sir Richard Burton, sick with fever in the interminable swamps of South Sudan, (Al-Sud) asked the same questions. His answer, "the Devil drives," rings true. The Devil is our ego that relentlessly drives us on with no regard for the future, or for our well-being. Our ego, our selfish self, only wants to inflate itself, to do more, to experience more. The real struggle in life, the one that matters, is to gain mastery of our ego and use it to benefit ourselves and our loved ones.

I flew from Vancouver to New Delhi to Leh. In a matter of a few hours, I had gone from 700 to 14,000 feet elevation. There had been some travel delays and we were crunched for time. I stood under a clear blue sky tasting the thin air. I thought, this ain't natural. Sure, enough it wasn't.

On day two in Leh we met our guide and three mules. All that day we hiked up and up, passing through a severely desiccated landscape. We saw not a single green shoot or green blade in this high elevation desert. We camped at 16,000 feet. That first night I barely slept, waking with a start each time I dozed off. My alert systems were activated. My body was warning me, "not enough oxygen." By noon the next day, at 18,000 feet it had become obvious that I was not doing well. The guide told us that the trail to the right ended at the Zanskar River, about three hours walking. On the other side of the river was a village where the new road that goes partway up the Zanskar River, ends. He said that there they may be able to help me. If not, about once a week a car came to the village. Philippe and the guide turned left to finish the trek, Karen and I went in the other direction. After six laborious hours, stopping to get my breath every few minutes, we arrived at the Zanskar River. The river was a torrent of wild white water crashing into the walls of a deep, rocky canyon. There was a bamboo basket attached to a cable that spanned the river. We gingerly got into the basket; it seemed pretty solid. A young boy, waiting to cross, helped to pull the basket to the other side. He knew the ropes. We could hear the wild waters of the Zanskar far below, with white caps battling each other to be the first to reach the Indus River. Halfway across the boy yelled "Car! Car!" Sure enough, a car was just entering the village. Upon reaching the other side the boy ran up to the road to intercept the car. Within five minutes a shiny new 4 × 4 Land Cruiser drove up. A big, six-foot-some guy got out, walked up to me and said, "how are you feeling?" I mumbled "I've felt better." I had just met a miracle named Doctor Lee. He was from the States, Buffalo NY. His expertise was high altitude sickness. He had come to Leh to present at a conference on altitude sickness. He was on a one-day outing to drive to the end of the new road up the Zanskar canyon. I was bundled into the back of the Land Cruiser, and we set off for the hospital in Leh.

I quietly worshipped Doctor Lee from Buffalo. His matter-of-fact ways reassured me that I would be just fine. It was just another temporary glitch. He left some instructions for the hospital staff and said he would be back in the morning to check on me. I was in a hospital room with six beds but only one other patient, an Indian army officer suffering severe shell shock. He had been in a battle with the Pakistani army, fought at 19,000 feet where they duel with exploding artillery shells. It is hard to imagine the hardship of the bitter cold, barely being able to breathe, with exploding artillery shells landing on your camp. Karen lay down in an empty bed and stayed. A nurse set me up with an oxygen drip, a small tube dribbled oxygen into my mouth. It wasn't enough oxygen. Sucking hard on the tube did not help.

Dr. Lee came in the morning and checked me out. "You have pulmonary edema and will have to stay here for a few more days. I'll be back tomorrow." The nurse swabbed the floor with kerosene. "Kills bacteria," she told me. It also killed my sense of smell. The next day I was worse. I could only sit up straight so that the fluid in my lungs stayed put in one place and didn't spread out. To lay down was to drown. Another day and even sitting bolt upright I wasn't getting enough oxygen. I tried to turn up the regulator on the oxygen cylinder. It appeared to be set at a meagre five pounds pressure. I did this exactly how I would do it on an oxygen/acetylene cylinder in the shop back home. I first turned the valve on top of the cylinder wide open. The gauge shot up to a hundred pounds, and then the regulator exploded with a loud bang. Shards of glass flew across the room. The army guy in the next bed shot straight up out of his bed and tried to climb the wall. Pure oxygen poured directly out of the cylinder. I immediately felt better. A nurse came running in and berated Karen for tampering with the oxygen regulator. She brought in a new oxygen cylinder and before leaving she shook her finger in Karen's face and said, "do not touch! Do not touch!" I smiled in spite of being back to a measly five-pound drip of oxygen.

My breathing slowly got worse. On the fourth night I sat up all night desperately trying to get enough air. I tried everything. Deep breathing, shallow breathing, fast breathing, slow breathing, meditating on life and death. Nothing made any difference. I knew that if I got even a thimble less oxygen I would die. "Is this the end?" I wondered. When I thought about not seeing Sjoukje again, I felt so sad, and my breathing was instantly worse. I was drowning. I realised that emotions use up oxygen. I thought about the Somali mother who couldn't afford the indulgence of grieving for her dead child for more than one day. I was drowning. For the rest of the night, I kept my mind blank. Any thoughts that came to me were immediately squashed. I was a drowning man breathing through a straw and paying the price of attachment. Dying is surprisingly prosaic.

With the coming daylight my breathing improved. It seemed to verify the old stories of sick people surviving a crisis if only they could hang on till daylight. Come morning Dr. Lee said, "we have to get you to lower elevation." He was flying to Srinagar (at 6,000 feet elevation) in six hours and would arrange for me to be on the same flight. Karen and I went to the airport. An hour before the flight, we were told that the airport manager had given my seat to someone else. Karen immediately went to his office, walked in, put her hands together over her heart, the Indian way to say that your spirit is involved, and said, “my uncle will die if he does not get on this flight.” He ordered her to leave. She stood her ground and repeated her mantra over and over and over. He finally got up and walked out. Karen was two paces behind him repeating her mantra. Suddenly he turned around and abruptly said, “he can go,” and briskly walked off. My niece saved the day and saved my life.

Once in Srinagar at 6,000 feet, I immediately felt better. Doctor Lee’s driver took me to one of the fabled houseboats on Dal Lake. This was where the British colonials would come to escape the brutal heat of the North Indian plains and wile away the summer, relaxing in a luxurious houseboat, floating in the cool breezes of Dal Lake. My stay was less conscious. I slept for 32 hours straight. I awoke a new man, or better yet, the same old man. Shrinigar was shut down because of martial law. The off-on war with Pakistan had been revived. There was a curfew with armed soldiers posted every thirty feet along the streets. There had been bombings. I heard some gunshots. I stepped outside and took a deep breath. I had seldom felt so rejuvenated. Everything about life: martial law, the curfew, gunshots in the night, all of it was relative. After a lifetime of various deprivations and close calls, simply getting enough air trumps everything.

Number Twenty-Two: Life or Death, a Fine Line it is

I was driving fast on a seldom-travelled back road. It was a shortcut. It was nearly dark, and I was missing Celeste. We were newly married, just ten weeks before. In Celeste I had found a kindred soul. She was an entrepreneurial outsider with little regard for society's "civilised" conventions or legalities. I had found an outlaw wife. I couldn't believe my luck!

Celeste and I were engaged in some nefarious activities which involved driving a lot of these back roads that cross the US/Canada border unnoticed. I had been checking out a new crossing and was on my way back, eager to tell Celeste that I had found a really good one. I had hit paved road and was driving fast, thinking about her cosy warm house and her lovely, cosy warm self. I looked down at the speedometer, it read 150 km/h. Too fast! I let up on the gas and at that moment the wheels hit a patch of black ice and the car was travelling sideways. That is all I remember. I woke up in a hospital bed not knowing anything and sore all over. Days later the events slowly came into focus.

The rental car had rolled over eight times before coming to a stop. I wasn't wearing the seat belt and was thrown out through the windshield, the cops figured that happened on the third rollover. I landed in a dense shrub of willow bushes. A single car coming from the other way had just enough fading daylight to see my car hurtling through the air. They didn't stop, but they did alert the sheriff. The sheriff came on the scene to find me in bare feet, covered in blood, walking around the open field. I evidently answered his questions before he called for an ambulance. I had no memory of any of this, but Celeste and I had some real fears about what questions had been asked or answered.

The ambulance took me to the hospital in Colville, Washington. The doctors called Celeste to say that if she wished to see her husband again, she needed to come right away. After assessing my injuries, they realised that they couldn't keep me alive with their limited equipment and expertise. An evacuation by air ambulance to Seattle, the site of the number one trauma ward in the USA, was next. Three days later I came to.

The first thing I saw was the worried faces of my daughter and wife, not sure if they should smile or cry. I was monitored around the clock for the next five days. On my bedside table was a stainless-steel tray of shiny surgical instruments ready for an emergency tracheotomy. My throat had a purple swelling so large that it could block my ability to breathe at any moment. I had a punctured lung and eight broken ribs with severely bruised muscles and torn ligaments across my upper back. I had dislocated my right shoulder, which they didn't notice in the face of all the other injuries until much later. It seemed that my back and shoulders hit the ground first. It felt like I had just come off a medieval torture rack that stretched everything, feeling like the tendons and muscles in my upper back had torn free from their moorings. There were some head injuries as well, and in a mirror, I saw a shaved head with a row of steel staples across the top. I had the look of Frankenstein's monster and was able to frighten small children just by taking off my tuque.

Men with shiny black shoes had come to the hospital asking a lot of questions about me while I was unconscious. Why was I on those remote back roads in a car rented for only one day? Why were there walkie talkies in the vehicle? (Thank God that's all that was in the vehicle). Celeste knew how to talk to these people. She kept her answers super friendly, polite and bland. They all left, but Celeste and Sjoukje couldn't stop looking over their shoulders.

Our stressful visitors and the mounting medical costs for someone with no insurance led us to push hard to get out of the USA as soon as the doctors would let me go. Five days later I got an early discharge and we drove to Vancouver with me lying in the backseat of the car. I was on the couch at Dirk's house for the next three weeks with the curtains drawn. I could not stand any light, or any noise. Mostly I was asleep for the entire time. A kinda unconscious experience.

Eventually, I drove home to the Kootenays where I reflected on the cost to me and those close to me for so readily taking chances. Me, as an individual human being, is an illusion. Humans survived for a million years because we lived in family groups. Family groups who protected each other, who cared for each other. I survived to see eighty years only because others were there when I needed them. We all live and survive and thrive because, from the very day of our birth, we receive support and help and care from others. This is the true grace we all inherit when we take our first breath, and it stays with us till we breathe our last.

Turning down the Middle Path

Enlightening Mongolian Monks

In 1988 I joined the Canada Tibet Committee (CTC), which was, and still is, dedicated to the quixotic mission of freeing Tibet from Chinese occupation. I joined not for my dedication to Buddhism but for Tibetan freedom. I am a bred-in-the-bone freedom fighter. For the first five years of my life, we lived under German occupation in the Netherlands. My father risked his life, and the lives of his family, by joining the Resistance. I grew up on stories of "the War" and the heroic exploits of the Frisian resistance and the brutally sad stories of German retaliation for those exploits. Resisting overbearing authority is embedded in my bones. In the end it's Che Guevara, not the Dalai Lama, who is a role model. I was living in Vancouver with Sjoukje and about to go to Ethiopia for my first project with MSF when my CTC friends introduced me to a Tibetan lama named Zasep Rinpoche. My friends thought I should have Rinpoche's blessing before leaving on my first MSF mission. A deeply ingrained scepticism about religion had me doubt the efficacy of spiritual protection; however, I was also deeply pragmatic and happy to accept any help I could get.

The Rinpoche was a stocky, well built, handsome Tibetan guy with a black moustache, a ready smile, and a gentle sense of humour. We soon discovered we had something in common. We were both immigrants, me from Friesland, and him from Tibet via India. We talked about our common experience as immigrants to Canada, and the experience of being an outsider in a foreign land. We spoke about how that experience insists on concessions to new realities. I came away from that meeting thinking of how very different Rinpoche's experience of life as a lama and a revered tulku was from the rigid Calvinist workaday world I had come from. Dutch immigrants to Canada and the USA gained acceptance in a new world through their work. Rinpoche was accepted as a teacher and spiritual mentor rather than a worker, but we did meet as immigrants, as men who had negotiated life in a new and unfamiliar world.

We both agreed that, over time, we have become indistinguishable from "them" externally, but an inviolate core, like the heart of Joan of Arc, remained unchanged, creating a living, breathing, dichotomous being in both of us. He did blessings for my journey with MSF, and we parted ways.

Five years later I was walking down Baker Street in Nelson, some 600 kilometres from Vancouver, when I literally bumped into Zasep Rinpoche. He said, "what are you doing here?" I replied, "what are **you** doing here?" Our simultaneous answers of, "I live here," were like an echo of each other. I was living in a 100-year-old farmhouse in Queens Bay, 35 kilometres north of Nelson. The Rinpoche had a house and a gompa on Sproule Creek, 10 kilometres south of Nelson. We went to the Dominion Café to have a coffee and catch up on five years of semi-nomadic living.

It became apparent that neither of us were homebodies. We both spent more time away than we did living in our homes. Zasep Rinpoche was a true twenty-first century pastor, ministering to spiritual communities in Vancouver, Toronto, Indiana and Australia as well as assisting Buddhist monasteries in Tibet and Mongolia. Sometimes he was just travelling the world for fun. I was working on MSF projects in far-flung, out-of-the-way places, (or just travelling the world for fun) and only coming home to regenerate for another fling out into the wider world. We both took immense joy in the seemingly magical finding of like-minded company, and in such wonderfully improbable proximity. The meeting in Nelson was the beginning of a long and continuing friendship.

Some years later, Zasep Rinpoche invited me to go with him to Mongolia. I agreed to go but asked him to find something for me to do there, a project, rather than being a tourist. He came back to me two weeks later with a request from Mongolia to electrify a Buddhist monastery in the Gobi Desert. Gaden Relief, a Buddhist charity, would pay for the system.

Mongolia has a long history of Buddhism. When it was swept into the Soviet empire in the 1920s, Buddhism was brutally eliminated, but now that Mongolians were free of the Soviet Union they were bringing back their Buddhist practices and institutions. Delgeruun Choira Monastery had been completely destroyed by the Soviets in 1939. It had been the seat of the great Buddhist scholar and teacher Zava Lam Damdin (1867–1937). In the year 2000, a 25-year-old monk was recognized as his reincarnation. The new Zava Damdin Rinpoche was reviving and rebuilding Delgeruun Choira Monastery.

The role that emerged for me was to design and install a solar-powered lighting system for the monastery. Monks had been using candles to read and study at night, and the desire was to have LED lamps for them to use, as well as to light the temple for ceremonies.

I designed a solar-powered electric system from an 8 × 10 black-and-white photograph of the site. The monastery was a work in progress. There was a new traditional Tibetan temple with upturned roofs, a much larger sixty-foot diameter yurt (ger) that served as their temple for large gatherings, a small house for visiting lamas, a scattering of yurts and some outbuildings left over from Soviet times. From the photograph I made rough measurements of the distances the power needed to travel from the battery bank to the various buildings, guesses as to how much electricity was needed, and made a list of the components needed. I planned to buy these in Beijing.

Rinpoche was first going to travel to Tibet to visit his home monastery in Kham province on the headwaters of the Mekong River at 14,000 feet elevation. He was received there as the living embodiment of the eight previous revered masters of this monastery. I was going directly to Beijing to buy twelve 200-watt solar panels and other electronic components. We were to meet in the Three Happiness Hotel in Beijing on August 2, 2006.

Once in Beijing, I hired a translator, a very dressy young Chinese woman in five-inch high heels. We had a long day checking out various places, and prices, for solar panels. She was intensely interested in what I was doing, with questions like, "is this a good business?" "Is there a lot of money to be made?" I explained that I planned to install a solar system to light up a Buddhist monastery in Mongolia. "You must be well paid for doing this work?" I told her that I do not get paid to do this, that this work is for my soul. She began to ask questions about Buddhism and was completely baffled by my explanations, a society where people live by a belief that does not include the pursuit of money? At day's end, the taxi pulled up at the hotel. I prepared to pay her. We had agreed on $100 US for the day. She seemed embarrassed, muttered something in Chinese, and abruptly said, "no! I too will support a monastery. I do not wish to be paid." She turned on her high heels and walked away. I was left to ponder, did she just have a change of heart, or an upwelling of old collective cultural memories of a time when the sacred mattered? Was she superstitious and investing in abstract spiritual help? I was impressed that even in a money-oriented new China, people could still be moved to assist in a good cause.

The next day Rinpoche arrived from Tibet and we met in the Three Happiness Hotel. He had a thigh bone trumpet. The bone had a beautiful, soft, cream-coloured sheen. It looked ancient, with the patina one sees on a mammoth tusk. The bone had two rounded knobs at the knee. There was a small hole drilled in both knobs. This made the bone a trumpet. The bone had been ever so carefully covered with a tight-fitting black leather skin. Three inches of bone had been left exposed in the centre.

Rinpoche's uncle, who was a lama at Rinpoche's home monastery in Tibet, had given him the thigh bone trumpet. It is important to know where a bone to be used as a trumpet came from. It must be the thigh bone of a woman. It may not come from one who committed suicide or died some other violent and tragic death or one who died of TB. This bone had come from the old lama's niece. She had died in childbirth at age twenty-three. The thigh bone trumpet is in fact a gift from Rinpoche's deceased cousin.

The old lama took her body up the mountain for a traditional Tibetan sky burial. Her body was placed on a flat burial rock where vultures could come and eat the flesh. Most of her bones were then pulverised and thrown to the wind. The lama kept one thigh bone and buried it for one year in the ground. After digging up the bone he cut off the hip ball, made round holes in the two knee knobs and cleaned out the marrow. The bone was air dried for six months, and then whiskey was poured into the hollow bone as a kind of final antiseptic. He then meticulously covered the bone in paper-thin black leather with stitching so fine one could not see where the piece of leather ended.

Rinpoche blew on the trumpet with a mighty blast. A loud, clear, haunting Tibetan tone echoed through the Three Happiness Hotel.

We boarded a train to Ulaanbaatar. We loaded the twelve solar panels and hid them under the two unused bunks in our four-person sleeper cabin. We hoped to avoid paying the Mongolian duty on Chinese goods. I was pleased to see that a Rinpoche was willing to take some risks and is not so bound to legalities as his profession would suggest. Our friendship deepened.

When we arrived at the train station in Ulaanbaatar we were greeted by robed monks and a flurry of blue and yellow ceremonial khatas. Bowed, shaved heads softly conferred heaven's blessing upon us. We were driven in a black Mercedes to our base in Ulaanbaatar, a palatial four-story house in a walled compound. This was the house of Guru Deva Rinpoche. He was a 97-year-old, highly venerated monk. He was also the beloved teacher of Zava Damdin Rinpoche. The monks that lived there were waiting for our arrival in the grand foyer, each with a khata draped across extended arms, bowing their heads and murmuring blessings. The reception took place under a massive, thirty-foot chandelier with a thousand twinkling crystal lights. The watts this one chandelier used up was equal to what our entire solar-powered electrical system would produce once installed.

Guru Deva Rinpoche had done for Tibetan Buddhism what the Irish monasteries had done for Western civilization. During Europe's descent into barbarism in the dark ages, monks saved and copied Greek and Roman texts ensuring their survival into the Renaissance.

When Tibetan monks and lamas, along with the Dalai Lama, fled the Chinese invasion of Tibet in the winter of 1959, they left their books and libraries behind. This, combined with the Soviet destruction of everything associated with Mongolian Buddhism, could have meant an immense loss for Buddhist learning, scholarship and history except for an ironic historical quirk. During the late nineteenth century, wealthy Russian aristocrats, with the assistance of the Czarist government, had organised large and well-funded expeditions to Central Asia and beyond. They brought back enormous amounts of everything exotic. There was an enthusiastic interest in Europe and Russia during the mid and late nineteenth century for the religions of the Orient. The extensive and growing collection of Buddhist books, art and statuary were housed in a library in St. Petersburg. During the Soviet era when they were busy destroying Buddhist temples, artefacts and written materials across the empire, the KGB had ignored this Buddhist treasure trove and library because it did not fit the definition for "enemies of the state" in St. Petersburg.

In the 1960s, Guru Deva Rinpoche began to reprint Buddhist sacred books, many copied from the archives in St. Petersburg. He widely disseminated these texts to Buddhist monasteries sprouting across all India and Nepal, began by these newly arrived Tibetan refugees, ensuring that the millennia-old teachings survived.

We were ushered up a grand curved staircase to our rooms, bedrooms with maroon and gold embossed wallpaper, exquisitely carved furniture and hand-woven Tibetan carpets on the floor. Rinpoche's room was similar to mine except that his had a shrine with gold statues and a throne draped with gold, red and yellow brocade that also served as a bed. Rinpoche was a tulku, a recognized reincarnation. As a tulku he was granted a level of honour above regular monks. He could also wear yellow robes as well as the more common maroon monk's robes. Monkish servants brought our meals, robed monks opened and closed doors for us. These digs were well beyond the opulence of a mere five-star hotel.

I came to the private conclusion that Buddhism is, among other things, another vehicle for hierarchy. An elevated spiritual rank automatically confers a high temporal rank as well as the externalities that come with this. A high lama receives a bright yellow (the colour of gold) khata instead of a blue one. They wear heavy gowns embroidered with gold thread rather than simple red robes and sit on gilded thrones surrounded by stunning shrines with rows and rows of bejewelled gold statues.

The entrance to our temporary house was a grand foyer with a high vaulted ceiling. The larger-than-life golden Buddha framed by even larger, brilliantly painted, thangkas reminded me of the grandeur of the Notre Dame, made to mirror the glory of God to awe the "simpler folk." It was also to let them know where they stood in the hierarchy. The church, especially in mediaeval times, used the same means to designate and maintain hierarchy, as did the Incas, the Egyptians and the Romans. We human beings are programmed for heirarchy. It makes us feel safe to know our place.

Once having glanced an entrenched hierarchy I then saw it everywhere. I admit to a well entrenched personal prejudice when it comes to hierarchy, authority, or being told what to do, which had been instilled in me by my early experiences with Calvinism and from being raised in a Frisian family. Friesland never adopted Europe's feudal system. The saying, "every Frisian is a nobleman" reflects our history and mindset. Rinpoche said that my attitude was merely an expression of the ego. Perhaps all the exposure to monks and Buddhism would diminish my attitude. However, I saw that Rinpoche and I shared some of this mindset. As a visiting lama he had to live in special VIP housing with windows and thrones and brocade coverings while he would much prefer to live like other monks in simple windowless gers. He also was caught up in the web of protocol.

Before heading into the Gobi, we visited the Amarbayasgalant Monastery in the north of Mongolia. This was where an eleven-year-old Zava Damdin Rinpoche had first gone to study Buddhism. Amarbayasgalant is a large walled monastery with dozens of temples all built in classic Manchurian style with upswept roofs, elaborate curved entrances and brightly painted pillars and doors. The buildings inside the wall were spared during the Soviet purges of 1938/39 for the same reasons they saved the Winter Palace in St. Petersburg: to demonstrate to the people the opulence of the rulers and thus justify the Soviet revolution. In Mongolia they preserved this to demonstrate the excesses of Lamaism. Russia excels in propaganda and official lies to this day.

Mongolia was the first country to join the great Soviet socialist experiment, in the 1920s. All of Asia was in turmoil. China was a violent, chaotic mass of warlords all vying for power in the midst of an unpredictable civil war with shifting alliances and brutal, backstabbing betrayals. This spilled over into a thinly populated Mongolia. Mongolia did not have the military resources to stop the sporadic invasions and depredations visited on their people. Attempts to negotiate with Peking came to nothing. As a result, in the story told to me by my hosts, the government of the Bogd Khan decided to ask for help. Sukhbataar, a young military hero, rode his horse over 500 miles to Irkutsk where he caught the Trans-Siberian railway to St. Petersburg. He presented himself to Lenin. Lenin was happy to help. A fully equipped Soviet army was shipped to Mongolia on the new Trans-Siberian railway. The Russian soldiers hunted down and killed every living Chinese they could find in Mongolia.

One man's story tells of three thousand starving and exhausted Chinese soldiers who were camped in a small valley a mere thirty miles from the Chinese border. The Russian military was alerted, and they surrounded the valley in the dead of night. A nomad herder crossed the valley later that day. He described the incredible carnage of thousands of dead and dying men. He brought water to those crying out for a drink until it was too dark to see. He was so horrified by the human brutality that he went to Delgeruun Choira Monastary and became a monk. He learned to write, and hence his story survived.

The road south to Delgeruun Choira through the Gobi was a series of braided tracks in a semi-desert landscape. When the road got rutted, during a rain, they simply drove around the ruts and voila, another track. In low-lying places there were a dozen or more tracks. There were no road signs. Every so often a track veered off. Our driver never hesitated. Without a local on board, one would always be lost.

After seven hours we arrived at Delgeruun Choira to an ecstatic welcome. A dozen boy monks were waiting along the side the road. They ran next to the car waving blue khatas, and laughing with sheer joy, till we came to a stop. Zava Damdin Rinpochewas was there to greet us along with his mother "Amala" and some local nomads. A flurry of blue khathas were exchanged, the two rinpoches touched foreheads in an intimate expression of love and respect. We went to a large ger where Amala had laid out food for the hungry travellers.

The monastery was truly in the middle of nowhere. There was a collection of small gers set up in a bleak, windswept landscape. In the middle of all this was a most incongruous lavish temple with swooping upturned Manchurian roofs and a huge, 60-foot ger serving as another temple for public ceremonies. The monks of Delgeruun Choira were young boys ranging from seven to fifteen years old. They wore raggedy maroon robes tied at the waist with a piece of rope and sneakers with no socks. They were all smiling.

Our welcome at Delgeruun Choira

The very next day, five boy monks and several nomad guys were hanging around an ancient relic of an engine. The archaic engine powered a generator that ran the electric pump that pumped water for drinking. They hand-cranked the engine for a good 20 minutes. It finally started and instantly poured out thick clouds of black smoke that completely enveloped the engine and the boys. Thankfully, it quit almost right away.

I took a look and was quickly immersed in the workings of this haywired-together piece of old Soviet technology. I got my tools, electrical tape, epoxies, and a multimeter and proceeded to connect up loose wires, tape up exposed wiring, tighten or replace the rusted bits and pieces and generally tidy the thing up. The boys were enthralled; I worked in a tight circle of them, gathered close around, with ten willing pairs of hands eager to hold my pliers, pass a screwdriver, or hold a spool of wire exactly like young boys everywhere wanting to fix things, to do things, to learn things. They followed my every move and hung on my every pronouncement, muttering "goddamn junk" even though they understood not a word. I was the Pied Piper of Delgeruun Choira. These children would follow me anywhere.

When the engine restarted it no longer smoked. It ran the generator with some old V belts, and we had a stream of cool, crystal-clear fossil water. Two years ago, Gaden Relief had paid to have a 400-foot-deep bore well drilled. This well tapped a deep aquifer that delivered clear cold water to the monastery.

Because the Russian engine was not so reliable, Gaden Relief had donated a new 15 KW Kubota generator. The new generator worked for a short while before it refused to start. After a puja for the Kubota the monks went back to what they knew, their old Russian engine.

I later managed to get the Kubota running. It immediately spewed clouds of thick black smoke, quit running and refused to restart. I spent the next few hours messing with it, to get it going again. The air filter was completely clogged. They ran it during a sandstorm until it had quit. The water trap was half full of water. We ended up using a nylon stocking for a temporary air filter. It ran like the brand-new engine that it was. We filled our water bottles. Tough karma for one fine Kabota generator to end up in the Gobi Desert. They wanted to do a puja to make sure it kept running. I suggest they do a puja for me. I needed it more than the Kubota. They thought that was very funny.

The monastery complex was not what I thought it was going to be from the photo. The distance between the buildings, and therefore the distance electricity would have to travel, was more than double what it appeared in the photo. As well, they occasionally moved the residence gers. Some were no longer where they were in the photo, others were gone all together and then there were new gers, added in a random fashion.

I had planned to light nine buildings: there were now fourteen, and that meant that the electric load had near doubled. Among other things, the well had an electric pump I hadn't known about. This alone added 1,200 watts to the system. However, the pump was only turned on twice a week. It could still all work.

It was obvious that the 12-volt solar system I had come to install simply would not work for them. I did some calculations, measured everything, made a to-scale map of the place, thought and re-thought possibilities, came up with a possible plan and made a shopping list. I was not sure how this new system would look in the end, or that I would even be able to do this, but it was clear that we would need to return to Ulaanbaator. I talked to the rinpoches, and they told me that this was possible, but the trip could not happen for two weeks. I spent the time measuring and planning the layout of the new, expanded, solar system and exploring in and around the monastery.

I decided to use a one-room, old stone building as the powerhouse. It sat at a central location and would serve as the apex for a spider web of wiring to all the buildings we needed to connect. The building was used as storage for boxes and boxes of priceless religious artefacts, Tibetan books (hundreds of sutras), exquisitely painted boxes, carved wood printing blocks, brass statues, ancient thangkas, old leather amulets, brass cymbals, thigh bone trumpets, silver bells, a silver embossed conch shell, wood carvings, miniature ceramics and much more.

When the monastery was destroyed by the Soviets, local nomads had spirited away these artefacts and buried them in the desert. With the reincarnation of Zava Damdin Rinpoche returning and the building of a new temple beginning, local people came bearing treasures that their grandfathers had rescued from the monastery and hidden away 70 years ago. My monkish helpers emptied the building and moved the artifacts to another stone building. It was an emotional task for them to handle these ancient sacred objects from the time of the first Zava Lam Damdin, when Buddhism ruled life in Mongolia. Rinpoche and I spent hours looking at these thangkas, the writings in delicate calligraphy, the exquisite protector statues, the lovingly crafted, hand-painted boxes. It was a profound way to connect with the Delgeruun Choira of the past.

I had noticed a bent-over old woman who could sometimes be seen hobbling around, clutching her walking stick. She lived by a small cluster of huts beyond a nearby rock outcropping. The monks brought her soup in a small plastic pail each morning and some dried dung for her fire. They said that she had lived in these same few huts long before they had arrived. She had a small herd of goats then but now had only one young goat left. Zava Damdin Rinpoche and I went to visit her. She was mostly blind and peered out at us from under a coarse black cloth wrapped around her head and shoulders in a way that made her look top heavy. After our greetings I asked how old she was. She looked in my direction and shrugged her shoulders. An eloquent gesture, clear in its meaning. What does that matter? I asked if she was here the day the soldiers came and destroyed the monastery. She nodded her oversized head. What did you see? She bowed her head and several minutes later began to talk, all the while looking at the ground. She told us that they came at the day's end, at dusk, with many big trucks. Soldiers were jumping out of the trucks, yelling and screaming, running into the temples, driving all the monks outside, beating them with their guns. Huge, fierce dogs kept the monks standing in a circle. Big bright lights on the trucks made the monastery like it was daylight. No one could get away, soldiers forced monks to empty the libraries, beating them as they ran with arms filled with scrolls and books. Big piles of sacred text were set on fire with the flames reaching to the heavens. Our peaceful monastery was a frightful place with bright searching lights, yelling, screaming, barking dogs, gun shots, dead and dying monks, blood on the steps of the temple. Tears rolled down the creases of her flat leathery cheeks. She said, "I cannot talk more," and turned away and shuffled into her house. I was left speechless. We had touched on a piece of history that seared my soul.

Zava Damdin Rinpoche later told me that the Soviets forced the younger monks to raze their monastery to the ground with not a single brick left standing. They wanted to destroy even the memory of this place. A totalitarian dictatorship cannot allow a religion that recognizes its own "truth." The young monks were inducted into the army. Monks from Delgeruun Choira undoubtedly took part in the epic battles in 1938 when the Russian army defeated the Japanese on the Mongolia–Manchuria border and changed history. When the Japanese army failed to win the great natural treasure house of Mongolia the Japanese turned to the navy, who had their own disastrous solution for securing resources for a newly industrialised Japan. The attack on Pearl Harbour. Much of history is dictated by fortuitous chance.

One day the rinpoches decided that we should all go on a picnic. About a half-hour drive south of the monastery we came to a wall of house-sized boulders. At one point there was a narrow entrance flanked by two enormous boulders. This defile soon widened into a grove of aspen trees, a rare sight indeed in the Gobi. The leaves were just beginning to turn the soft golden yellow of autumn. Past the grove of trees we came to a grassy meadow, about a city block wide, with walls of enormous, rounded boulders on either side. The meadow curved to the left and ended up against a wall of rounded rocks. A trickle of water coming from a spring hidden under the rocks ran along the meadow floor to the grove of trees. It was a hidden Shangri-La completely protected from the dry searing winds and sandstorms of the Gobi Desert.

After we picnicked on dried sheep's cheese, dumplings and dried mutton, Zava Damdin Rinpoche offered to show us a holy place. We walked into the grove of aspen trees to stand by a small wooden cabin. Before Buddhism came to Mongolia this grove of aspen trees was known as a sacred sanctuary where killing was not allowed. If a hunted person could reach this place he was safe no matter what he had done. The Greeks, Romans and Medieval Europeans had similar sanctuaries where a fugitive could not be harmed. Mongolia shared in an ancient human impulse to protect a persecuted person. The idea of sanctuaries is once again gaining attention in today's world where we see huge numbers of stateless migrants and refugees fleeing oppression, hunger and climate catastrophes.

Centuries earlier, a small temple was built there, where a cabin now stands. Monks from the Delgeruun Choira would go there for retreats, to meditate, to pray, to find peace for their souls.

When the Soviet soldiers came to destroy the monastery, they loaded the old monks onto trucks and drove them here. They were all shot where we now stand. In the following years army officers and their friends would come here with women from the capital to have drunken weekends of debauchery. One night, during such a "party," a bolt of lightning hit the temple and burned it to the ground. Justice had the last word. Zava Damdin Rinpoche said, "this history is also a part of why this ground is sacred."

After the two weeks had passed, we left for our trip to Ulaanbaatar to get more electrical supplies and, on our way, we took a detour to the ruins of Karakoram two hundred miles straight west. Karakoram was the capital city of Genghis Khan. In 1268 he invited monks, priests, philosophers, shamans and spirit wrestlers from the world over to come to his new city. Everyone who came was invited to present his religion to the great khan seated on his throne in a giant ger. After hearing from all comers, Genghis Khan called everyone together and told them he had heard them all, had considered everything they had told him. He declared that of all the religions of the world, the Mongolian worship of the eternal sky was the most believable and therefore the most enlightened religion, but everyone within his empire was free to worship however they wished.

We know a lot about the details and descriptions of Karakoram and the Mongolian summer of religious debate from the journals kept by a priest, William of Rubruck from Belgium. He stayed in Karakoram for an entire year. It seems that when someone travelled a great distance in 1268, they were not in a hurry to repeat the long, hard journey to get back home.

Our journey to Karakoram included myself, Zasep Rinpoche, Zava Damdin Rinpoche and Bilgoon, the great jolly Friar Tuck monk as our driver. Zasep Rinpoche planned to leave at the end of this road trip. I was to stay on in Mongolia on my own.

We drove straight west in our Nissan 4 x 4 through the great unfenced open range of the central Gobi. On the first day we drove for ten hours and met three vehicles: one old Mercedes and two Russian jeeps. Each such meeting was an occasion for both vehicles to come to a stop, have a conversation, mostly questions about the road, before we all moved on in our different directions.

We encountered herds of sheep and goats, horses, and occasionally herds of shaggy Bactrian camels with their distinct twin humps. I tried to count the horses in one enormous herd. It gave up when they thundered off and disappeared in a cloud of dust. A thousand hoofs hitting the ground all at once shook the very earth we stood on.

During the entire drive we didn't see a single fence or road sign or so much as one tree. The land is vast, unbroken and enormous. You can see forever. The horizon is so distant that Rinpoche remarked that "here you can really see that the earth is round." One is not so much taken by the hugeness of the landscape as by the overwhelming size of the sky, a clear, deep-blue canopy that dwarfs the vastness of the landscape. Travelling through the great steppes of Central Asia, it is clear why Genghis Khan and the Mongols worshipped the eternal blue sky.

At dusk we arrived at Karakoram. There was an old temple. The two rinpoches are extremely interested in temples. We got an enthusiastic and ceremonial welcome and then a guided tour of the temple. They paid special attention to the shrines that contain gilded statues, colourful thangkas, incense burners, rows of brass balls, and protector pictures draped with khatas. Buddhism has no end of ceremonial "stuff."

We continued our drive to Ulaanbaator the next morning. Once we arrived I was introduced to Gerlee, my guide and translator. She was a Mongolian woman with black hair and a quick, ready sense of humour. She immediately told me that when I was in Ulaanbaatar I was in her care. She gave me a cell phone and said, "you must have a mobile while you are here in Ulaanbaatar, then I cannot lose you!"

The next morning Gerlee picked me up in an extremely beat-up little green car. We were on a search for electrical stuff. Switches, connectors, breaker boxes, fuses, light fixtures, different gauges of wire, 600 hundred feet of 100-amp underground wire. She spoke good English and was very quick to grasp what was needed and to contact the right people to help find it. It seemed that she knew everyone. I was somewhat apprehensive about our chances driving this haywire little green car that rattled through the chaotic swirl of Ulaanbaator traffic, but Gerlee was a fearless driver. When she picked me up the next morning she had a piece of the front grill in her hand: "our car is having a revolution," she said with a laugh. I took a handful of zip ties out of my toolbox and secured every loose piece of the grill to its neighbour, to the car frame, to the fenders, to the radiator frame, to other zip ties and declared "we no longer allow revolutions." Gerlee was delighted by this instant fix. She said, "very anti-Soviet you are."

For three full days we scoured the city, going to stores and industrial outlets and getting advice and directions from people Gerlee found. These ranged from electrical engineers to city planners. We went to Ulaanbaator's famed black market where everything under the sun seemed to be available. Gerlee was a firm bargainer, using humour and her ready laugh to coax vendors to reduce their prices. Everything we could find was Russian-made. In the end we managed to get everything, with some substitutions thrown in here and there. Gerlee was a fountain of information, smart and attractive. The three-day shopping trip with Gerlee was fun and for me a bit of a relief to be away from the-all male company of monks. We talked about the collapse of the Soviet Empire and how that happened in Mongolia. Gerlee, who was in university at the time, described those euphoric, heady times when they got a glimpse of a different world of democracy and new freedoms. "Hope and optimism was in the air we breathed." Her stories were similar to the ones I heard from our national MSF staff in Georgia and Azerbaijan.

Ulaanbaatar had a most effective public transportation system. People wanting to go somewhere stood on the curb and extended an arm. When a car stopped, you told the driver where you wanted to go. He, or she, took you to your destination. You paid them an approximate taxi fare. Anyone with a car can make a bit of extra money whenever they wish. In the city centre when the movies or theatres close you can see a dressy woman in high heels and a fur coat hailing a ride, or a young girl needing to get home from a night shift. I was seeing an early and more informal version of today's rideshare apps, without the apps.

We had an extra day, a free day, in UB before I left for the Gobi. We went to the palace of the Bhod Khan, a huge, unadorned square building surrounded by a high wall. The Bhod Khan was the head of the theocracy that ruled Mongolia. He was their God King. He ruled over a country of far-flung and superstitious nomads. One story about the Bodh Khan. He had a car brought to Mongolia. It was of little use with virtually no roads, but he came up with another use. Visiting nomads would hold their foreheads against the wall around his palace or lick the bricks as a show of devotion. He had someone wire the wall to the car battery and the ignition coil. The Bodh Khan would throw a switch; the pilgrims would get an electric shock similar to an electric fence. He found this most amusing. One can see that his demise was perhaps not such a bad thing.

The time came for us to travel back to the monastery. We said goodbye to Zasep Rinpoche, stepped back and bowed to him. It was kind of a joke because we never greeted each other this way. Rinpoche bowed and our foreheads touched. We stood for a moment, foreheads touching. My little joke turned to an intimate gesture of regard and affection.

Zava Damdin Rinpoche whispered me success and said that Amala (his mother) would take good care of me. Amala beamed and gave me a reassuring nod. Zava Damdin Rinpoche went on to say that he had observed me for a week and thought that I had strong Mongolian character and consequently the respect of monks. He told me that I could be in charge at the monastery in his absence and that the monks would do whatever I wished. I was not sure what all this meant or what it was that I had to live up to. It reminded me of the time in Ethiopia when Colonel Kedani, as he was leaving for a week, told me that he would give me a hundred soldiers who would die for me if I wanted. I wasn't sure what that meant either, but I still have occasional thoughts about the possibilities.

I met the translator who would travel back to the monastery with us. Her name was Gana. She was Zava Damdin Rinpoche's 35-year-old sister. During the drive I realised that Ghana did not speak English. This came as a bit of a shock. It turned out that she had lived in East Germany for four years and was fluent in German. We communicated in my broken German, after a fashion.

Once back at the monastery I simply worked all day, every day. It was late October and still nice weather but I knew it could change quickly. Siberia was a mere 200 miles away, and a sustained north wind could bring arctic conditions overnight. I had two boy monks as my main helpers, Erik and Tandzer, aged 15 and 16. Both were from nomad families living in the Gobi. They were quick, eager and willing to do anything. I first put them to work digging a 600-foot trench for the underground cable to carry the current from the powerhouse to five permanent buildings. The work was slow and difficult. The Russian electrical stuff we bought in UB was difficult and time-consuming to work with. Simple switches, light fixtures, breaker boxes were all hopelessly complicated in their construction with a zillion little bolts and nuts, where only a few clips would have sufficed. This is how we made these things back in the1920s.

I originally thought that I could probably finish in ten days, but I soon realised that I would be lucky to finish in three weeks. It got increasingly cold and windy. One day we worked in a wicked wind that sheared around corners of buildings as if they did not exist. I worked wearing a pair of Russian motorcycle goggles to keep sand and grit out of my eyes. We began to see sheets of ice in the water barrels. My helpers simply could not understand how, or why, I worked without gloves. They expressed their concern by finding a pair of gloves for me (too small) and later a pair of shoes to replace my torn sneakers (too small). They were amazed that I continued to work and didn't stop to attend to the cuts, scrapes, bruises that simply happen when you work with knives, hammers, screwdrivers, etc. Gana would attempt to bandage a cut finger while I worked but I mostly said, not now! Later! She finally resorted to stuffing band-aids in my pocket. The two young monks Erik and Tandzer told Amala that I would get a cut, refuse a bandage and the next day it would be healed up. In the end they figured that if someone tried to shoot me the bullets would bounce off. (There is a belief in Mongolia that some shamans have the ability to repel bullets.) There is no happy way to live up to this!

The winds now found all the little openings where the cover for the ger met the ground. The boys heaped dirt and sand all around the perimeter. My ger had a small berm all around to keep the wind out. Gana gave me an extra blanket and a generous pile of dried dung for the fire. My ger was my private, snug, warm retreat.

At night the sky was clear and cold with stars so brilliant it took one's breath away. The Milky Way was a band of light that swept across the sky from horizon to horizon. I could actually see individual stars. It seemed that one could almost reach out and touch one. The full moon turned night into shadowy day. The desert took on a ghostly appearance. I walked through a mysterious landscape where shapes, spirits and apparitions hovered at the edges of imagination.

The boy monks' cheerful natures were infectious. Gana stayed with us all day long, helping where she could, bringing us tea and sometimes hot soup. One cold and sunny day Erik and Tandzer wired up the LED lamp that I had made in my shop back in Canada. Sjouke, Celeste and John Cooper had decorated and painted these lamps until they were Kootenay works of art. Other boy monks would come by, curious to see what we were doing, and then want to help. They would hover just over my shoulder, watching every move I made, sticking their hands and fingers in to help. To hold something. To move something out of the way, to help turn a screwdriver. Drove me crazy. I had to send them packing with no explanation possible as to why I was unwilling to accept their help.

I showed the boys how to wire up a ger with wall plugs, off/on switches and light sockets. They began to measure out and assemble the extension cords for the various gers. Quick and nimble 16-year-old fingers flew to the task. They were soon quicker than myself at this finicky task.

It got colder and windier but most of the work was now inside. Wiring up lights, switches, wall plugs and the five separate breaker boxes. The two "boys" became more adept and did a lot of this work. They worked hard to get to spaces, above the ceiling, in the temple, to string wires, so that they were out of sight. They shimmied up support poles to hang wires and lights 40 feet up in the air. One day I gave them two lamps, an off/on switch, and 40 feet of wire without instructions and had them light up the ceiling of the ger temple. At the end of the day they showed me the entire installation and proudly pointed out that every single nut and bolt and connection was wired together exactly how I did it. I was proud of my young helpers. I hadn't realised how closely they had followed and remembered my every move.

Left: Wiring the system

Below: Building the frame to hold 10 solar panels. The boy monks had not seen a welder before.

A big find was this huge sledgehammer, big enough to drive a grounding rod deep into the flinty dirt.

Below: with my two helpers with completely installed solar panels

On the last day, we were planning on leaving for Ulaanbaator in the afternoon. The only thing left to connect up was the breaker box and two circuits in the big ger. By noon we were done. It was finished! We skipped lunch, and I did a tour of the entire installation with the two boys and Gana explaining how and why everything worked. I explained the electrical circuits in each of the five fixed buildings, how they were fused and where to look when a circuit failed. In the powerhouse it was all about how the solar panels connected in the junction box; how the charge controller regulated the current going to the battery bank of eight, 200-amp-hour batteries. I explained how the inverter converted 24 volts of electricity into 240 volts of lethal force that could evaporate the end of a screwdriver in a flash of blue flame. (When I demonstrated this with an old screwdriver their eyes became big and almost round.) I showed them how to monitor the watts and voltage and flow of electricity; how to switch the system from solar power to generator power and back to solar; how to troubleshoot and maintain the system.

By three p.m. the tour was done. I packed up my stuff and prepared to leave. However, Gana told me that Amala had prepared lunch and that I had to come to her ger. I wanted to leave in order to make the six-hour drive to Ulaanbaator in daylight. I emptied a big bowl of soup in one huge draught, stood up and said, “I'm ready, let's go!” They immediately poured another bowlful of broth and insisted that I sit back down and finish it. Five impatient minutes later a young monk in full ceremonial dress came in through the low door, walked over to me with arms extended, bowed and presented a blue ceremonial khata. I was completely taken aback. He stepped back with a huge smile. Another young monk came in with arms extended to offer a khata and then another and another and another all in their ceremonial red robes and yellow embroidered jackets. The ger filled to the walls with robed boy monks all wearing huge smiles.

My arms were piled high with sky-blue khatas. The last monks to come in were Erik and Tandzer, both dressed in their finest robes. They presented me with bright yellow khatas, usually given only to lamas. Erik's khata contained a small gold stupa, and Tandzar's khata contained a mala with wood beads. Not a word was said, but the smiles on our faces spoke louder than anything that could be said.

It was a long, slow drive. Just as daylight was fading we saw a herd of wild gazelles. They ran like the wind. Five hours into the drive it began to snow. Within twenty minutes the car did a slow, 180-degree spin. The monk driver was terrified. I offered to drive. Once behind the wheel I breathed a sigh of relief, locked the hubs, engaged the four-wheel drive and booted the Nissan Explore up to 60 clicks. It became a bad snowstorm with poor visibility. We drove into a tunnel of the driving snow on a slick, slippery surface. This was familiar territory for a driver from Canada.

We reached Ulaanbaator well after dark to an enthusiastic welcome in Amala's apartment. We had a late meal of mutton. Gana was cutting up a sheep carcass on the kitchen counter and continued to do this while carrying on an animated conversation with her mother. They talked, they laughed, they obviously delighted in each other's company. It seemed that I was the subject of much of the conversation, I understand not a word except Jon ... Jon ..... Jon ... We all went to bed at midnight.

The next day Gerlee came in her little green car to move me to the guest house. As we left, Amala said that I will be a heroic page in the history of Degeruun Choria. It seemed so over the top. I found all this hyperbole embarrassing and was happy to leave this adulation, settle into my room (comes with a hot shower) in the guest house and revel in my aloneness and nothing-to-do-ness.

I had time to wander around Ulaanbaator. The city had old Soviet infrastructure. The streets were potholed, the public buildings were unimaginative, massive authoritarian statements in concrete. The endless apartment buildings were all the same, all rectangular towers of crumbling cement with peeling paint and streaks of rust leaking down from where iron balconies were cobbled onto the outside walls. An enormous, and astoundingly inefficient, central heating plant with towering chimneys fired columns of black smoke into the once clear blue sky. There were miles of six-foot diameter steel pipes covered with thick asbestos insulation with chunks missing here and there. Some of the pipes were on the ground, some, where they crossed the street, were high overhead on massive steel and cement supports. These pipes carried hot water to all the apartment buildings in the city. The buildings farther away got only lukewarm heat. It was all so massive and looked like a parody of an industrial society gone bonkers. Like Baku or Yerevan, Ulaanbaator had the indelible stamp, and look, of a Soviet city.

Oddly enough there were advantages that came with living with the heavy-handed, inefficient, infrastructure and haywire technologies and distribution systems of the Soviet empire. People developed the habit of innovation, how to make things work. They learned to accept and deal with whatever came their way, and most importantly, people developed the habit of helping each other, sharing scarce resources with friends and family. This forced citizens to create strong and reliable support systems for themselves. These people living in shabby and haywire circumstances may in the end have been happier than people living our more comfortable life in the affluent West. I was reminded of my mother telling us, "there is too much money. During the depression, when there was almost no money, people needed each other and we all helped each the other."

I was left with the strong impression that Buddhism is, at its core, pragmatic and flexible and recognizes that as the world changes so Buddhism will also change to align itself with new understanding about the nature of reality. The Buddhist faith, or system if you like, seems to avoid the problems that come with our Christian "leap of faith" requirement to embrace beliefs that conflict with reality. Buddhists believe that all religions are trying to achieve the same thing, to get to the same place, and all have equal validity. However, they believe that the Buddhist way is the most effective way to reach this common goal. The religious wars in Europe, which created untold suffering, make no sense from this perspective.

Travels with Rinpoche

The following year Zasep Rinpoche and I travelled to the province of Zavkhan in far west of Mongolia. This was Gerlee's childhood home. Rinpoche had been advised by an oracle to set up a Buddhist retreat in Mongolia far away from the capital. During long midnight talks we came up with some ambitious plans for this far-flung camp.

During our time at Delegruun Choira Monastary we had discovered that we enjoyed travelling together. The rinpoche was good company. He had a lively sense of humour. We had some discussions on Buddhist beliefs, but I was more interested in how things work, e.g., how did they know who was a tulku? A tulku is a recognized reincarnation, usually of an important person in the Buddhist hierarchy. Rinpoche himself was a tulku. There are well-established methods to guide the search for a reincarnation. At the end of the search an oracle is consulted. He goes into a trance to verify, or not, the results of the search. Did they sometimes make a mistake? Did they ever pick the wrong person? Yes! The Rinpoche told me. Sometimes it would turn out that the tulku's actions in this life were quite out of sync with the sterling character of the deceased. When this happened, they shrugged their spiritual shoulders and hoped for a better result next time. In Buddhist philosophy, we experience thousands upon thousands of reincarnations, one missed or waylaid lifetime was not such a big deal in the scheme of things. There is a lot of slack in the system. My kind of theology.

In the beginning of this journey, I thought the rinpoche might become a spiritual teacher to me, but as it turned out, we ended up in a mutual exchange of ideas and as something more like friends. When he talked about Buddhist beliefs or practices I pointed out parallels in Christianity. He was not familiar with the history of the West, how the church and Christianity shaped Western civilization and where the brassy new evangelical churches (we had seen some in Ulaanbaatar) fit into the web of Christian thinking. The rinpoche was interested in this complex matrix of time, deeply held beliefs and human folly. These were fun conversations. He was quick to appreciate where the intersections of faith and political realities created a rich vein of irony in their wake.

Zasep Rinpoche, Gerlee and I flew from Ulaan Baanbataar to Uliastai, the capital of Zavkhan. A battered green Russian army jeep with a driver was waiting for us at the airport. Gerlee's classmate from secondary school was the governor of her home sum (county), Tsagaakhairkhan. He had made his jeep and driver available to us for the duration of our stay. We set off for Uliastai. Halfway to our destination the driver stopped for a car parked at the side of the road. It was the governor of Zavkhan along with three other men. The governor was a handsome stocky man in a black, pin-striped, corduroy suit. The other men were the mayor of Uliastai and the second in command for the province of Zavkhan. There were enthusiastic greetings and introductions, after which the governors asked for blessings. Rinpoche, resplendent in his special maroon robe with wide, sweeping, electric-blue cuffs, delivered the roadside blessings, softly chanting a mantra in Tibetan while holding an amulet to the top of the bowed heads. When it was over, they each presented Rinpoche with a blue Kata and a green, 1000-Tubrick note (about $1 US). We agreed to have lunch together in town. The governor's car took off in a cloud of dust. The jeep was a temperamental starter, but when it coughed to life our driver showed his stuff. Using all gears, expertly dodging ruts and potholes, we caught up with the governor's car. As soon as the road widened, we roared by, leaving the governors in a cloud of dust. I liked this driver.

Uliastai was a small city situated in a valley where two rivers converged creating a large flat basin. The town was cradled by mountains on all sides and boasted a population of 18,000 souls. Considerable for a thinly populated Mongolia. Uliastai had wide streets and shabby drab Soviet-era architecture. In a concession to Mongolia's' nomadic ways the town was ringed by gers, each one on a generous-size lot surrounded by fences made of slab wood with the bark still showing. These outer city dwellers come and go. They can pack up the ger and move somewhere out into the steppes and return to town when it suits them. In the town centre there were raised wooden sidewalks, hitching posts and men on horseback wearing the long Mongolia deel (a long garment worn by both men and women) held at the waist with a wide yellow or orange sash and felt hats. It had the feel of an exotic version of Gunsmoke's Dodge with automobiles, overhead electric wires and cell phones grafted onto the old west.

In Uliastai, Rinpoche was approached by three more men, all related to the governor, also asking for blessings. When the parking lot blessings were done, we all piled into the jeep and set off for Gerlee's home. Before we left one of the governors presented me with a khata and a note for 400 Tubriks wrapped up in it. There seemed to be some confusion as to where I fit into all this. I think he was simply covering all his bases.

We left the wide river valley of Uliastai, and the road began a slow climb. It looked like Montana with sweeping open grasslands and enormous treeless hills. We stopped at the top of a low pass with a *toovoo* at the summit. A *toovoo* is a holdover from pre-Buddhist times and consists of a cairn of rocks replete with offerings. This one had coins, single cigarettes, pieces of brightly coloured cloth, a rusted knife blade, an empty vodka bottle, a sun-bleached horse skull, and an upright wooden pole swathed in raggedy blue banners standing in the middle of the pile of rocks. The *toovoo* is a shaman's nod to the spirits of the land. For a Buddhist, all religions are a way, a system, for getting to the place we all want to arrive at. For a Mongolian Buddhist, the *toovoo* is just one more way to acknowledge the supremacy of spirit and therefore offers another pebble on the path to enlightenment. We walked in a clock-ways direction around the *toovoo*, and each of us added the traditional three stones to the pile.

We descended into the valley of the Shiree River and stopped at a small wooden temple fenced off with upright slab wood. The temple had a hand-made, home-built look. It would have fit right in back home in the Kootenays. An old woman with a wrinkled, weather-beaten face came out of a smallish ger next to it. A lifetime of facing into the winds of Mongolia had made her skin the colour and texture of a well-worn buckskin shirt. She was wearing a patched maroon deel and gumboots. Behind her, three small barefooted children with dusty faces and raggedy clothing looked on. She unlocked the gate into the slab wood compound and removed the padlock from the heavy wood door. Inside we saw two rows of wood pillars made of peeled, sanded and laboriously fluted logs. These were painted red and black with yellow stripes and framed a walkway leading to the altar. Hand-painted thangkas hung on the walls all the way to the altar. At the back of the temple we saw protector statues of sun-fired clay, some carved in wood, as well as incense burners, butter lamps and framed, black-and-white photos of the famous lamas of Zavkhan and a colour photo of the Dalai Lama all draped in blue katas. The interior of the temple was meticulously clean.

In 1989, after the fall of the Soviet Union, a seventy-year-old monk came to this remote valley and built this temple. From here he served the spiritual needs of the area for the next eleven years. Their lama had died six years ago. They all hoped that one day a new lama would come to live here and pick up where he left off. Rimpoche thought this opportunity was made for me. He said he would show me the basics and give me one of his monk's robes. I think about what that life would be for the rest of the drive but soon realise that I am already moving on.

As we left, the woman asked for a blessing for herself and for her grandchildren. Rinpoche performed a blessing ceremony laying his hand on all the bowed heads. The old woman presented me with a faded blue khata. I later found a 100 tubrik note folded into my khata. I was undone by this gesture. I wanted to go back and … do what? Rinpoche said not to worry, "You have done many generous things for others."

The hills came together, making a choke point. This was the end of the bigger valley and the start of a narrow opening, flanked by two enormous black boulders, into the much smaller valley where Gerlee's mom lived. Her home was a small, four-wall ger set up against some dense willow bushes bordering a branch of the Shiree River. There were two other gers close by, forming a small community.

Like the Aluet kayak, the Mongolia ger represents human ingenuity at its best. Both are simple adaptations to the particular needs of a people. Neither of these adaptations could be improved on. The ger is perfectly suited to a nomadic life and the extreme variations in the wind and temperature on the Mongolian steppes. It can be transported on one camel, can be taken down and set up in less than an hour and is easily repaired with local materials. Gerlee's mom's ger was a good example. The walls and the ceiling poles were made from willow sticks and a carved block of wood called a tovo where all of the poles meet in the centre of the ceiling. All fastenings and the door hinge were made from leather. Over sixty years old, it was as sound and usable as the day it was first made.

It was approaching dusk. The sheep and goats were coming home. By the time we had tea and a meal of mutton broth the area in front of us was carpeted with sheep and goats. Must have been 500, all bedded down close in to the three gers. Two huge mastiffs circled around the herd. These sheep were going to be food for humans, not for the local wolf pack. We also bedded down for the night. Gerlee slept with her mom, Rinpoche got the other bed, I slept on the floor behind the stove. Gerlee's sister Doya slept in the neighbouring ger.

In the morning we got a good look at the place. The sheep and goats were just leaving. The front yard was well fertilised. Doya was milking the two cows with long, shaggy black hair. They looked like they were park Yak. The neighbours had a bigger ger with a solar panel attached to the roof. A Russian motorcycle was parked off to the side, and an ancient Russian flat-deck truck with the hood up was a little ways off. The neighbours were family, cousins. Three children were playing a game on the deck of the truck with hard, round, sun-dried sheep turds. We sat around, drank tea and waited. It felt a lot like Kootenay time, only more so. Eventually Rinpoche and I went for a walk. We found the sheep on a hillside a mile or more from the gers, the two mastiffs lay close by in the shade of a small leafy tree.

Back at Gerlee's mom's ger, time had slowed to a crawl. At four o'clock, a thin lanky man of fifty or so with one long, yellow tooth showed up with three horses for us to ride. He was a true raggedy Mongolian cowboy. He had a patched and worn deel held at the waist with a rope, a brown felt hat, boots with upturned toes and leather chaps. Our guide had a lopsided grin that exposed his one, exceptionally long tooth. We set off to explore on horseback. Rinpoche rode a brown horse, Gerlee was on a grey one and I doubled up with the guide on the smallest horse. Life is not always equal. We rode through open meadows and along narrow paths through the willow bushes as we crossed and re-crossed the meandering streams. At the valley's end, the horses climbed up a giant sand dune.

From the top we saw we were at the edge of a Lawrence of Arabia desert. Looking south, it was hills and valleys of yellow, drifting sand reaching all the way to China. Looking back the way we had come we could see the entire valley. The Shiree River split into three smaller streams that braided their way along the floor of the valley. The valley bottom was about a kilometre wide and mostly flat with dense willow bushes along the winding streams. Between the streams it was flat and green with grass. We saw the three gers as well and beyond them, the end of the valley, flanked by the two black, pyramid-shaped rocks that guarded the entrance. It was truly a hidden valley.

For Gerlee's mom and her nephew, this small valley was theirs. There is no private property in Mongolia and no fences to demarcate land ownership. Wherever you place your ger, that is your land until you leave. The first private property in Mongolia came about after the fall of the Soviet Union, when more people moved to Ulaanbaatar. The government gave a free lot to anyone moving to the capital. Consequently, the city is surrounded by ger "suburbs." Each lot has some kind of fencing and a big mastiff-type dog to guard the premises.

To our left mountains soared up into the blue sky. Two jagged peaks loomed over the valley. To our right we saw where our valley floor met enormous sand dunes. Between a bend in the river, two hills curved to make an open space between them. We could see what appeared to be a small, hidden plateau. We had to go and check this out. A 15-minute horse ride and we were there. It was a small, elongated field of bunch grass wedged between a bend in the river and the foot of the sand dunes. It was about eight acres of flat ground cut off from the rest of the valley by a bend in the river. Eureka! This was it! We had found our meditation centre, our own Shangri-La.

We returned to the ger bubbling with enthusiasm and happiness. It was infectious. Gerlee's mom sang as she prepared supper. We were barely seated when they began to arrive.

"They" were the first of an ongoing stream of people who had heard the news: There was a lama in "mom's" ger. They had come for a lama's blessing and divinations. For themselves, for their children, for their ageing parents, for their work, for their livestock, for their new venture, for their hopes and dreams.

Mom's ger, with the sheep at home.

First an old man, with only two teeth showing, had lost two cows. He asked if he would ever see them again. Rinpoche asked how long they had been gone and from where did they disappear. They had been gone for two months and disappeared from a summer pasture quite far from his ger. Rinpoche bowed his head, closed his eyes, and rocked back and forth. All the while he held a closed hand, holding a single dice against his forehead. He then lowered his arm, blew into his closed hand and dropped the dice into a silver cup. He repeated this three times. The *mo* is good, he explained. The cows are alive. They have not been slaughtered and are far away. He needs to ask around and ask questions with a faraway place in mind. Rinpoche was presented with an offering of a ten-tubrik note. The next man's father had lung problems and his heart was not good. "How old is your father?" "Seventy-two" the dice was dropped: 1, 2, 3. The *mo* is medium, not good, not bad. He is already old and his life is winding down. He should not use much salt, bad for high blood pressure. No oily food. It's all he can do. He will be OK for the next year. It is very good that you look after your father and repay your father's kindness. This is good karma for you. This man presented Rinpoche with a bottle of vodka.

Gerlee's second cousin then approached, a quite small, pretty young woman with a worried expression. She had come with her boyfriend, a big handsome guy who looked like he could lift a horse. She was pregnant and wanted to know how strong the relationship with her boyfriend was, what kind of future was there for this new baby. "How old are you?" "Twenty-three." "How far along is the pregnancy?" "Two months." "How long have you been together?" "Six months and twelve days." "Does he have work?" "Yes, he is a physical education teacher at the school in the Soum Centre." The relationship is strong. Your pregnancy is good and healthy. However, it is important that you look after yourself well, that you do not drink, that you do not smoke and also avoid secondhand smoke. It is important that you relax your mind. I will write down a mantra for you.

Next was a very carefully dressed woman wearing a new deel, with three silver barrettes in her long, shiny black hair and an extra-wide yellow sash. Her husband and her two oldest sons were taking a herd of cattle to Ulaanbaatar to sell on the cattle market. She was concerned with how well this would go. "How long ago did they leave?" "Three and a half weeks." "How long is the journey?" "Two months or more," the dice fall 1-2-3. The *mo* is not great. Get rid of the animals, otherwise there will be problems. He should get the cattle on a truck! Impossible says the woman. Rinpoche asks how many cows? Four hundred. I see Rinpoche straighten up. Four hundred head of cattle on a thousand kilometres cattle drive, holy smokes! Rinpoche tells her they need to be vigilant, to keep a sharp eye out for sick cows and as much as possible keep the herd away from other cattle. She should also arrange, and pay for, a special puja at the temple in Ulestia. Rinpoche recommends a specific puja. The woman eagerly agreed to do this and sat back looking resolute.

Next came a tall, big-boned woman with dark skin and heavy features. She looked like she carried the weight of the world on her broad shoulders. Gerlee told Rinpoche that this woman, one of her classmates, had a difficult life. She was a recent widow and now was alone. Her first and second husbands both died of liver disease.

(This is an enduring legacy of Soviet life: a mind-boggling amount of alcohol is consumed. Vodka was super cheap and could be bought anywhere for less than a dollar a bottle. This was how the people of the Soviet Union, living impoverished and restricted lives, sought some measure of solace. In Mongolia, men commonly died of liver disease in their forties.)

She lived in the Soum Centre and had five children, ages 4, 5, 8, 11, and 23. The youngest child worried her the most, crying all evening, every evening, I don't know what to do. She went on to explain that her father was a monk. He left many texts and protector statues behind when he died. Now she was afraid that she handled some of these things in a wrong way. Some of the dharma things had been stolen because there was no man in the house. The children had played with some of the books last week. Rinpoche said he would stop by her house tomorrow morning on our way back to Uliastai. He would do a blessing for the youngest child and have a look at the books and dharma things to make sure they were OK. She nodded and leaned forward, and Rinpoche laid his right hand on her bowed head.

In the corner by the door the newly pregnant woman and her young man were oblivious to everything. They were smiling, flirting, giggling, wrapped up in their own world. It appeared that Rinpoche's divination was already bearing fruit. The dogs barked, there was the sound of a vehicle outside. Seven people came in the low door. They were Gerlee's classmates come to see her. They were all wearing colourful dresses, skirts or new jeans. Her mom brought out a well-stashed bottle of vodka. Tiny one-shot cups, filled to the brim, were carefully passed out. The return of the Soum's prodigal daughter was toasted, once, twice, three times. "Nik Hoyer Koro."

The din, the banter, the laughter were infectious and filled the crowded ger. Thank God no one smoked. Rinpoche asked if anyone knew any songs,

Mongolian folk songs. This was a completely redundant question in Mongolia. However, it generated lots more suggestions, more talk and laughter, until one tremulous voice began. Soon everyone joined in. The women who sang first had a clear, precise voice. She sang a melody that wavered and undulated and filled the ger with magic. Gerlee said, "she's my music teacher, she's only two years older than us."

They all wanted blessings from the lama. One by one they knelt in front of Rinpoche and recounted their hopes and dreams and fears, and one by one they all received Rinpoche's blessing.

I was struck by the difference compared with our very private Western world. That evening, the innermost fears and failures of people were bared. Their private lives, and family lives, it all came out in the open. There were few secrets, no hidden and private places, no well-hidden insecurities that gnawed at the soul.

The door opened and a determined-looking woman wearing a deel and upturned Mongolian boots entered the ger with her man in tow. It was the one-tooth cowboy. He grinned, his one tooth reflecting the light from the candles. We hadn't given him anything for his services. I said "it's the horse guy, let's give him the bottle of vodka." Rinpoche nodded and handed him the bottle. The cowboy broke into a huge grin. Gerlee said they had a problem to ask Rinpoche about.

The woman knelt in front of Rinpoche and began to talk. "My husband, we have been married for 34 years, has a problem with alcohol. He drinks way too much, and this has made so many problems for such a long time. We could have had a good life all these years, but he ruined us with his drinking." There was a long silence. Rinpoche looked at the guy sitting beside his wife holding his bottle of vodka to his chest, who grinned and nodded. His wife was watching the lama. (I think, wow, Rimpoche put his foot in it this time.) The cowboy spoke up. "When I drink, I mean to have only one drink but after I have one drink I want to drink more until there is no more." The woman asked if the lama would do a *mo* to see if he will stop drinking.

Rinpoche said, "there is no need for a *mo*, that won't help anything." He talked directly to the guy: "what you must do is place the bottle of vodka I gave you on the altar in your house and make a vow that you will never drink this bottle of vodka. Every time you want to have a drink you will think of this bottle of vodka on your shrine, and of your vow. This will help you not to drink so much. I will pray for you."

It was after midnight by the time everyone left. We went outside to see everyone off and to make bets on how many people can fit into a Russian jeep. Rinpoche and I walked around the hunkered-down herd of sheep. The night air was chilly, the first bite of fall. It was the dark of the moon, but we could easily see to walk. In that dry air at 6,000 feet the night sky was luminous, lit by countless stars, each one its own spark of light. The Milky Way was a radiant band sweeping across the heavens, the firmament seemed so close, heaven seemed to be within our reach.

Back in Ulaanbaatar we had a long discussion about the Zavkhan Ger camp. Our ideas were too ambitious and well beyond what was needed. Also, this venture costed out at over a hundred thousand dollars, only to set up the camp. We got carried away. Our enthusiasm lifted our spirits but was not firmly anchored in reality. Rinpoche eventually went with a scaled-back meditation camp, closer to Ulaanbaatar. Rinpoche straddles two worlds with ease. Back home in Nelson he was just another guy on Baker Street. He belongs to the Western world of coffee shops, chatty conversations, fundraising, cars and international travel. In Canada he was more of a man among equals. To his followers and dharma students in the West, he was their teacher and spiritual counsellor. As such he was a respected and loved person. In Mongolia, Rinpoche was a revered personage, a national treasure. People from all walks of life, the wealthy and the poor, the influential city elite and the nomads and herders came to him for a lama's blessing, for counselling, for solace. In Mongolia, Rinpoche seemed to truly live his purpose.

As Rinpoche's friend, sidekick and fellow traveller, I didn't always fit the picture and wasn't always sure where I should fit. Some saw me as his attendant, but I didn't always express the distance and deference expected of this role. During the blessings/divinations, I was often presented with the same ceremonial khatas the rinpoche got, but with smaller bills tucked into the folds. Rinpoche had a large following of students all over the world: Canada, Australia, the USA, Mongolia. He was their teacher, they were his students, and this set the tone of the relationships. I was a different type of relationship. I believe that Rinpoche valued this difference. Everyone needs a friend.

Travelling with Rinpoche in Mongolia opened doors for me wherever we went. I experienced aspects of life in Mongolia that I would otherwise never have seen. It was a front row seat to Tibetan Buddhism, to religious life in a liberated Mongolia. I also had a front-row seat to practise humble patience. The rinpoche always came first. He was the centre, he rode in the front seat. I recall lines written 800 years ago by Rumi. “Do not try to be the sun. Be a dust mote.”

I left Mongolia on a cold sunny day with a heart warmed by the generosity and love shown to a stranger from the other side of the world. I have experienced the kindness and generosity of human beings wherever I have lived and travelled on our vast earth. Georgians living a civil war took us in, strangers in need appearing in the dead of night at their home. Azeri citizens who stepped between me and a gun pointed at my head. Somali nomads guided a Canadian lost in the Ogaden Desert to safety. An Ethiopian army officer, Colonel Kedani, offered three soldiers to escort me on an ill-advised trip into Somalia. The essential nature of humans, worldwide, is to be helpful and kind to others. Our need for love and friendship is more human than our inclination to hate and violence. Empathy lives in the human heart. It has always been thus. This simple truth is the key to our survival as a species.

Zasep Tulku Rinpoche

Presenting a khata to Zava Damdin Rinpoche at a second visit to Delegruin Choira Monastery (with electric light!)

The Nuns of the Zanskar

At the request of Gaden Relief, Rinpoche, myself and my wife Celeste travelled to Zanskar Valley in Ladakh. Zanskar Valley is remote and hard to get to, with only summertime road access. During winter, when temperatures drop to 40 degrees below zero, people walk out on the frozen edges of the fast-flowing Zanskar River. It's an extremely difficult and dangerous five-day trek.

In 1950, a courageous young woman from Zanskar Valley named Amrita (later she was known as Amala, Honoured Mother) made a long, formidable journey, mostly on foot, to Lhasa. She stayed for several years studying and was ordained as a nun at the fabled Drepun Monastery, where she was personally blessed by the Dalai Lama. She returned to her Zanskar community as a true heroine. She had a vision that her remote, inaccessible valley hidden away in the vast Himalayan Mountains would become a place dedicated to Lord Buddha's teachings. Because of her example and leadership, seven Buddhist nunneries were established in Zanskar Valley. These nunneries had fallen on hard times and were extremely impoverished. Our mission was to visit all seven nunneries and do assessments on what could realistically be done to assist the nuns.

The last 200 km of the Zanskar Valley route is a steep, one-lane dirt road skirting enormous glaciers. Vertical rock walls on the left contrast sharply with the thousand-foot drop-offs on the right. In places we had to clear the rocks and debris from a recent slide off of the road. The towering snow mountains, reaching five miles into the blue sky, the glaciers, the valleys are the exposed geology of our planet, on a scale that one experiences nowhere else on earth. We seemed tiny, like unto ants. The religions of Tibet are born from this overwhelming landscape. In Mongolia, one is dwarfed by an immense blue sky, a perfect blue dome that encompasses everything and makes even the vast steppes seem small, and so Mongolians worship the eternal blue sky. Tibetans make pilgrimages to the mountains, to Mount Kailash in western Tibet. In Indian mythology, Kailash is where heaven and earth meet. This is the throne of Lord Shiva. Mount Kailash is the source of four of Asia's major rivers: the Brahamputra, the Indus, the Karnali, and the Sutlej. The mountains store water for the high desert lands of Tibet and Ladakh as well as for all of western Asia. They are the source of life.

We arrived at the Karsha nunnery, which is the oldest nunnery in the Zanskar, with twenty-eight nuns – twenty in residence and eight away in Dharmsala for further study. Karsha was built partway up the mountainside on a rocky promontory with some of the buildings set into cliffside. From the village of Karsha, we climbed steps cut into the bedrock. I stopped counting at a thousand. After the last step, we saw ten or so one-room buildings with smoke coming out of the stone chimneys of five of them. The all-white buildings were connected by rocky footpaths. Some of the flagstones on the paths had rounded indentations where thousands of feet, walking these same paths for centuries, had worn away the hard Himalayan granite. A reminder, set in stone, of the nuns' devotion; quietly powerful, like the water that wears away these mountains. The Karsha nunnery was to be our base.

The temple was an all-white two-storey building built on a rocky ledge which was on the edge of a deep gorge, an enormous ravine worn away by the inexorable movement of water flowing along its depth. The ravine was steep and must have been over a thousand feet deep. On the other side of the ravine, at our level, were the all-white buildings of the much bigger Karsha monastery.

All the nunnery's food storage and preparation took place on the windowless ground floor of the temple building. There were fires burning in what looked to be huge, blackened clay stoves topped by three layers of foot-high open ovens for low, medium and high heat uses. They reminded me of the huge, wood-fired cook stove in our farmhouses with a warming oven heated by the chimney. The entire room was lit by the fire. The ceilings were a flat black from centuries of soot. The walkway through this large room was lined with piles of firewood and led to a door to the outside where we saw more piles of firewood on a rocky ledge. The nunnery's kitchen seemed mediaeval, wreathed in smoke and fire.

The second floor of the building was open and airy. Behind a carved wood door was the sanctuary of the temple. Colourful hand-woven hangings and thangkas graced the walls. At the back of the room, two rows of wooden benches were covered with small Tibetan carpets. A shrine on a raised dais at the front of the room had a standing Buddha and two Tara statues with multiple arms. The soft glow of a hundred flickering butter lamps created a sense of timelessness. Here the nuns' day began, at six in the morning, with their first puja.

We were ushered into a spacious room with a window looking out over the valley below. We were served their version of the fatted calf: a broiled sheep's tail. We were hungry after our long journey, and we dug in. We later learned that the nuns of Karsha lived on reduced rations for weeks to afford this feast, a feast they themselves did not participate in. This was our first glimpse of what Zanskar poverty, devotion and determination looked like.

The next day we went to Padum, the only town in the valley. Padum felt like a dusty ghost town from the old west. There was little there, a few fruit and veggie stands with hanging clusters of bananas that looked like the bruised survivors of a long bumpy ride from south India. Tibetan women selling turquoise, a few guesthouses, restaurants, tea stands and tiny crowded stalls selling prayer flags, cheap sandals, packaged soups, candles and homemade socks. Everything was covered in dust. The three restaurants in Padum all had the exact same photocopied menu. The Ibex guesthouse claimed that the menu was stolen from them. The hardware store had drums of kerosene and diesel fuel, from which they poured off a litre at a time into water bottles. Anything else you might want – tools, rope, tarps, etc. – was piled up in the centre of the floor. We had to rummage through this to find what we needed. Going to Padum was like a scavenger hunt.

We visited our first outlying nunnery, Zangla. It was on a flat plain not very far from the river. In sharp contrast to Karsha, this nunnery was a busy, bustling place. The nuns were mostly younger; some looked to be twelve-year-old girls, wearing long, red, rather raggedy robes. We met Laurel, a thirty-two-year-old, proud lesbian from Boulder. Laurel was dressed in jeans and a brocade jacket. She was bright, alert, and eager to show us around. She had lived there for three years and was fluent in Zanskari. We were taken on a tour of the nunnery. First to the greenhouse filled wall-to-wall with plants. Tomatoes, cucumbers, different cabbages, green beans, and a riot of flowers. In a separate room they had set up a food dryer powered by sunlight. Next, a large airy room where nuns were spinning wool and weaving cloth. Laurel showed us how they were experimenting with natural dyes. The temple was a little spartan compared to Karsha, with an altar decorated with a profusion of flowers and butter lamps. The room had the same feeling of a sacred stillness, a retreat from the hectic world. It seemed that the nuns were all busy, some working in the greenhouse, some building a new adobe one-room house or repairing the paths that connect the entire nunnery, others spinning wool and weaving cloth on a handmade loom. All the buildings here were relatively recent.

We were taken to see a dozen or more small, one-room adobe houses, all in a row, built on a long-elevated ledge with a narrow walkway connecting all the rooms. The nuns each had their private one-room house. We were ushered into Laurel's house. Inside, the walls were plastered white, and the cow dung floor was patted down to a hard brown sheen. She had a table, two chairs, a counter with an MSR camp stove, a double bed along the far wall, with Tibetan rugs on the floor and a shrine against the wall beside the bed. The room smelled of incense. A nun was sitting on the bed. Laurel introduced us to the shy, very beautiful young woman with rosy cheeks the colour of autumn apples. She glanced at us and then looked down at her feet until we left. Celeste wanted to know if we were witnessing accepted practice or forbidden fruit, but we didn't ask. Laurel was an enterprising young American woman who had introduced new ideas and ways of doing things that clearly had benefited this nunnery. We recommended a solar pump to bring water up from the river and some solar panels for light. Rinpoche gave a blessing to the nuns, who all collected together to see us off. We went back to Karsha with a basketful of veggies for our nuns.

The next day we picked up Laurel. She had agreed to be our translator. After twenty-five miles back toward the way we had come, we arrived at the newest nunnery in the Zanskar. The Manda nunnery sat on five acres of land donated by the nearby villagers. The Manda nunnery was started when some of the nuns at Zangla decided to have their own place. The nearby villagers donated the five-acre field, and the nuns got to work. With borrowed tools they made an elevated platform and built a small wooden temple with a separate kitchen attached. When we arrived, the nuns were digging small canals to direct rainwater into a catch basin. Next, they planned to begin building one-room houses for the nuns. Hard work all of this. These were nuns with the calloused hands of a construction worker. The local people donated some building materials, firewood and occasionally a day's labour. Most of the nuns still lived at home, and others worked for local farmers in trade for food and building materials or to make some badly needed money for the nunnery. The nuns who stayed slept on the floor in a room in the temple. There was no heat in the temple. The family of a novice nun would often build a room for her. Until then she stayed living at home.

We toured the nunnery with all eight nuns in tow. The nuns would eagerly tell us of what possibilities they saw, and what they hoped for; an expanded alter with room for a thousand butter lamps. There was a gasp at such an exalted idea. A garden because the lay of the land would funnel water to here. A porch on the front of the temple. A shed for chickens here, we think we have enough grass for a cow. The excitement and enthusiasm of these young women was infectious. Celeste wanted to stay, to pitch in and help get'er done. For Manda we recommended a solar electric system and money to buy building material and tools. Back at Karsha, we were welcomed like long-lost relatives who had stepped out into the wide world and returned safe and sound.

We visited four more nunneries. These nunneries were all more established than the first two we visited. Each had their own particular needs. The nuns were mostly older women from fifty to eighty-seven years old. They lived on meagre diets and endlessly repaired their clothing.

The last place we visited was the hard-to-get-to Pishu nunnery, on the other side of the Zanskar River. It was getting windier and colder by the day. Sometime in September it would snow, and the road in and out would close for the eight months of winter. The only way in or out of Zanskar Valley in winter was to walk on the ice that formed along the edges of the river. The entire journey on ice is at the bottom of a deep gorge (the Grand Canyon of the Zanskar). This would be an arduous and dangerous five-day trek.

Pishu was located on a vast dry slope that ended where it met the mountainside. To get there we crossed a long footbridge suspended on steel cables over the rushing Zanskar River. Laura was with us, as well four of our nuns from Karsha, who by now wouldn't let us out of their sight. Three nuns from Pishu were waiting for us with three small Tibetan horses covered with threadbare, colourful, hand-woven saddle blankets, mismatched tack and string for reigns. They had learned of our coming from a visiting nun. They would wait at that footbridge all day if needed. Patient, humble, unquestioning, unhurried, deeply devoted Zanskari nuns.

For Buddhists, time flows like the waters of the Zanskar River. It has no beginning and no end; nothing is permanent. We are all mere specks swept along in the flow of time, here only to continue on our path to enlightenment, to earn some merit, to hope for a better rebirth. There is no competition, no judgement, no convincing another of the rightness of your path. We are all on our own path, we create our own sorrows. The Buddha taught that attachment creates sorrow. I have struggled with this idea for a long time. No attachments means what? I cannot imagine. Does it mean no children, no family, no striving to make things happen? I know that this isn't what Buddhism is actually saying, but understanding and knowing are quite different things.

It was an hour-long horse ride to the nunnery from where the nuns had met us. Rinpoche, Celeste and myself clambered onto our little horses. We set off across this gravelly moonscape dwarfed on either side by two ranges of towering snow mountains, with the nuns leading the way, their red robes flowing in the wind. We could have been a caravan out of Arabian nights. The rinpoche, taking the reins from his nun, trotted off with his yellow robes and tall orange hat bouncing across the colourless landscape, which made us howl with laughter. These horses don't gallop but only trot, very fast, causing the rider to bounce up and down like a pogo stick. Our two nuns followed Rinpoche's example and soon we were all bouncing up and down and singing "yippee yai yea!" The nuns loved all this hoopla.

An hour later we arrived at a cluster of low mud and stone buildings set into an indentation into a near-vertical mountainside. We were welcomed by a reception line of beaming nuns with white khatas to place around our necks. We were invited into the temple and given butter tea and cashews.

The following is Celeste's description of Pishu nunnery. Her touching, vivid description captures the essence of this humble little nunnery far better then my poor attempt to do so.

The temple is similar to the others we have seen. They are dark, incense-saturated, sacred sanctuaries draped with brocaded, colourful fabrics, quilted around detailed paintings depicting Taras, Buddhas, protectors, and a mind-boggling array of deities, so old that the gorgeous raw silk is tattering. The inside walls around these rooms are softly undulating mudded walls over rock, with every square inch intricately painted with more Buddhas, goddesses and deities. Some of the thangkas, paintings and Buddhas are over a thousand years old. Around the perimeter of the temple are rows of cushions covered with heavily sculpted Tibetan carpets. In front of each of these are small low rectangular tables, each carved with demons and dragons and symbols painstakingly painted in primary colours. During pujas (prayers), the tables are used for tea, candles, and incense braziers. In the centre of the room is a decoratively embossed tin "box" with glass sides for butter lamps. There is a small flu that goes out the top of the temple. Along the wall is the altar, resplendent with more thangkas and butter lamps, intricately painted cabinets in bright primary colours that hold candles, and silk-wrapped prayer books in Tibetan script. Buddhas of every description in gold, silver, wood and clay reflect the age and wealth of the temple. All are smoky, ancient and faded with time. The wooden posts that hold up the structure are heavily sculpted, painted and covered in more ornate fabrics. There is not one inch of space in the temple that is not ornately decorated or draped. The room is lit by a small, raised centre ceiling ringed with small windows that let in a soft light. The entry door is, as most of their doors, so low you must bend in half to enter. It is a place that feels so sacred, a place that feels so ancient. We have entered an inner sanctum from another time. I sit and take it all in. I feel I am in another dimension. I marvel at the detail, I marvel at the antiquity, I marvel at the sacredness, I marvel at these hidden cave-like places of worship that in some intimate sense rival the great cathedrals of Europe. I marvel that they are so removed from the bigger world; a world that has no knowledge of them. I marvel at my fortune to be in this sacred place.

Celeste en route to Pishu

Pishu is in a difficult and remote place. Their only water source, a spring at the foot of the mountain, is drying up. Climate change reaches every corner of the earth. In the winter they melt snow. In the long term, we did not believe it would be possible for the nuns to remain here. This was a heartbreaking reality. This ancient temple with its exquisite artefacts will one day stand abandoned and empty, another reminder that life is ever changing, nothing is permanent.

We recommended a new wood stove, more solar lamps, and to pay for making a water saddle (two water containers fitted to a horse so that they can transport water from the river five miles away). Laurel would look into why the government of India's small annual stipend is not coming through. We later learned that the man in Leh responsible for doling out this money was siphoning off the top. We think he took more from nuns that were remote, less educated.

The nuns did not even know how to use a bank account. The other nunneries also reported less than they should be getting, and Pishu, already poorer than most, received nothing. The nuns economised by having no-food days. The problem was that they were timid, they were afraid to appeal to the government, afraid of doing business with the outside world. It was scary for them, they felt helpless.

The monks and monasteries were getting the lion's share of money and support. The monks and monasteries prospered while the nuns got minimal support. They were seen as less important and less deserving, solely because they were women. Monasteries were built for the monks, leaving them more time for study and religious practice, whereas the nuns often were engaged in hard physical work of building and maintaining their nunneries. The places may vary, but the problem of seeing women as somehow lesser beings is sadly familiar to us all. If the nuns had received an equal level of support, the problems we were looking into would not have existed

The nuns we met live lives of contentment and meaning in truly marginal circumstances. They found unrestrained joy in welcoming strangers into their lives. It seems that living with all our wealth and abundance has deadened us to some of the essential human empathy that makes us complete. Georgians have a saying: "a guest is a gift from God." For the nuns at Karsha our presence was a gift, and the pure joy the nuns displayed during our entire stay was as precious a gift to us.

Celeste and The nuns at Manda Nunnery

With the Nuns from Karsha

Number Twenty-Three: A Buddhist Nun to the Rescue

The nuns at Karsha had taken us under their wings. They didn't let us out of their sight. If one of us went for a walk, a nun stayed close by in case we fell or got too close to the cliff edge. This was especially the case for me because my left foot was in a cast. I had bunion surgery right before leaving home. A big, sturdy nun, with the arms of a lumberjack, took on the role of my personal guardian. Anytime I walked the rocky footpaths she was right there, holding my left arm and pointing out all possible footfalls. She commented on the landscape with sweeping gestures and on the uneven path pointing out obstructions. I understood not a word, but I was happy to follow this cheerful, confident voice.

We had one last project to complete before we left. This was to finish Karsha's water delivery. Water for the nunnery was carried up a thousand vertical feet from the village of Karsha on a nun's back. Starting at the nunnery, a more or less level footpath was made along the mountainside following the gorge. After about two miles, the bottom of the gorge came up to the level of the footpath. A one-inch plastic pipe had been laid out along the path connecting the nunnery with the bottom of the gorge. There was water running along the bottom of the gorge that sporadically dribbled into the end of the pipe. What was needed was a collector box similar to what we had on the creek for my house in Queens Bay. We headed up the trail along with eight nuns carrying plywood, bags of cement and an assortment of tools. Rimpoche received a horse to ride because he is a rimpoche, I rode a horse because I still had the plaster cast on my foot. My protector nun took the reins and walked out front leading my horse. It was a festive parade of red-robed nuns, Celeste wrapped in a blanket, and two men on horseback all singing their own songs. At one point the trail skirted a huge overhanging boulder on a steep hillside, with a hundred-foot vertical drop just a few steps away. My nun handed the reins to another nun and walked beside the horse.

I had to lean way forward in order to get under the overhanging rock. The horse saw this as an opportunity to get rid of his rider and leaned into the angled rock face. I was brushed off the right side of the horse. My sturdy nun caught me in her arms and carried me like I was her baby until we were out from under the overhanging rock. She set me down on the ground to a mighty cheer from all the other nuns. I have never seen such a huge grin on such a happy face. She had publicly accomplished her mission, keeping me safe and alive. It would have been a bone-shattering landing after an almost vertical drop off that ended a hundred feet down had those great strong arms not caught me.

We built a proper Kootenay collector box about fifty feet above the level of the water line to create water pressure. On our return we celebrated with many retellings of the story of how Mr. John was saved by a Karsha nun. A stream of cold clear water ran out of the open end of the water line outside behind the temple. The water then ran down the hillside, into the gorge to eventually reunite with the source, the stream at the bottom of the gorge. Our water had come a full circle. In Buddhism a full circle is a symbol for perfection. The next day two nuns moved some rocks and set up a wooden bench where the water line ended. This place became a special meditation site for the nunnery.

It's All About Conservation

The Brittany Triangle: A Hidden Treasure

In the southwest corner of British Columbia, on the Chilcotin plateau, two mighty rivers, the Chilco and the Taseko, drain the melt waters of the enormous glaciers and icefields of the Coast Range. From their sources many miles apart, the two rivers eventually converge to become the Chilcotin River, which in turn empties into the Fraser River several hundred miles east. The land between the two rivers is called the Brittany Triangle. It is 155,000 hectares of wilderness, a large foothills plateau at 5,500 feet elevation. Part of the homeland of the Xeni Gwet'in people, the Brittany Triangle is thirty-five kilometres wide at its base, defined by Tŝ'ilʔoŝ Mountain, and seventy kilometres from there to the apex of the triangle. A substantial piece of wilderness this.

Roads to log the pine forests of the Brittany were never built. It was deemed too costly to build bridges across these big wild rivers so the loggers leapfrogged the Brittany and carried on doing what they do until they reached the coast. Consequently, this remained a piece of untouched wilderness with a full complement of mostly undisturbed wildlife. Besides moose, elk, whitetail deer, mule deer, wolves, cougars, grizzly bears, black bears and eagles, the Brittany has a population of about 250 wild horses. The landscape is forested (mostly lodgepole pine) and dotted with hundreds of grassy meadows up to 80 acres in size. These meadows support the wild horses. The horses survive despite a full complement of predators and 40-below temperatures. They are completely integrated into the ecosystem of the Brittany. Unlike in the USA where wild horses are culled when their numbers get too high, the Brittany wild horses are a naturally regulated and stable population. They are possibly the only wild horses in North America living this way. Evolution's selection process has made for horses that are hardy and exceptionally smart.

Horses evolved in North America, spreading to other continents before becoming extinct in the Americas at the end of the Pleistocene (about 10,000 years ago). Horses returned to North America with the Spanish in the late 1400s, and over the centuries a few horses escaped here and there. The Pueblo Revolt in New Mexico in 1680 drove out the Spanish who left behind several thousand horses. The Pueblo turned the horses loose and it is believed that this event played a large part in expanding native horse culture, spreading horses throughout North America. Horses, after a ten-thousand-year absence, were once again back on the great American plains, where they survived and thrived. Within a hundred years there were millions of horses back in their evolutionary homelands. Horses arrived in Alberta somewhere around 1720. We do not know how they got to the Brittany, but horses were there by the early seventeen hundreds. The Xeni Gwet'in are a horse culture that have lived with Brittany horses for over three hundred years.

What follows historically makes one think that the Brittany Triangle must have some specially favoured karma. Accidents of geology and history played a big part in the shape of the landscape and in protecting this triangle of wilderness. As the glaciers melted after the last ice age, the cascading meltwater carved out the riverbeds for the Taseko and Chilco rivers. In the land between the rivers, the retreating glaciers left behind hundreds of potholes. These became shallow ponds or bogs that over ten thousand years slowly filled in to become meadows. The peat soil left behind was too acidic for the surrounding pine forest to colonise, so the grassy meadows remained meadows.

In the nineteenth century, the Chilcotin was the site of BC's only Indian war. The Xeni Gwet'in people of the Nemiah Valley (in the southern part of the Brittany Triangle) attacked and killed some members of a survey party that were bringing smallpox to this remote corner of the Chilcotin Plateau. This, among other events, inspired young warriors in some other regions of the plateau to drive out the white settlers. Believing that they were going to discuss a peace settlement with colonial officials, eight elders from the Tsilhqot'in nation (of which the Xeni Gwet'in are a part) travelled to Barkerville to negotiate an end to the war. The eight elders were immediately thrown in a jail. The next day the native men were put on trial. While the trial was in progress, gallows were being built in front of the courthouse. At day's end six the elders were found guilty and five were hanged from the new gallows[2]. A stark message for all that the new colonisers now ruled life and death in this land.

At the time, settlers were staking their claims and creating ranches in the rich grasslands of the Chilcotin. However, because the Xeni Gwet'in people of the Nemiah were considered hostile, this region of the Chilcotin was bypassed. What this meant for the horses of the Brittany was that their bloodlines were not diluted with those of escaped ranch horses during the ensuing years. Genetic sampling, done in the 2010s, shows that the dominant DNA of the Brittany horses is that of the Spanish Barb Horse brought over by the Conquistadores. This was a sought-after horse at the time with its Moorish and Iberian bloodlines. The light build and quick and alert posture of the Brittany horses points to their ancestry.

In the twentieth century, the two rivers on either side also protected the Brittany Triangle from a rapacious logging industry. There was diminishing timber supply for the sawmills in Williams Lake, and the Brittany caught the eye of Tolko Industries. With cutting permits, from the provincial government, in hand they prepared to move road-building equipment into the Brittany. In the summer of 1989, the entire native population of the Nemiah Valley camped in front of and on the new bridge at Henry's Crossing. Tolko was stopped dead in its tracks. After a fifteen-year-long legal battle, on June 16, 2014, the Xeni Gwet'in received title to most of their traditional homelands, part of which includes much of the Brittany Triangle.

The Brittany was completely unknown to me until a September day in 2003 when I heard an interview with Wayne McCrory, the legendary wildlife biologist and conservationist, on CBC Radio. Wayne talked about the forest fire that had recently swept through this remote corner of the Chilcotin. The fire was now under control, but it had ignited the peat in the meadows of the Brittany

---

[2] The five Tsilhqot'in leaders executed on October 26, 1864 were named Klatsassin, Piell, Tellot, Tahpit, and Chessus. A sixth, Ahan, was hanged in July 1865 in New Westminster.

Triangle. Since the peat fires only smouldered, the Forest Service, when asked to help, said, "no flames, no fires. We are done."

Wayne and his nephew Sean were putting out the peat fires with just the two of them. I hadn't met Wayne McCrory but knew of him. He was a local hero, a bear biologist and environmental activist who was known nationally for his conservation work. I talked to Wayne by telephone, offering to help, and got a set of complicated directions to where he was. I recruited a strong young local guy, Shiloh Grelish, and we loaded up the 4 × 4 truck with camping and firefighting gear and headed out for Williams Lake. Wayne's directions took us onto a series of seldom used 4 × 4 roads, climbing steep hills and crossing fast-running creeks. Deep into the hinterlands of the south Chilcotin, we drove into a blackened and burned landscape with smoke heavy in the air. We discussed the wisdom of continuing farther into this desolate land of smoke and blackened spires. It looked like we were driving into Dante's inferno. Shiloh pointed out that we could well be on the wrong track. He refused to call it a road. After hours of driving steep, rutted jeep trails, we came to our first meadow. Two guys, black with soot, were digging out smouldering peat (unbeknownst to us at the time, we had arrived at Upper Place). Wayne and his nephew Sean putting out peat fires seemed like a modern version of Joseph Campbell's hero's journey Just the two of them on a quixotic mission, battling a force of nature. The smouldering fires moved slowly, but inexorably, across the meadow, exposing the rocky detritus left behind by the retreating glaciers and thus setting the meadows back ten thousand years. Without intervention the fires would smoulder away under the snow throughout the winter. By spring there would be nothing left but rocky, barren fields. These would in time become pine forests. This would spell the end of the Brittany horses by eliminating their food source.

To put out a peat fire one has to dig down below the level of the smouldering peat and make a trench in front of the burn. This deprives the smouldering fire of fuel and stops it dead in its tracks. This is easier than it seems because peat is soft, no rocks or gravel, only many thousands of years' worth of peat build-up. The fires are mostly started by stallion piles (in order to mark their territory, stallions shit in the same place till there is a pile the size of a bushel basket). A fast-moving grass fire races across the meadow and doesn't have enough time to fire the peat, but it can set a pile of dry horse shit on fire, which, as it smoulders, generates enough heat to set the peat on fire. The smouldering peat fires burn in expanding circles. The older the fire the bigger the smouldering, smoking circle, until two circles join up. This makes for long sinuous lines of smoke. Fire fighting equipment isn't needed, it takes only a shovel and a strong back.

Wayne took us to a cabin that belonged to David Williams at "Far Meadow," a half hour farther down the 4 × 4 road. Dave was the original advocate for the Xeni Gwet'in and their long land claims fight, which was finally settled in their favour by the Supreme Court of Canada in 2017. This land claim settlement, where the Nehemiah band received title to 1,700 square kilometres of their traditional lands, was an historic precedent in Canada's long path to reconciliation with indigenous people.

For the next two weeks we dug peat from dusk to dawn. Historically appropriate, a Dutchman and an Irishman digging peat side by side. This is how our ancestors, in both Ireland and Friesland, heated their houses. We put out Black Stallion Meadow, Triangle Meadow, Lost Wayne Meadow, and a dozen more unnamed meadows. Wayne badly burned his foot when he stepped into a deep trench, where glowing coals fell into the top of his boot. He left for Williams Lake hospital. Shiloh and I stayed for another five days. Chilcotin winter was coming on, and it turned cold. To survive the frost, the peat fires burned lower into the ground. In Triangle Meadow we dug trenches four feet deep to stop the burn.

Just as we finished Triangle Meadow it began to snow. Alarm bells went off. We were a day's drive into serious backwoods territory. No one would venture in here until spring or summer. We loaded the pickup down with rocks to give us more weight and set off. The truck slid and slithered but got enough grip to make it up the steep pitches. In places the road was on a severe slant. The fear was that we could slide sideways into the trees. The truck would then stay right there until spring, and we would have faced a long, cold winter walk. After eight hours of clenched sphincters, we arrived at Twin Lakes and the beginning of a proper gravelled road. We remembered how good it was to be driving at 50 mph. We both agreed that we would be back.

What neither Wayne nor I knew at the time was that, eighteen years later, we would be sitting in a cabin we built at Capt. George Town, Wayne writing his book on the wild horses, me writing this story. We had gotten caught up in the wildness of this place, the uniqueness of this hidden plateau, and the remarkable presence of wild horses and had bought a 240-acre property in 2004, which became a wildlife preserve.

The history of Captain George Town involved a native guy who had been a policeman. He had homesteaded the valley and raised his family there. His one-room log cabin became known as Captain George Town. In the summer of 2003, we built a new log cabin. The cabin sits 100 feet from Elkin Creek. In September, chinook salmon make the incredible journey from the Pacific Ocean, up the Fraser River, up the Chilcotin, up the Taseko and finally up Elkin Creek, coming all this way to spawn. They come one thousand kilometres, force their way through the wild waters of Hell's Gate canyon and climb 5,500 feet to complete their life cycle here at Capt. George Town. The big chinooks are the only salmon strong enough to make this incredible journey. This place is the ultimate metaphor for the survival of our natural world and by extension the survival of humanity itself.

The cabin has become our wilderness retreat where we escape the increasingly complicated and intrusive world out there. The cabin is also used as a base for wildlife research. Sadie, the Wolf Lady, has spent two winters snowshoeing, by herself, across the frozen landscape to document the habits of the Brittany wolf packs. She found that during the winter, horses make up 80% of the wolf diet. For years we've collected DNA samples, from horsehair snagged on the rough bark of spruce trees, to puzzle out the ancestry of the Brittany horses. What we discovered is that the Brittany wolves dine on Spain's sought-after Moorish horses.

Unspooling the Landcruiser's winch to get out of a muddy spot in the "road"
Below: Digging out the peat fires in Triangle meadow.

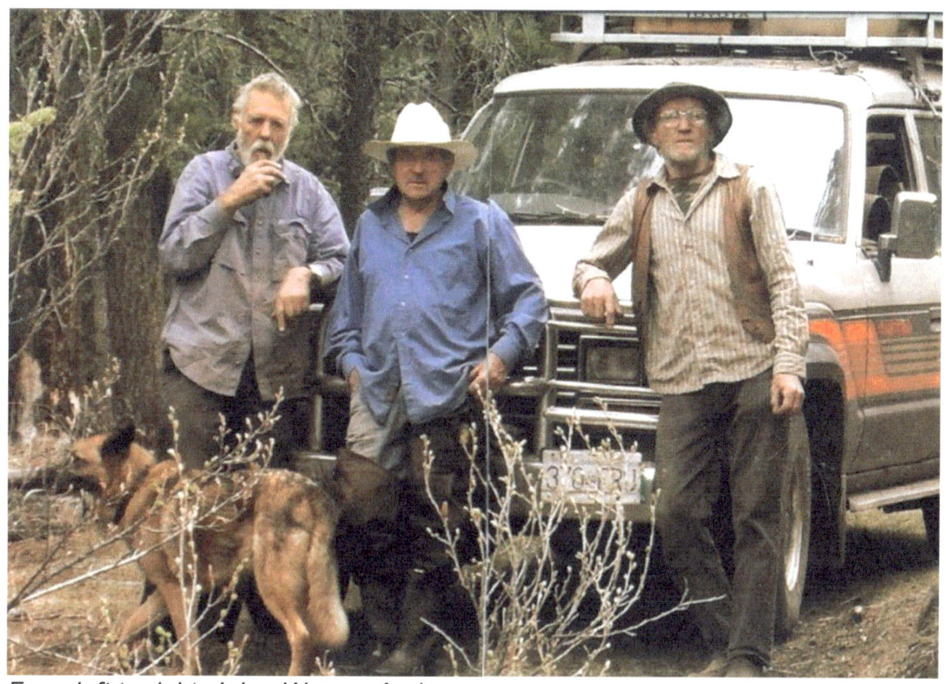

From left to right: John, Wayne, Andy
Below: Building the cabin at Captain George Town, summer 2013

Number Twenty-Four: Wild Horses Couldn't Keep Me Away

Evelyn, Andy and myself were at Upper Place, thirty acres of meadow and swamp. A dilapidated log cabin is all that's left of the long-since-abandoned native homestead. Some of the Xeni Gwet'in people from the Nemiah valley had built a huge log corral covering several acres, with clear cold water from a creek running through one corner. The corral was built to capture wild horses. Using salt blocks to lure them in, the Xeni Gwet'in have caught and tamed Brittany horses for over two hundred years. The meadow fronts a long boggy flat of grassy hummocks, willow bushes and pools of swampy water (moose pasture we call it). We've come from the Elkin Creek Valley (Captain George Town) a half hour away on a quad. We were taking the day off from building a log cabin. We were at the heart of the pristine, untouched, roadless, Brittany Triangle and its abundant population of undisturbed wildlife.

As we approached, we could see three wild horses on the outside of the corral and several more trapped inside. Andy said, "they're visiting their friends in jail." There were four trapped horses: a stallion, a mare and two yearlings. I cannot abide to see wild critters locked up. Two hundred years ago Blake wrote, "robin red breast in a cage, puts the whole world in rage." Wild horses in a cage could start a war. We herded them into a small holding corral, 40 feet by 80 feet, shut the gate back into the main corral and opened the holding corral's gate to freedom. The horses, bunched up against the logs at the far end of a small corral, were unable to see the open gate from there. I went into the corral. I couldn't resist the opportunity for some close-up photos. I would never again be this close to wary, wild, Brittany horses. The corral was about forty feet wide, and I was slowly moving towards the horses, right up against the logs of the far side of the corral. The four horses, all bunched up against the fence, watched my every move. They were on high alert, nostrils flared, ears up, with all eyes on me, a predator. As I inched my way along the logs, slowly getting closer, the stallion moved to stand in front of his little herd. After fifteen minutes of my slowly inching closer, the horses suddenly made a move. They galloped along the far log fence forty feet away. When they were directly across from where I was standing, the stallion turned and came straight at me going full tilt. I was trapped between the fence and this furiously protective wild stallion. Suddenly he saw, with his remarkable 350-degree vision, that his mare had found a way out, and he turned 180 degrees at full gallop, showering me with clods of mud and dirt. By the time fear hit me, the episode was already over. The four horses crossed the uneven ground of the bog, with hummocks and treacherous pools of quicksand, at a full out gallop as only wild horses could. They didn't slow down until they reached the trees on the other side of the bog, a half kilometre away. The four horses were once again wild and free and back in their own familiar world. Near death notwithstanding, our hearts felt bigger for opening a cage door. We left Upper Place with a new spring in our step. Back at camp, Wayne had the campfire going. “You trained them,” our resident

wildlife biologist said, “those horses will never again be lured into a corral.”

The three just freed horses racing across the peat bog.

Aerial photograph of Elkin Creek
Below: Crossing Elkin Creek by Landcruiser.

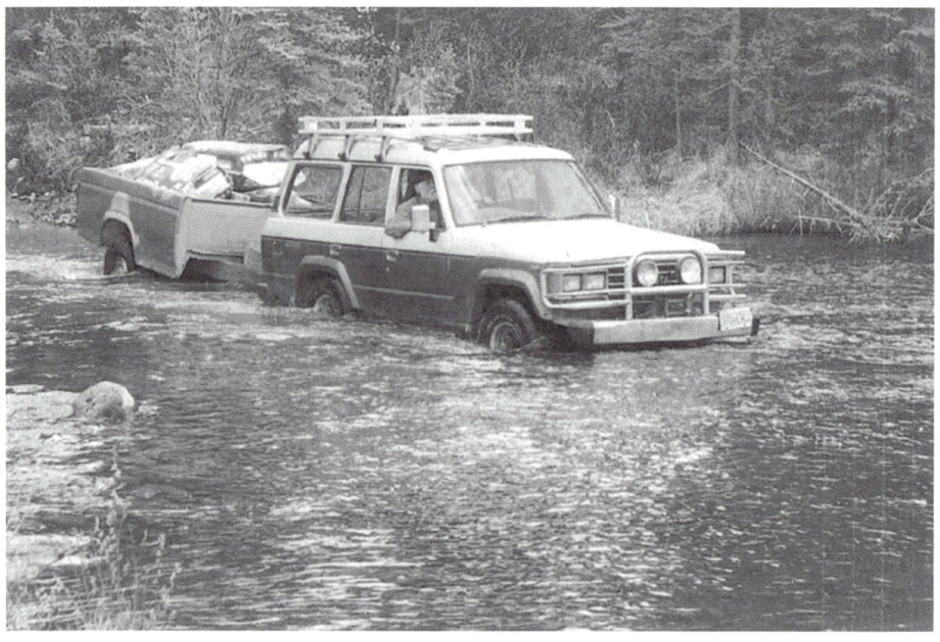

Mother Earth, Father Time

My experiences in the Brittany brought me to write this ode to the rhythms of life in the area.

Year One

We drive the old 4 × 4 wagon road through miles of lodgepole pine forest. A million pine needles rustle softly in the breeze, the smell of pine resin hangs in the air. We breathe in the perfume of the Brittany. Arriving at the cabin we are bubbling with excitement. We have a week of immersion in this pristine untouched wilderness. Next morning it's time to explore. We wander all day following horse trails. These are well-defined paths winding through the forest that always, eventually, lead to a meadow. We approach a meadow tiptoeing, in complete silence, like a stalking cougar, hoping to see a band of wild and wary horses and perhaps the magnificent black stallion. It's a magical wonderland that harbours the mysteries of another time. This wilderness, untouched by human hands, also harbours an ancient truth that allows subdued emotions to silently take wing.

Year Two

The 4 × 4 wagon road leads us ever farther on into the Brittany. Smoke is everywhere, hanging thick in the air. It is an ominous feeling to drive miles of burnt forest. The landscape is one of blackened spires, some still smoking, and a forest floor of smouldering stumps and grey ash. We travel in sad silence watching the apocalypse unfold. Shiloh says, "whoa! We need to turn around." We keep going, eventually getting to a meadow. We see long, sinuous lines of smoke curling up from the ground. The fires have ignited this meadow. The peat fires will smoulder all winter long under the snow, leaving behind bare gravel and rocks. Armed with shovels, we dig out the slow-smouldering underground peat fires. In the next three weeks we put out a dozen meadows. Our aching muscles sleep the deep sleep that comes with hard work. If these meadows go, so do the wild horses of the Brittany. We leave the cabin as the first snow flies, happy and content.

Year Three

We drive the slow wagon road into the Brittany. The road is rough and bumpy. It is late spring, and the world feels alive. The burnt snags stand stark against the clear blue skies. What was once forest floor is now miles of two-foot-high yellow grass as far as the eye can see. The tall grass moves back and forth in the breeze like unto the swells of the ocean. It is a breathtakingly beautiful sight. We come to the first meadow. It is transformed. The meadow is now a small lake with masses of red flowers floating on the water. Seeds that lay dormant for a half century were patiently waiting for the lake to return. With millions of trees missing and no longer pumping up groundwater, the water table has come up. Our spirits soar at the sight of the magical rebirth of our beloved Brittany. We do not see horses. They now have such a rich bonanza of grass, they do not need the meadows.

Year Seventeen

Driving the rough 4 × 4 road into the Brittany, as far as the eye can see, millions of small pine trees all about 15 feet high. A few black snags still stand, a silent reminder of what was. It's a wondrous rebirth. When we step out of the truck, we once again smell the scent of pine resin and hear the breeze sighing through the pine needles. The tall yellow grass is gone, overwhelmed by the new forest. The trees are so densely packed that it is not possible to stroll through this forest. These trees face years of competition with each other to thin themselves out. The water table has dropped. The lakes have reverted to meadows. The gorgeous red flowers are once again dormant seeds patiently waiting out the years. The horses are making new trails and once again inhabit the meadows. The logs of the cabin are a shade darker, but it still stands as sturdy and welcoming as ever. We still recharge our souls by coming here and seeing the Brittany go through its changes. This wilderness, untouched by human hands, reveals an ancient knowing that along with the wild horses, we too belong to nature

Life and Death

Brother Melle

My older brother Melle was between George and myself in age. George was born with a deformity and was fated to grow into a severe hunchback. He spent his younger years enduring multiple surgeries in Toronto Hospital for Sick Children to straighten him out. When he was thirteen, he was in a full body cast for the whole summer, with his left leg, in its own cast, suspended from the ceiling with a length of rope. Consequently, Melle took the place as the responsible elder brother. Melle was the reliable one who could always be counted on do what was needed, to do what was right. My brother Melle had a heart the size of Mount Loki. Melle and I had done a fair bit of travelling together, kayaking in the Queen Charlotte Islands (Haida Gwaii), treeplanting in the wilds of BC, and so many other places. After my time in Ethiopia with MSF I had wanted to bring Melle, a devout man, to experience the ancient Christian culture there.

I invited Melle to go with Celeste and me on a January 2019 trip to Ethiopia. Our purpose was to be in Ethiopia for Timkat, the grand outdoor festival commemorating the baptism of Jesus by John the Baptist. Timkat was Ethiopia's biggest annual celebration.

Ethiopia became a Christian country centuries before Europe. They practise an ancient Christianity with deep roots back in time. Public celebrations like Timkat, with services conducted by robed priests walking with tall staves, swinging incense braziers, hark back to European mediaeval times. Their deep, ancient faith had survived seventeen years of dictatorial communist rule.

We also planned to visit the unique, rock-hewn churches in Lalibela. Melle said to Celeste, "This is the trip of a lifetime." Melle had celebrated his eightieth birthday a week earlier. Fasil, my friend in Addis, was our driver and our guide.

We picked Melle up at the Addis Ababa airport, and the next day we went to see a church famed for its medieval murals depicting scenes from the bible. After a two-hour drive, we arrived at the church to find it was closed for the next hour. Fasil suggested lunch at a restaurant a little ways back. The restaurant offered a traditional Ethiopian meal of injera and goat meat, ready to serve in a half hour. We decided to use the half-hour wait to see a bridge built by the Portuguese 500 years ago. After a ten-minute walk, Melle and myself were standing on the edge of a drop-off looking down at a jeep trail just a few feet below us and beyond that a wide valley where we could see a stone bridge crossing the river. The bridge looked quite unprepossessing, quite small in fact, and not worth clambering all the way down to see close up. We decided to just enjoy the view. The river winding its way along among the big bare hills that defined the valley and the oddly shaped terraces dotting the hillsides wherever it was less steep showed how Ethiopians used every bit of land that could produce something.

I said, "I need to pee." Melle replied, "you'd better go then." I walked fifteen feet away to relieve myself. As I turned to walk back, I saw Melle was no longer standing there. Fasil, and the other three Ethiopians with us, were yelling, "John! Come here! Melle has fallen." It was a cacophony of noise with people yelling over each other so I was thoroughly confused, but I walked towards Fasil. He said, "Melle is hurt, he fell, they are bringing him here." Four guys came up the jeep trail carrying Melle. They laid him on the ground under a small bamboo shelter. I kneeled down beside him. Melle looked up at me. His eyes had a 'not there' distant look. He said "I can't feel my legs. John, can you raise my head?" I carefully raised his head a few inches and put a folded-up shawl under his head. He said, "that feels better." Those were Melle's last words. He never spoke again.

One of the Ethiopian guys ran to the restaurant to bring back our van. Celeste came running up, knelt beside Melle, and proceeded to give him mouth-to-mouth resuscitation. A few minutes later a man and a woman showed up. They had been at the restaurant when the guy coming to bring our van told them what had happened. The man took Melle's pulse then opened an eyelid and shone a small flashlight directly into the eye. He said to Celeste, "I am a doctor from Germany, it is no use, he is gone."

We loaded Melle into the back of the van. A still warm body. Where is the line between life and death? A short period ago he had been my brother, talking, alive and then suddenly a dead, lifeless body was lying in the back of the van.

During the long, sad, two-hour drive back to Addis, it became real. My beloved brother Melle was gone, dead, just like that, without even a goodbye, with no opportunity to tell him how much I had always admired him, how, for all of our lives, he had set the example I at times tried to live up to. I spurned his way but, in spite of that, he was my moral compass. I owed Melle such a huge debt, and now it was too late to say any of that to him.

We drove to the hospital, to a grubby back entrance leading to the morgue. They laid Melle on a gurney. We waited. Celeste had shown the presence of mind to stick her hand under his clothing and find Melle's hidden money belt. We waited. They wheeled the gurney into a room. I followed along and saw, through an open door, that it was a room with a cement floor covered with blood. There were bodies laying on stainless-steel tables, some cut open with gaping, bloody midriffs. Then the steel door shut with a clang. We waited.

We were a long time waiting, leaning against a dusty cement-block wall. Celeste didn't speak but smoked one cigarette after another. I was envious that she had something to do. I was called over to the outdoor corridor that led to the morgue room, the butcher room I couldn't help thinking, where a man wearing a blood-stained white smock and a pair of bloody rubber boots told me my brother had died of a broken neck.

Fasil drove us to our hotel. The two women at the front desk welcomed us with tears in their eyes. They held our hands as they expressed their sorrow at what had happened. They had a huge bouquet of flowers for us and asked if we needed anything. Fasil insisted that he stay with us and took Melle's room. That was the end of Melle's one and only day in Ethiopia.

The next day we had to go to the police for a "Cause of Death" certificate, to the tourist bureau to register the death, to an undertaker to prepare the body and supply a coffin for the flight home, and to Air Ethiopia Cargo Division to arrange, and pay for, transport of Melle's body back to Edmonton. We called the Canadian embassy to get some help facilitating the transport of the body. An Ethiopian man from the embassy stayed with us for the next three days to complete all of the complicated arrangements. He and Fasil did whatever could be done to guide us, to take care of us, to see to it that we received all the support we both needed. At the Air Ethiopia Cargo Division, we were asked to identify the body. A hearse pulled up, they opened the back door, inside was a red coffin. Someone opened the lid of the coffin to reveal Melle, unwashed, completely naked with blood stains on his belly. This was the last time I saw my brother.

The steps to have a body repatriated from Ethiopia can take up to two weeks. We were confirmed on a flight, with Melle's body in the cargo hold, on the morning of the third day, thanks to everyone's help. When we went to retrieve our suitcase, the owner of the hotel, a well-dressed man, was there at the front desk with his wife. They were in their late fifties. They expressed their sorrow at the death of my brother with tears in their eyes. They would not take any payment for our entire stay. They gave me an Ethiopian cross, a special Lalibela cross and left us saying "God gives, and God takes. Blessed be the name of God."

Fasil was with us the entire time, driving us where we needed to go, taking care of everything. In the end he would not take any money for his time or for the use of the van. The genuine love and care we received from Ethiopian people, in our time of trouble, was true to the Christian ideal of helping those in need. Melle would have understood these very Christian responses with his whole heart.

I miss my brother. I miss his voice. Melle always answered my telephone call with a loud and enthusiastic, "Hello John!" Now that I'm writing about long ago times I want to pick up the telephone to ask Melle about his recollections. He remembered our past much better than I ever did. Melle paid more attention; he was not so given to hurrying on to the next thing.

For me, the Ethiopia trip was going to be an opportunity to talk to Melle about some of the things that happened during our growing-up years. Much is lost with Melle's passing. It is a stark reminder that time's winged chariot is hurrying near for us all. If we want to do, or say, something, the time to do so is right now.

I think about you Melle, and about how we brothers were so much a part of a larger family and of a larger Christian Reformed immigrant community. Outsiders in a strange land. With each passing of one of us, these memories fade and can no longer be shared and revived. You were the last brother with whom I could talk about these times. Your passing leaves me more alone and stranded in a future that I do not feel at home in, with less and less connection back to who and what we were. I think about the warmth of our shared family. Sitting around the table in the warm, cosy living room, the old log-cabin part of the farmhouse in Forest, Ontario. "Echt gezellig" (authentically warm and cosy). Mem was knitting or darning socks, Heit, wearing glasses much too small for him, reading a book and us boys playing a boardgame. It was simply companionable. What comes to me is the memory of how each of us was a living part of all of us, and this living stream of human contact is now diminished. With you jumping into eternity, it's become a trickle.

However, we don't get to choose how the lives of our families unfold. We pay our money and take our chances and live with the results, whatever they are. Life is unpredictable, life is precarious, life is precious, life is to be lived to its fullest.

Brother Melle in Queen's Bay

Life Goes On

A story of a death should be followed by a story about a wedding. My last story is one of continuity and community. I was recently honoured to be asked to officiate at the wedding of Erik and Ariana. I am a longtime friend of the Brinkman family. I first saw newly born baby Erik in his crib and over the years watched him grow from a most rambunctious youngster into a great strapping man whose love of life and his enduring love for those around him is simply infectious. I first met Arianna when she was a stately young woman. She, along with Erik, came to visit me in the Kelowna hospital when I was gravely ill. I quietly blessed her name, when she held my hand, while I lay in that hospital bed. What follows is part of the speech I delivered at the occasion of their union.

Marriage, the coming together of a man and a woman, is our most ancient and durable institution, with deep roots into our human past. Today we link with all our ancestors.

Erik and Arianna, we have watched the growing love you have for one another and for your new family. You laugh and joke and enjoy each other's company. You have a clear respect for each other. This is a very good beginning. This joy and admiration will sustain your relationship when the difficult times in life come, as they always do. Times of pain, sorrow and frustration can be enriching, and strengthening if faced together as a shared experience by two people who truly love each other.

Marriage is the miraculous mystery when two people become one and yet maintain their own unique selves. Marriage, and the creation of a family, is the physical, emotional and spiritual union we enter into so we may explore and experience the transformational power of love. Marriage on a more practical level is a partnership, where you both work together toward a common goal. For this partnership to work, to be a success, you must each willingly and generously do what needs to be done. You will know what this is when the time comes. The old metaphor of a marriage being likened to two people rowing a boat together is fitting: when only one person rows or pulls harder on the oar the boat only ever travels in circles. When you both pull equally the boat travels straight and can steered to its destination

Through your marriage, and the raising of your family, you will learn that putting the well-being of others ahead of your own needs is not difficult. Through this marriage, both of you will become complete.

However, this marriage is more than just about the two of you. It is also about your family, and your community. This larger community stands behind you, to enjoy you, to witness your life's trajectory, to watch your family grow, to support you, to be there for you when life overwhelms. In the words of the seventeenth-century poet John Donne: "No man is an island."

So, in the late evening of my life, I am honoured to speak words that celebrate the continuity of life and to honour an ancient tradition that secures our future. True solace is found here, for one hearing time's winged chariot drawing near. I am out of words to describe how spirit mingles in today's events.

The Wedding

Number Twenty-Five: One More for the Road

Note from John's daughter: An early morning email in spring of 2023 contained this message and story: "Dear Sjoukje, at the venerable age of 83 I am still capable of doing really dumb things. With trepidation and much love from your dad."

At age 83, the grim reaper had on more swat with his scythe. He missed.

There was a brisk new tang in the air, leaves were just beginning to turn. The trees would soon be resplendent with the bright yellows of fall in BC. As I walked I stopped to pick four good-sized mushrooms. They were beautiful, with a soft, pale-yellow cap and a dimpled surface. I carefully nibbled at one to test it. I've known for over twenty years that if the tongue tingles when you nibble on a mushroom, it's suspect. Not to be eaten. However, there was no sensation, no tingling tongue, so I had four safe and edible mushrooms to put in my bag. Having known about the tingling tongue test for such a long time lent this "fact" its own veracity.

Once in my kitchen I sliced up three mushrooms and carefully sautéd the heavenly morsels in butter. I savoured three very tasty mushrooms. Twenty minutes later I began to feel less well. Something was not right. Another twenty minutes passed and then I was really sick and began throwing up. It seemed that my oesophagus had rebelled and would only allow a liquidy green bile to pass. No sought-after purging of a poisoned gut, just endless retching, each bringing up more bitter bile with short breaks in between.

After two long hours of this I was seriously sick, very sore, and bone tired. I staggered to my bed to lie down, thinking about an article in the previous day's *Globe and Mail* about a woman in Australia who made a meal with mushrooms for her three guests. All three dinner guests enjoyed a tasty meal and then sickened and died. I decided to stay awake thinking that if I fell asleep I may never wake up.

My body refused, and it seems that I fell asleep soon after my head hit the pillow. I woke up at ten in the morning, surprised to be alive and wondering if I had only had a bad dream. The uneaten fourth mushroom on the kitchen counter dispelled that notion.

Conclusion

To look back over eighty-plus years of life is humbling. The certainties I lived with for the better part of my life have mostly evaporated. I no longer know what I once believed I knew. So much of life was an illusion. I grew up in an age when men were men, and a man knew what he knew. We walked with a firm step guided by certainties, not knowing that these certainties were the temporary, flawed beliefs of the age. In the brave new twenty-first-century age people celebrate new, more abstract, digital certainties that are equally delusional. The world I grew up in has changed so much, so fast. At times I feel lost in my own human home. For the first time in all of human history, the majority of people are divorced from the natural world. Our touchstones, the places where we find solace, are more and more found in techno gadgets. Not reliable allies, these. I feel we are standing on shifting sands. Over two thousand years ago the Buddha looked out over the shifting sands of time and saw impermanence, that nothing remains as it is. Impermanence is now accelerated to a point where our natural world is not able to adapt to such rapid changes. We humans are ultimately as much a part of the natural world as the wild horses of the Brittany. Our unsustainable ways of living are threatening their well-being and survival, as well as threatening the well-being and survival of our own children and the unborn generations that will follow us.

However, history shows us that human beings are extraordinarily adaptable. Our ancient tribal ways are rooted in an evolutionary mandate for survival. These imprints have guided us to believe that conflict and war is the only way for the family, the tribe, or the nation, to survive. The global changes and the resulting shocks coming our way may be a necessary prelude to leave our tribal thinking behind. A truly global catastrophe could force us to realize that all human beings are the same and that we must work together, in concert, to survive and to create a sustainable way to live on this earth. It will be our next evolutionary leap of faith that will transform us and our earth. I am sustained by my lifelong motto. Nothing is Impossible.

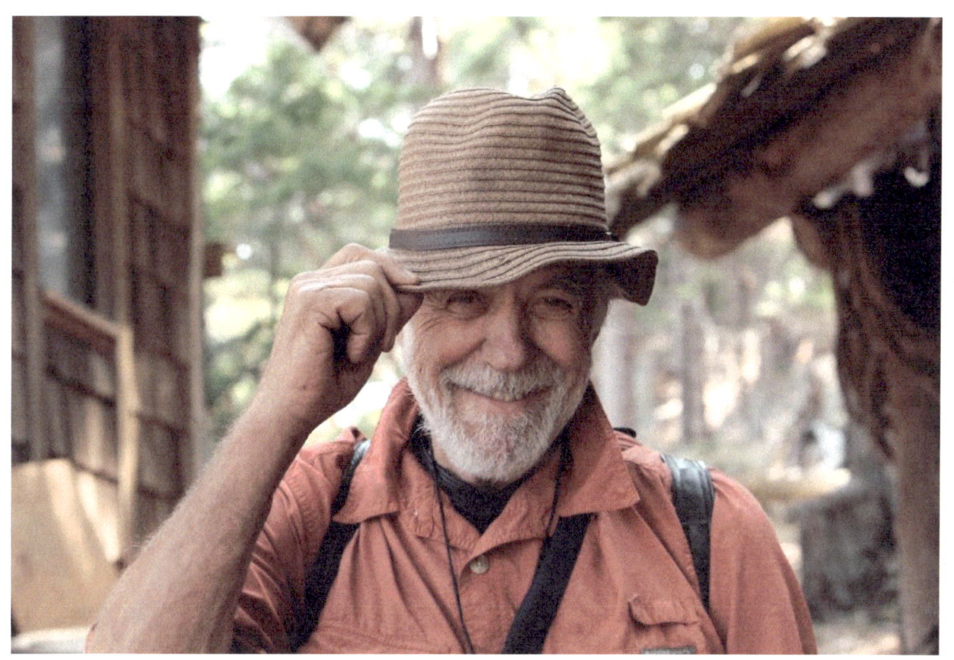